AMERICAN ANTICOMMUNISM

The American Moment
Stanley I. Kutler, Editor

The Twentieth-Century American City
Jon C. Teaford

American Workers, American Unions, 1920–1985
Robert H. Zieger

A House Divided:
Sectionalism and Civil War, 1848–1865
Richard H. Sewell

Liberty under Law:
The Supreme Court in American Life
William M. Wiecek

Winning Is the Only Thing:
Sports in America since 1945
Randy Roberts and James Olson

America's Half-Century:
United States Foreign Policy in the Cold War
Thomas J. McCormick

American Anticommunism:
Combating the Enemy Within, 1830–1970
M. J. Heale

The Culture of the Cold War
Stephen J. Whitfield

M. J. HEALE

American Anticommunism

COMBATING
THE ENEMY WITHIN
1830–1970

•

THE
JOHNS HOPKINS
UNIVERSITY PRESS
BALTIMORE AND
LONDON

© 1990 The Johns Hopkins University Press

All rights reserved

Printed in the United States of America

The Johns Hopkins University Press
701 West 40th Street
Baltimore, Maryland 21211
The Johns Hopkins Press Ltd., London

∞ The paper used in this book meets the minimum requirements of
American National Standard for Information Sciences—Permanence of Paper for
Printed Library Materials, ANSI Z39.48-1984.

Library of Congress Cataloging-in-Publication Data

Heale, M. J.
American anticommunism : combating the enemy within, 1830–1970 / M. J. Heale.
p.   cm. — (The American moment)
Includes bibliographical references and index.
ISBN 0-8018-4050-3 (hc). — ISBN 0-8018-4051-1 (pbk)
1. Anti-communist movements—United States—History.   2. United States—Politics
and government.   I. Title.   II. Title: American anti-communism.   III. Series
E183.H43   1990
973—dc20   90-36391   CIP

For my wife, Lesley

CONTENTS

•

CONTENTS

Editor's Foreword

•

THE DECLINE of communism has been the signal political event as the twentieth century neared its close. Powerful, entrenched communist governments fell like dominoes in Eastern Europe, and even in the Soviet Union the Communist Party surrendered its monopoly of power. Failure abounded. And the result significantly reduced the likelihood of confrontation between Russians and Americans, the military paladins of rival economic ideologies.

The Marxist vision of a classless, socialist society never appealed much in the United States, even to racial and newly arrived ethnic underclasses. Yet for nearly a century and a half, anticommunism has been a divisive, painful sideshow of American politics, exploited by political and economic elites who characterized Marxism as a frightening threat to American ideals of boundless opportunities and riches.

British historian Michael Heale offers a special vantage point to the political history of anticommunism in the United States. His account is cool and detached, yet the analysis and understanding are especially insightful. He recognizes that anticommunism has been more than a response to the Russian Revolution of 1917 and that it appears as a constant thread in the American political and social fabric since the late nineteenth century. Heale exposes the cynical rhetoric and purpose of anticommunism, but always with a keen appreciation of its impact. Communism no longer threatens the United States; sadly, however, anticommunist rhetoric persists in our political language, as witnessed by periodic controversies over flag desecration, fluoridated water, and school prayers, among others. It remains to be seen whether the new post-communist age will purge such an anachronism from our symbolic politics.

Stanley I. Kutler
THE UNIVERSITY OF WISCONSIN
MADISON, WISCONSIN

PREFACE

•

FOR MANY PEOPLE in the modern world, one suspects, "the American moment" in human history is associated with a deep hostility to that form of communism inspired by Karl Marx. For several decades the United States has made the containment of international communism its primary global mission, while the celebrated antipathy of many Americans toward communistic movements at home has also seemed like a statement about the national purpose.

It is this domestic anticommunism that is the subject of this book—the American preoccupation with the red enemy within. From the mid-nineteenth century to the late twentieth century there have been Americans who have held "communism" to be not only a foreign ideology but one that has so far invaded the United States as to threaten the unique experiment in republican freedom. On some occasions such perceptions have become so pervasive as to constitute a Scare, most spectacularly exemplified by the Haymarket Affair of 1886–87, the Palmer Raids of 1919–20, and the McCarthyism of the 1950s. The term *anticommunism* is of fairly recent general usage, but it can usefully be applied to a phenomenon with deep historical roots in the United States.*

From the beginning American economic and political institutions have been broadly dominated by men who were propertied, white, and Christian. In the American context these attributes were possessed by the many as well as the few, so that those philosophies that held that free enterprise was "the American way," or that the genius of American institutions had been imparted by the Anglo-Saxon race, or that the American mission had been blessed by God had popular as well as elite dimensions. Class, race, and religion, in a host of intricate ways, have generated overlapping ideological and institutional formations that have provided a congenial context for anticommunist politics.

The relationship of American capitalism to anticommunism is complex, for big businessmen tended to be cool toward Senator Joe McCarthy's red-baiting crusade, while many trade unionists were committed champions of the free enterprise system, but the pervasive business

---

*Consistency, according to Emerson, is the hobgoblin of small minds. Nonetheless, in the following pages such terms as *communist* are not normally accorded a capital C except when referring to the Communist party or its members.

values of the United States hardly fostered a tolerant attitude toward the Left. The peculiar racial and ethnic configurations of American society also left their imprint on the anticommunist persuasion. Black slavery, racial segregation, and restrictive immigration laws have all at various times been represented as bulwarks against red revolution. The role of religion in shaping American anticommunism remains difficult to assess, for particular denominations have often absorbed their political and economic values from the larger society, but most Americans have been eager to avow a belief in God, and religious leaders have frequently denied "atheistic" socialism or communism a place in the United States. Most of those Americans privileged with property, white skin, and religious faith, of course, have not been admirers of Senator McCarthy and his ilk, and some of them have been avowed Communists, but the vigor of anticommunism has owed much to its capacity to tap the dominant values of American life.

The imperatives of class, race, and religion have had to be worked out within a political system sometimes called "republicanism" and sometimes "democracy." From the Revolution onward, Americans were warned of the fragility of republican institutions, and this belief that the United States is dangerously vulnerable to subversion has survived into the twentieth century. The insecurities inseparable from a capitalist economy and a democratic polity doubtless contributed to this widespread conviction that the American republic was forever imperiled by enemies within. No single interest could long monopolize power, and a challenge to the preeminence of a particular class or group could be interpreted—or represented—as a form of insurrection.

The insecurities of elites in the republican polity, with its weak tradition of deference and limited powers of coercion, have been matched by the anxieties of its citizens. Told that the republic was theirs to preserve, some of them on occasion have been dismayed at its failure to sustain their own interests and values and have banded together to combat the insidious influences they believed were denying them their inheritance. The republican tradition of an active citizenry, pressed though it has been into some highly questionable forms, has served the anticommunist cause well.

The unusual origins of the United States, together with the variegated nature of American society, have also placed a peculiar burden on political ideology. Americans were united more by shared values than by ancient traditions or powerful institutions. Republicanism—or Americanism—has done something to give a diverse and restless people a sense of commonality, and an instinctive awareness of this has perhaps made Americans nervously sensitive to forms of ideological subversion. They have regularly turned to their own revolutionary heritage to rebuff doctrines of alien pedigree, naturally adapting their patriotic faith to changes in the social and economic landscape. Even before the publication of *The Communist Manifesto*, the political, economic, racial, and religious experiences of the United States were interacting to conjure up for many Americans an idealized image of a Christian republic of self-reliant white men, ensuring a suspicious reception for Marxist socialism.

Businessmen were early inveighing against the "communistic" and un-American effrontery of labor groups, seeing them as destructive of the fundamental American principle of equality of opportunity, and the relentless course of American economic development, within the frail framework of republican government, served greatly to strengthen the patriotic claims of anticommunism. It is tempting to trace a trajectory from the anticommunist expostulations of local businessmen in the mid-nineteenth century, through the capitulation of an urban community to red scare emotions after the Haymarket bombing in Chicago, to the recourse of state and federal governments to counterrevolutionary measures during and after the First World War, and finally to the global crusade of the United States against international communism in the mid-twentieth century.

The historical record, of course, reveals no such tidy and ineluctable progression, but the sequence may serve as a warning against accepting those interpretations of anticommunism that emphasize its hysterical, irrational, and aberrant features. The red scares that punctuated American history were necessarily shaped by changing American and international environments. First manifested in what Robert H. Wiebe has called the "island communities" of the nineteenth century, it took the growth of a national economy and the strengthening of federal political institutions before anticommunism could impinge significantly on national politics.

Part 1 of this book examines the evolution of American anticommunism during the era of industrialization between about 1850 and the 1920s, when a racking class conflict supplemented by nativist apprehensions about immigration generated fears of violent insurrection. Yet "the nationalizing of American life" had not been completed even by the time of the Big Red Scare, which some politicians hoped to use to enlarge national authority. The political system was nonetheless gradually adjusting to the pluralistic demands of an urban-industrial society, as when political parties yielded some of their influence to pressure groups, some of which functioned as vigorous outlets for patriotic impulses. Extensive safeguards against class revolt had been put into place before the credibility of Industrial America was strained by the great

PREFACE

crash of 1929, but the subsequent growth of government at home and the disturbing specter of the Soviet Union abroad served to revive and redirect anticommunist discontents.

Part 2 examines the period from the 1930s to the 1960s, when the United States became a global power and intense party competition allied to the bureaucratic impulses of the national security state made possible the second Big Red Scare. The vigilante activities of an earlier day had largely disappeared (Senator McCarthy caused offense not so much by searching for Communists as by reviving the arbitrariness of vigilante justice), and class conflict too had abated, but the political and bureaucratic classes, more than was the case in some other countries, had their own reasons for embracing a zealous anticommunism.

The American polity operated so as to magnify the threat of red revolution, but the insecure elites and patriotic citizens who perceived it had not normally taken leave of their senses. Hardheaded calculations and coherent ideological perspectives were closer to the heart of red scare politics than was mindless hysteria. It usually needed both the conspicuous and indisputable presence of some radicals in the United States and communistic successes abroad to give the anticommunist cause much buoyancy, particularly in turning the middle class and respectable working class people and elements of the intellectual community against those reform alignments that sometimes afforded radical minorities a little protection. It was the misfortune of the American Left not only to be linked—apparently—to international revolution but also to be large enough to be noticed yet small enough to be crushed. The periodic destruction of anarchists, socialists, and Communists, and the harassment of labor and liberal causes, may raise questions about the morality of American anticommunism, but it does nothing to impugn its rationality.

.

Like other books in this series, this one has benefited from the suggestions and encouragement of Stanley Kutler and Henry Tom. I am also very grateful to my British colleagues John Thompson and Tony Badger for reading particular chapters, and to my exemplary typist Linda Persson. This book is dedicated to my wife, without whom it would have been completed either earlier or, more probably, not at all.

AMERICAN ANTICOMMUNISM

PART ONE

THE RED MENACE
IN INDUSTRIAL
AMERICA

•

From the 1850s to the 1920s and beyond, the dominant image of the red menace within American society was one of violent insurrection. As this image suggests, the principal motive force of anticommunism in those years was class conflict or, to put it another way, the insecurities experienced by propertied elites. In the United States democracy of a kind had arrived before industrialization, and the respectable classes not only were denied complete political control but also had to live with a system in which government power was exceedingly limited. For the most part they approved of limited government, not least because positive state action tended to be associated with the interests of labor, and the ideology of republicanism became part of their weaponry in the class war. The fraternal egalitarianism of the American republican heritage, with its insistence that rights and opportunities were available to all, enabled collectivist doctrines to be repudiated as un-American. If labor organizations and the like could be represented as incompatible with republican ideals, not only might the limited resources of the state be turned against them but, perhaps more important, active citizens might also be aroused to defend their republic.

Socialism was said to be imported to the United States by those immigrants who had succumbed to its promise in the class-ridden societies of the Old World. The propertied classes' fear of revolt was thus deepened and broadened by a nativist distaste for the unassimilated foreigner. The mob activity, assassinations, and revolutions that punctuated European history as the United States was industrializing kept alive fears that the Old World's disorders might be carried to the New. This perception of the radical alien as the personification of the threat initially underlined the powerlessness of the respectable classes, whose writ did not run much beyond their local communities; but as a national economy emerged to place greater responsibility on the federal government, it eventually became possible to fashion a logical response. The republican tradition of an active citizenry continued to be deployed against the red menace, but government also provided for its elimination by excluding undesirable aliens from the country.

1

AN AMBIGUOUS LEGACY (1830–1870)

•

AMERICAN society, it is often said, is suffused with an ideology of anticommunism. However true this may be of the twentieth century, it is not a charge that could be credibly leveled at the nineteenth-century United States, which could hardly predict either the Russian Revolution or its own superpower future. But if some of the conditions that would shape American anticommunism were not present in Abraham Lincoln's world, others were. Even before the Civil War there were Americans who saw something both alien and sinister in what was already called "communism," and the economic and political environment they inhabited would make its contribution to the anticommunist tradition. That tradition, of course, had yet to emerge, and there were features of American society working against it. The United States in the midnineteenth century possessed the potential for a pervasive antiradicalism, but it also nurtured radicals of many kinds, and it was a favored refuge for the harried followers of Karl Marx.

Communist refugees, if not exactly popular, were at least tolerated in a society that had itself been born in revolution and in which egalitarian doctrines were strong. Important features of American political culture were conducive to radical ideas and experiments. Yet the individualistic thrust of American political ideology, the entrepreneurial imperative of the economy, the religious and moral zeal of a Christian people, and the patriotic values of a proud republic already sat ill with the collectivist and materialist doctrines widely imputed to socialism. The course of

American history in the nineteenth century would greatly strengthen the basis for antiradicalism.

Revolutionaries and Refugees

For much of the nineteenth century no country was more receptive to radical and revolutionary ideas, even to socialistic and communistic ones, than the United States. Its own revolutionary tradition disposed it to look with favor on revolutions abroad, and the democratic course of its politics proved a rich breeding ground for egalitarian ideologies. America has been a refuge for the oppressed since its colonial beginnings, and nineteenth-century European socialists were made no less welcome than seventeenth-century religious dissenters. From colonial times, too, the North American continent had served as a kind of laboratory for experiments in social and political organization, and in the 1840s more new settlements were being established than ever, many of them claiming to practice forms of "communism." These experiences meant that the Americans of the mid-nineteenth century were not uniformly hostile to political radicalism.

A nation that had been born in violent revolution could not easily deny the legitimacy of attempts to overthrow government by force. Revolutionary movements directed against monarchy and despotism readily engaged the sympathies of nineteenth-century Americans, who offered their own republican system of government as a model for peoples everywhere. Americans saw in the Greek and Latin American struggles for independence replications of their own epochal fight for freedom, and the revolutions that detonated across Europe in 1830 and 1848 were hailed as the products of that liberty the United States had been nourishing since 1776. From this delusive perspective, it was the American republic that was inspiring a species of world revolution, albeit only by example. The revolutions of 1848 in particular seemed to promise constitutional alternatives to absolutism, and President Millard Fillmore and countless newspaper editors expressed their sympathy for the risings.

The Hungarian revolt against the Habsburgs most readily commanded the attention of Americans, for it too could be seen as a national war for independence against an imperial power, and the short-lived Hungarian republic was proudly described by Daniel Webster as the "American model at the Lower Danube." When the "governor-president" of the defeated republic, Louis Kossuth, visited the United States, he was greeted by the president, the secretary of state, and large numbers of the American people. "Wherever we go," wrote one of his companians, "bells are ringing, guns roar their salvos, the streets are decked in festive colors, banners flutter, and the population throngs in the streets." Kossuth failed in his attempt to secure military and financial support, although some Americans believed this was an occasion when the United States should depart from its tradition of noninterference in European affairs; but the public sympathy he aroused could not be mistaken. Americans of this generation looked with favor on revolutionary movements, at least those they could identify with their own.

If revolution was favored by the American political tradition, so was the radical doctrine of equal rights. The Declaration of Independence had held it to be "self-evident" that "all men are created equal," and two generations later Alexis de Tocqueville was still taken aback by the "unbelievable outward equality in America." Yet commercial and industrial growth was producing a more stratified society in the United States as in Europe, and in the 1830s and 1840s radical members of the Democratic party railed against the wealthy in the name of equal rights with as much vigor as any Marxist. They denounced "the pampered parasites of ill-gotten wealth" and "the blood sucking cormorants of capital" and pointed out that "in the past and present organization of society, the pecuniary interests of capital and labor are *antagonist*." Some of them looked for ways of creating a society in which there would be not merely equality before the law, but also an actual if rough equality of economic condition, with all households possessing much the same wealth. To this end the Democratic writer Orestes Brownson in 1840 proposed the abolition of the inheritance of property, so that all Americans could start life "even" and with "nearly equal chances of success." Brownson was disowned by his fellow Democrats, but that such an idea could be advanced from inside a major political party, rather than by some fringe group, is an illustration of the extent to which a radical egalitarianism agitated American political life.

Even outside radical circles the majoritarian principles derived from the American Revolution commanded widespread support. In 1848, the year *The Communist Manifesto* looked to an "independent movement of the immense majority," somewhere between 70 and 80 percent of white men in the United States actually turned out to vote in the presidential election. For the moment it was less the writings of Karl Marx than the egalitarian example of the United States that concerned some Old World authorities. In Queen Victoria's England there were men who regarded American republicanism in much the same light as some Americans were later to regard Soviet communism, and in 1866 a proposal for Harvard to send a visiting lecturer to Cambridge University was turned down in part on the grounds that he might infect the students with a subversive "love for democratic principles."

While the United States nurtured radicals of its own, it also continued to serve as an asylum for the oppressed of other nations. There was no scrutiny of the political views of immigrants, and European revolutionaries were not made unwelcome. German radicals had begun to arrive in the United States in the 1830s, and after the failure of the 1848 revolution in Germany four or five thousand more made their way there. Playing a role in that revolution had been the Communist League, of which Karl Marx and Friedrich Engels were members, a movement of workers from several countries with its headquarters in Cologne.

Among those who had helped to organize the League in Cologne in 1847–48 was Joseph Weydemeyer, who in 1851 accepted Marx's advice to settle in New York. Radical newspapers had been suppressed in Germany, and Marx was looking to New York, which already boasted a German-language press, for a new outlet for his writings. Weydemeyer's *Die Revolution* did not long survive, but it did publish Marx's *The Eighteenth Brumaire of Louis Bonaparte*, and its collapse was the result not of suppression but of insufficient support from New York's German community. The German revolutionaries who settled in New York showed little interest in proselytizing Americans, since for the most part they remained preoccupied by the prospect of a new revolution in Europe, and their proceedings were conducted largely in German. Their influence was slight even among other German immigrants, although Communist Clubs did appear in New York and a few other American cities in the 1850s.

A few German radicals did attempt to adapt their politics to American conditions. One was Hermann Kriege, who became enraptured by the idea of free land, and another was William Weitling, who developed the idea of a labor exchange bank (so producers could swap their products) and who advocated an American "republic of the workers." Such ideas did not always make them popular, but this handful of German Communists, socialists, and revolutionaries, who were often at odds with one another, were at least tolerated. With the outbreak of the Civil War, Joseph Weydemeyer even managed to reconcile his Marxist preachings with his duties as an officer in the Union army.

Tolerated too were a variety of experiments in communal living. The United States, unlike Europe, provided an environment in which socialism could actually be practiced, and in the first half of the nineteenth century a large number of communities settled in its open spaces that were communistic or socialistic in that they experimented with various forms of collective ownership. "We are all a little wild here with numberless projects of social reform," wrote Ralph Waldo Emerson in 1840. "Not a reading man but has a draft of a new Community in his waistcoat pocket." The Marxists were to dismiss these communities as "utopian," but they attracted quite a lot of attention and served to introduce many

Americans to socialistic ideas. In the 1820s the industrialist Robert Owen, of New Lanark in Scotland, chose New Harmony, Indiana, as the scene for his attempt to establish a "Community of Equality," and he was privileged to expound his socialist ideas in Washington before an audience of congressmen and government officials, including the president himself. In the 1840s the ideas of cooperative industry of the French utopian Charles Fourier were effectively expounded in the United States by Albert Brisbane; they won a small but enthusiastic and even respectable following and animated several short-lived communities. The utopian experiments were not necessarily inspired by imported ideas. The Reverend Adin Ballou established the Hopedale Community near Milford, Massachusetts, which drew up a constitution for "Fraternal Communism" and became celebrated as a "Christian republic." Even better known was the Oneida Community founded by John Humphrey Noyes in central New York, which practiced "complex marriage" and "Bible communism." The community's rejection of the monogamous family caused greater offense to other Americans than its communism.

The utopian communities were sometimes harassed, and the German radicals were on occasion denounced for their revolutionary ideas, but in the mid-nineteenth century members of the Communist League and other European refugees could find homes in the major American cities, and collectivist experiments were being made in the countryside. Labor groups articulated ideas ranging across equal rights, universal education, the equalization of property, and land reform, and even influential members of the Democratic party were drawn to doctrines designed to level the American social order. The United States also possessed its share of reactionaries who looked with horror on all these developments, but a pervasive antiradicalism had not yet taken shape and the tendency was held in check by a political culture that cherished both the tradition of refuge and the legitimacy of revolution.

An Antiradical Potential

Yet even in these years the American environment was less favorable to political radicalism than the sprinkling of Communist Clubs and socialistic communities and the feting of Kossuth might suggest. Already the promptings of class, religion, and even race were predisposing many Americans to be wary of anything that could be labeled communistic, as were the cluster of ideas and practices known as republicanism. The American political tradition itself offered an attractive alternative to socialism, enabled foreign ideologies to be denounced as subversive, and demanded that citizens actively avow the republican cause.

The republican heritage, with its commitment to individual liberties and representative government, encouraged people of all ranks to identify with the great American experiment. Even labor movements when they emerged attempted to define themselves with language and ideas drawn from the republican tradition. Although it could inspire workingmen, this heritage nonetheless could be turned with particular force against any idea or movement that served the interests of a fragment at the expense of the larger society. The very word republic, as Tom Paine had pointed out, meant "the *public good*, or the good of the whole," and conservatives—and liberals too—regularly employed the ideal of harmony against those unpatriotic enough to set class against class. Even political parties had initially been denounced as unrepublican in that they poised the interests of a part against those of the whole, and class-based movements attracted a similar opprobrium. The fraternal promise of republicanism would always be used to deny legitimacy to more exclusive fraternities.

The republican impulse to regard the common good as indivisible was also related to the American tendency to hunt for subversion, a tendency encouraged by the insecurity many felt in such a fluid social and political order. From the eighteenth century onward Americans have feared the enemy within. The Revolution itself had occurred when colonial leaders became convinced that the British government was plotting to deprive Americans of their liberties. The belief that the republic was in imminent peril helped generate the political parties of the 1790s, those hitherto unacceptable forms being justified by a yet greater menace, and Americans continued to mount watch for the domestic enemies of republican government. In the 1820s some perceived such a menace in the institution of Freemasonry, when they reasoned that Masons in government were conspiring to advance the interests of other Masons and hence undermine the principle of equal rights that was said to be the basis of republicanism.

In the 1830s and 1840s many native-born Protestants directed their suspicions toward Roman Catholics, who were said to give their first loyalty to their church and not to their country. With Catholic immigrants pouring into American ports from Ireland and Germany, Catholicism, like communism in the twentieth century, seemed to some a species of international anti-American conspiracy. Samuel F. B. Morse, just before turning his prodigious imagination to the invention of the telegraph, warned of a giant conspiracy masterminded by Prince Metternich, the pope, and the Austrian emperor, to use the "unlettered Catholic emigrant" to seize control of American institutions and crush the cause of liberty.

The suspicion that the republic was being subverted was no paranoid fringe fear. Even the major political parties continued to function on the premise that their opponents represented some kind of antirepublican conspiracy. Democrats denounced the Whigs for fastening a financial aristocracy on the country and were in turn accused of subverting the republic with the spoils system. The abiding conviction of the fragility of the republican experiment was not altogether misplaced. If such fears animated the political parties, they also divided the great geographical sections. Antislavery agitators accused the Slave Power of bending government to its despotic will, and southerners charged that abolitionism was the product of a British plot to divide and destroy the republic. Indeed, the Civil War could be said to be the product of northern perceptions that the South represented the very negation of republican liberty, a mighty cancer in a republic of free men, and of southern perceptions that northerners were bent on reducing the South to colonial dependency. American public discourse in the mid-19th century reverberated with accusations of conspiracy and subversion, and while for the moment Catholics and slaveholders were more prominent targets than socialists or communists, those charges kept alive the belief in the frailty of republican forms and the imperative need to locate any enemies within.

The need to preserve the republic from its enemies enjoined on its citizens an active vigilance. Indeed, the republican emphasis on limited government, on the capacity of people largely to govern their own lives, encouraged Americans to be alert to their civic duties. Americans were a nation of joiners, which Alexis de Tocqueville attributed in part to the absence of a hierarchical social order and the weakness of traditional habits of deference. Among the associations they joined in the nineteenth century were the great political parties, which assumed responsibility for educating citizens in republican principles. Strikingly high turnouts characterized presidential elections from the 1840s, and barbecues, rallies, parades, and mass meetings evinced a great popular interest in political affairs. "What a sublime spectacle," marveled one editor in 1844. "Millions of men rushing to the polls under the full impression that the weal or woe of the nation was hanging as it were upon their individual act."

Here was the active citizenry upon which republican government depended. If few blacks, newly arrived immigrants, propertyless transients, and paupers participated in these republican rituals, countless family farmers, skilled workers, and small householders did, sustaining the notion and their own belief that this was a people's government. Other voluntary associations, such as the temperance and antislavery societies, supplemented the work of the political parties in creating a tradition of energetic citizenship. This tradition, together with the weakness of government, also gave some legitimacy to the vigilante groups that appeared before the Civil War, particularly in frontier areas, when private citizens banded together to defend order and property in the name of the community. For the most part those citizens who joined political parties, temperance societies, and even vigilance committees were drawn from the "respectable" classes, those who owned at least a modest amount of property, enough to seal their commitment to the American system of republican government and, perhaps, to jump to its defense when its enemies were glimpsed.

Those enemies, real or imaginary, have played an indispensable role in American political life, not least in helping to define that identity for which Americans were being invited to fight. American republicanism took shape in contrast to European aristocracy, and for much of the nineteenth century Britain not unnaturally represented everything that the United States was not. In presidential campaigns propagandists went to considerable lengths to brand opposing candidates with English roots, connections, or sympathies, rather as in the mid-twentieth century candidates might be charged with being "soft on communism." John Quincy Adams was said to have married an English wife, Martin Van Buren to use an expensive English coach, and Franklin Pierce to be descended from the noble Percy family of medieval England. The insecurity implicit in the experimental nature of the republican mission reinforced this tendency to define "Americanness" by identifying a polar opposite. American political culture seemed to require an enemy without as well as an enemy within, supplying the inverse image of the American character. In due course the Soviet Union would perform this function even more convincingly than aristocratic England.

The awesome duty of preserving and cherishing the republic was assumed by men who were propertied, white, and Christian. The United States enjoyed the most favorable ratio of arable land to people in the world, and though significant numbers were excluded from this domain, a majority of white men held some kind of stake in society, and the extraordinary territorial and commercial expansion of the first half of the nineteenth century whetted their appetite for more. The small farmers and businessmen of this nation aspired to be masters of their own destiny and were unlikely to welcome any doctrine that deprived them of their estate. They, along with southern planters, were also united by the bond of race. As the aristocratic planters of colonial Virginia had earlier discovered, many men of modest fortunes could be induced to support the prevailing political and economic structure by the privileges it accorded to whites generally. In the nineteenth century there were men of Anglo-Saxon stock who came to regard the American mission as their particular inheritance and who feared the subversive effects of immigration and the alien political ideas that were thereby introduced. Racial and ethnic instincts were reinforced by religious impulses. Foreign visitors commented on the religious enthusiasm of Americans, who boasted of their large number of churches, clergymen, and church members and attributed the republic's good fortune to the approval of Providence. In short, American republican traditions had to be accommodated to these economic, social, and cultural forms. The collectivist and rationalist doctrines of European socialism were not readily compatible with the popular image of the United States as a Christian republic of small self-supporting producers.

The republic had been launched by a revolution rooted in individualistic and libertarian values. The Declaration that had pronounced all men to be created equal had also referred to their rights to "life, liberty, and the pursuit of happiness," a substitute for the more familiar phrase "life, liberty, and property." It had been threats to property rights, in the form of tax demands, that had initially alerted Americans to the arbitrary thrust of British policy, and the notion of individual liberty—freedom from dependence on others—remained closely associated with the possession of property, which conferred such independence. The egalitarian strand in the American political tradition enabled American radicals in the mid-nineteenth century to call for the equalization of property, but they rarely contemplated the abolition of private property. Radicals had to bow to the individualism of American culture and to the largess of nature. The American radical tradition was essentially agrarian in character, and political rebels tended to look to the land for remedies to social ills, as did the labor reformer George Henry Evans, who proposed that each citizen be granted a portion of the public lands. Agrarian radicals could sometimes make common cause with socialists, but the agrarian coloring of so many American reform movements served to enhance the alien image of socialism and communism.

This respect for human and property rights qualified the American affirmation of the legitimacy of revolution. For much of the nineteenth century revolutionary movements abroad for the most part appeared to be directed at replacing monarchy with some kind of liberal democracy, and with these Americans could empathize. They were less enchanted by revolutions accompanied by widespread violence, the destruction of property, and the elevation of "the mob." The American Revolution had cost lives, mainly in confrontations between Americans and royal forces, and it had furthered the democratization of American society and politics, but massive and bloody upheavals had been avoided, and though some loyalists had lost their lands they did not lose their heads, as did luckless aristocrats in France a few years later. The French Revolution itself was at first welcomed by most Americans, who saw the French people as following the trail of liberty they had recently blazed. But the execution of Louis XVI and the Jacobin "reign of terror" caused many to recoil in alarm.

The emerging Federalist party in particular saw in the French terror an example of liberty descending into lawlessness, and they feared that American politics might take the same ruinous course. The continued, if anxious, sympathy of Jefferson and the Republicans for the French Revolution merely deepened Federalist apprehensions, which were not quieted when French Jacobins and Irish rebels took refuge in the United States and joined the Republican party. From the Federalist perspective, radicalism was being imported into the American republic and threatened to subvert it. For the first time in American history an equation was made between being an alien and being a revolutionary, and in 1798 the Federalists introduced the Naturalization, Sedition, and Alien acts, which extended the period over which naturalization could take place, made malicious writing against the government punishable, and enabled the president to deport any alien deemed "dangerous to the peace and safety of the United States." Unlike somewhat similar measures in the twentieth century, the Alien Act was not enforced, and it soon expired, but it illustrated the limits to which American conservatives at least could endorse revolution and their readiness to assume that radicalism was somehow un-American.

American politicians and newspapermen responded in much the same way to later upheavals in Europe. Like other Americans, Horace Greeley of the *New York Tribune* warmly welcomed the outbreak of the revolutions of 1848, but he recoiled from the violence in Paris in June when the workers rushed to the barricades. Although he conceded that their motives may have been good, he termed the laborers' uprising "criminal" and praised the general who crushed it. Similarly, though Americans turned out to cheer Louis Kossuth, the German communist refugees after 1848 arrived without fanfare, and when some of the Fortyeighters began to expound their radical ideas they were denounced for bringing class warfare to the United States. These events again demonstrated that the American endorsement of revolution did not extend much beyond constitutional and liberal change and reinforced the apparent connection between radicals and aliens.

The propertied and commercial classes were rather easily disturbed by portents of mob rule and were anxious to deploy the elastic ideology of republicanism against the unpredictable lower orders. The economic and social elites were rendered insecure by the system of representative government, for they could not be sure of winning elections, and they resisted the tendency to equate republicanism with democracy. In their eyes republicanism implied a respect for the individuality and property rights of all citizens and a popular willingness to entrust the reins of government to "the better sort."

The potency of American conservatism has sometimes been underestimated, and even in the second quarter of the nineteenth century, when egalitarian currents were at their strongest, there were conservatives trying to hold them back. When radical Democrats advocated measures that would promote a roughly equal distribution of property, Whigs denounced them for their "equalizing and mobocratic doctrines," which were sometimes likened to those of the godless French revolutionaries. The American conservatism represented by the Whig party replaced the aristocratic yearning of the Federalists with a vision of a meritocratic society, but this merely provided a republican legitimation of the acquisition of wealth. It also implied that the unsuccessful were without merit and increased middle-class suspicions that ungrateful American laborers could be turned against the capitalist system.

The extraordinary entrepreneurial and corporate thrust of the American economy through the middle decades of the nineteenth century did deepen class divisions in the cities, where both trade unions and employers' associations made their appearance. From the beginning businessmen and conservative editors, with their allies in local government, the courts, and the pulpit, saw something both alien and anticapitalist in labor agitation. They invoked the patriotic language of republicanism, with its promise of rights for all, against these signs of class unrest. In 1836 a New York jurist denounced labor combinations as "of foreign origin" and inconsistent with American conditions that ensured that "the road to advancement is open to all."

When New York workmen formed cooperatives and staged strikes in 1850, the *New York Herald* inveighed against the "vast importations of foreign socialists." Three years later the *Boston Daily Transcript* damned a wave of strikes as part of an international conspiracy that had "commenced in England" and aimed at the overthrow of sound government and private property. When hunger demonstrations and flour riots disturbed the peace of New York during the depression year 1857–58, the leading philanthropic organization of the city blamed "the ultra communistic radicals, who openly advocated pillage and plunder, . . . and other foreigners." It explained that the doctrine of the "rights of labor" originated in Old World conditions, where dependency was the norm, and had no place in the United States, where "no one man has rights which are not common to all, consequently no one has a right to demand work and wages from another." An antislavery newspaper denied that the flour riots represented the "real feelings" of working men: "Their style of proceedings and spirit have a flavor of communism about them; they suggest a foreign origin." The early attempts by labor and the urban poor to organize were thus immediately branded as both socialistic and foreign inspired, incompatible with the American philosophy of equal rights and equality of opportunity. To fervent believers in this version of the republican dream, business and patriotic values were inseparable, and labor organizations could only be perceived as offensively un-American.

The distaste of many Americans for political radicalism was reinforced by the belief that theirs was a Christian republic. The revolutionary hero Tom Paine had been expelled from the American pantheon for his attacks on Christianity, and even many Jeffersonian Republicans had cooled toward the French Revolution as it acquired a reputation for infidelity. Whatever part Protestant evangelists played in calling slavery and other moral evils to account, the thrust of their political and economic teaching was conservative, as they disavowed Jacksonian democracy, trade unions, and communitarian socialism. A redeemed soul, they believed, made one whole, responsible for one's own destiny, and the mutualist ethic of labor movements often seemed to them to be subversive of the individual's moral accountability. Revivalists insisted on the early conversion of the young in order to "get the start of error, infidelity, Socialism, anti-marriage, anti-property, anti-legal fanaticism, anti-Sabbath and anti-Christ." Church membership was high in the mid-nineteenth-century United States, and evangelical Protestantism, in identifying itself with patriotic, self-help, and individualistic values, helped immunize Americans to the lure of socialism.

Further, the republic itself was invested with a providential purpose, and despite the constitutional separation of church and state, attempts were made to cement republican forms with a civil religion, as when legislatures appointed their own chaplains and presidents proclaimed prayer days. What particularly aroused clerics were the agnosticism and rationalism that such socialists as Robert Owen and the German Forty-eighters avowed, not to mention the "free love" experiments of some of the utopian communities. The vibrant Puritan heritage was not the only religious obstacle encountered by free-thinking radicals. Immigrants were swelling the ranks of urban Roman Catholic congregations, where they sought reassurance in traditional teachings. The Irish in particular, the most reluctant of exiles, cherished the age-old values of Mother Church. Zealous Protestants and pious Catholics may have nursed mutual hatreds, but both were hostile to the infidelity and hedonism widely imputed to socialists and communists. The resolute Christianity of most Americans would long remain poised against any political ideology that dispensed with God.

In these decades, too, another source of long-standing hostility to political radicalism and reform took shape. The great majority of those citizens of the young republic who were so sensitive to their political rights shared a common heritage of race, ethnicity, and language. In the mid-nineteenth century the American capacity for self-government was sometimes attributed to the innate qualities of the Anglo-Saxon race, a claim that seemed to be vindicated by the failure of the Latin American republics to sustain liberty. The tendency to delimit rights by race was, of course, already deeply ingrained in American political culture, a consequence of white experience with black slavery and Indian "savagery." Even northern whites had reacted with horror to the establishment of the black republic of Haiti in 1804, which became a byword for bloody anarchy and despotism, a horrifying example of the misapplication of the revolutionary creed of the rights of man. But it was the South that most anxiously attempted to reconcile American republican doctrine with racial privilege. As sectional antagonism between North and South deepened in the middle decades of the nineteenth century, southern slaveowners came to regard almost all political and social agitation as menacing the society they dominated. Any attack on slavery, or on the southern system of race relations, they rightly perceived to be a challenge to their rule.

Poor southern whites, sensing a threat in freed blacks, closed ranks with their political and social leaders, ready to resist any form of egalitarianism that might disturb the prevailing racial patterns. Socialism was early perceived as one such form. For the most part the German radicals who settled in the United States were hostile to slavery. In San Antonio, Texas, such Germans were publishing antislavery bulletins by the 1850s, and in 1853 Adolph Douai, who was later to emerge as a leading Marxist, began to publish an antislavery newspaper there, only to be driven out of town. In the North too, many Forty-eighters supported the antislavery cause, the Communist Club of Cleveland in 1851 resolving to "use all means which are adapted to abolish slavery." The planters not unnaturally came to regard such forms of radicalism as inherently opposed to their peculiar institution, one function of which, it was said, was to protect the South "from the demands for Land Limitation . . . anti-rent troubles, strikes of workmen . . . diseased philanthropy, radical democracy and the progress of socialistic ideas in general." Even before the Civil War white southerners had come to regard socialism as a threat to the South's system of race relations, a conviction that was to endure for generations.

In 1848, at the behest of the officers of the Communist League, Karl Marx and Friedrich Engels completed and published *The Communist Manifesto*. The next major milestone in the history of Marxist socialism was reached in 1864 with the creation of the First International in London, when Marx joined with British trade unionists and representatives of European workers' groups to form the International Workingmen's Association to try to guide the international labor movement. This variant of communism was thus emerging at a time when some aspects of American political culture were tolerant and even protective of self-proclaimed revolutionaries and collectivist ideas. The American endorsement of revolution and the egalitarian thrust of American politics, the United States' receptivity to utopian experiments, and its acceptance of political refugees provided some basis for a tolerant attitude toward the revolutionary communism prophesied by Karl Marx.

But there were already powerful forces in American society that could be mobilized against any manifestation of Marxism or related doctrines. The broad configurations of class, race, and religion generally militated against the success of such ideas, and if wealthy businessmen, slaveholders, and church leaders were naturally antipathetic to economic and political theories that questioned their privileged status, the distributions of property, Anglo-Saxon genes, and religious convictions were so extensive as to ensure that millions of Americans shared their perspective. Perhaps more important, the republican heritage itself could be used to repulse communism, and business, religious, and even southern spokesmen proved ingenious in fusing their own values with those of the nation.

The cult of self-help, so gratifying to successful businessmen and politicans, pervaded American culture. "The idea instilled into the minds of most boys, from early life," said *Harpers Weekly* in 1853, "is that of 'getting on.' " Such self-regarding values were being promoted by the most powerful currents in American life in these decades. Conservative Americans had always fiercely resisted the leveling tendencies in American political culture, and a conservative construction of American society and politics was made more plausible by the fast-emerging industrial revolution, which separated employers from wage earners and encouraged the propertied classes to see labor organization as alien and communistic. Even in the Democratic party political radicalism was fading by 1850 as mainstream leaders accommodated themselves to the burgeoning commercial ethic.

That polarization that had existed in American politics from the 1790s on between hierarchically inclined conservatives and leveling radicals was being replaced by a consensus on political economy, which allowed no room for socialism. A new polarization was of course opening up between North and South, but the intensification of racial fears served only to leave a strong antiradical legacy among southern whites. The other major force of these years, an expansive evangelical Protestantism, also tended to stiffen values that were generally inimical to collectivist and rationalist doctrines. The American traditions of revolution and refuge, long compromised by the American preoccupation with property and individual rights, could not easily resist these tendencies. One figure to discover this was the remarkable Scotswoman Fanny Wright, who had excited widespread interest in the United States in the 1820s when she had first propounded her ideas, but the popular mood turned against her as she became the personification of socialism, atheism, feminism, and antislavery, and as early as 1836 she was stoned for her "disorganizing principles and precepts."

If antiradicalism did not yet suffuse American political culture, the potential was there for it to become at least a powerful force. The principal target of anticommunist rhetoric in the mid-19th century was the nascent labor movement and the related hunger demonstrations in the major cities. Employers, editors, and the propertied classes were already equating socialism with foreign influences and denouncing it in terms of the sanctity of private property and the equality of rights and opportunity afforded by the American system. The presence of German and other foreign radicals in the cities lent a spurious plausibility to the charge that the doctrine of the "rights of labor" was of alien pedigree. But while the labor movement remained weak anticommunist rhetoric remained sporadic, and the political convulsions of the mid-nineteenth century even seemed to offer such working-class socialists as there were some middle-class allies. The prodigious evil of slavery tended to divert radicals from the failings of capitalism, and many Forty-eighters were drawn into the antislavery movement and thence into the new Republican party, where they made common cause with northern evangelicals and businessmen. By the end of the Civil War the Communist Clubs that had been formed in the large cities had generally disappeared. In the Republican party, alongside the conservatives and moderates, there clustered men owning a variety of radical philosophies.

The Radical Republicans, led by middle-class veterans of the antislavery crusade, emerged in the mid-1860s as an influential force in American politics, determined to make the United States over in accordance with their equal-rights ideology and prepared to use government to this end. The more conservative elements in American society gave ground before this ideological onslaught. In Congress the Radical Republicans used their powers to try to displace the old white ruling class of the South. Businessmen were discomfited when Radicals attacked the concentrated power of wealth and monopoly, and the self-help ethos of American culture was gradually eroded by Radicals prepared to make some use of government to regulate social and economic conditions. Their egalitarian zeal and their willingness to extend the power of the state gave the Radicals something in common with the growing labor movement, which had been revitalized by the industrial expansion consequent on the Civil War.

Labor issues invaded local governments and state legislatures, and many Radical Republicans showed some sympathy for workers' demands. In Massachusetts in 1865–66 influential Radicals lent their support to labor demands for an eight-hour day, and in the United States Senate in 1868 the most determined advocates of an eight-hour bill were a group of Radical Republicans. This incipient alliance between middle-class Radicals and American workers never fully crystallized, but Radical sympathy at least afforded the labor movement some protection from those who saw it as communistic and alien. The heady Radical ambition to restructure American society was a mark of the revolutionary political impact of the Civil War. The libertarian and egalitarian principles of the American Revolution had been given a new vitality, and the Radicals felt they were aligned with the cause of progress throughout the world. As long as this optimistic vision retained its credibility, the forces of antiradicalism would remain at bay.

2

THE
SPECTER EMERGES
(1870–1900)

•

In the spring of 1871 the American press for the first time dwelled on the lurid horrors of a "red" revolution. The occasion was the Paris Commune, described by the *New York Herald* as a movement by "reds" to "uproot society and 'organize hell' in France." Newspapers were soon speculating that the conflict between labor and capital was such that even the United States might not be immune to "a sudden storm of Communistic revolutions." In the remaining decades of the century labor disputes regularly erupted into violence, and the menace of communism became a staple of American public discourse. The great railway strike of 1877 demonstrated the rebellious potential of American workers. The Haymarket Riot of 1886, when a number of policemen died as the result of a Chicago bombing, proved that "anarchists" were as great a danger as "Communards," and it reinforced the identification of communists—of any variety—with foreigners. The avalanche of immigrants from the more suspect parts of Europe in the closing years of the nineteenth century kept alive the fear that revolution was being imported. President McKinley's assassination by a professed anarchist in 1901 seemed to come close to the fulfillment of a prophecy.

Between the Paris Commune and the assassination of McKinley the United States became the world's leading industrial nation. The tonnage of steel ingots and castings produced increased over 180 times, the production of crude petroleum increased over 13 times, and the number of Western Union telegraph offices multiplied nearly fourfold. As this industrial and commercial colossus was erected, the small firms that at first characterized the economy were eventually joined by giant corporations representing millions of dollars of capital and employing thousands of workers. The disruptive effects of industrialization were felt particularly in the chaotically growing cities, which came to produce over 90 percent of factory output. The proportion of Americans living in urban areas swelled from about a quarter to 40 percent, and more ominously perhaps, the number of large cities—those with populations of over 100,000—grew from fourteen in 1870 to thirty-eight in 1900. Their working-class districts were increasingly peopled by strangers from abroad. The old networks of community relationships broke down as rapid expansion fragmented the cities into discordant class and ethnic neighborhoods, and as Lord Bryce observed, they became a byword for bad government.

It was the twin processes of industrialization and urbanization that accelerated the growth of anticommunism, the product of class conflict and the insecurity felt by the propertied orders. The proliferation of industrial enterprises created an expanding and powerful class that commandeered the libertarian heritage of the American political tradition, elaborating an ideology of acquisitive individualism that vindicated the capitalist reliance on the market. But it was also an insecure class because business failures were high; overproduction, massive competition, and remorselessly declining prices put a premium on controlling labor, and in almost every industry there were attempts to reduce wages. Workers often sought protection in collective action of some kind, whether in fraternal societies, labor unions, strikes, or boycotts, nurturing a mutualist ethic that could spell ruin to the employer. Many harried businessmen doubtless did believe that they were confronted by "communism" when their workers organized against them, and in any case it served their interests to identify labor resistance with a violent and un-American creed, for they might thereby win support in crushing it. The republican tradition itself, with its reliance on an active citizenry and limited government, virtually invited them to espy red revolution.

The struggles between capitalist and laborer were usually fought out in the cities, whose uncontrolled growth was in any case generating fears for social order. The conflict between capital and labor was paralleled by urban tensions between the propertied and the lower classes. Businessmen and professionals had readier access to city councils than did labor leaders, but labor representatives were sometimes elected, and machine politicians often forged alliances with immigrant groups. The will of employers and the respectable middle classes did not necessarily prevail in the cities, and they could not always look for assistance to the state legislatures, where rural interests often viewed industrialists as well as urban workers with distrust. A sense of insecurity aligned the urban middle classes for the most part with the employers. In 1872 the city missionary Charles Loring Brace, in *The Dangerous Classes of New York*, located the major threat to social order in the multiplying and dispossessed urban masses. Many respectable citizens, having little direct contact with urban workers or with newly arrived immigrants, scanned the streets for portents of insurrection.

The Specter of the Commune

The news of the Paris Commune sent a flicker of unease through the propertied classes of all Western nations. In March 1871 Parisian workers, with the support of the National Guard, established their own government and called for a federation of communes, the confiscation of property, and the guarantee of freedom for all. In the bloody days that followed, property was requisitioned, an attempt was made to abolish debt, and the archbishop of Paris and other clerics were shot without trial. In May the insurrection was ended, but already the Commune had become infamous in the eyes of respectable people everywhere. It stood as a fearful warning of the instability of the modern city, the potency of labor, and the revolutionary nature of socialism.

The American response to the news from Paris was perhaps not quite as uniformly hostile as was the response elsewhere. Americans had long been paying homage to the right of revolution, and egalitarian ideals had recently been reinvigorated by the Radical Republicans. A few middle-class radicals did express support for the Paris workers, and the former abolitionist Wendell Phillips deified the leaders of the Commune as "the purest and the noblest patriots of France," the libertarian heirs of "Vane, Sydney and John Brown," who "from their scaffolds call out . . . 'Be of good cheer, Brothers; the seed your blood has planted shall not die.' "

But Wendell Phillips was embarking on a career as a labor agitator, and most Radical Republicans were not prepared to follow him on this questionable course. Already Radicals who had emerged from the Civil War with some sympathy for labor aspirations were beginning to believe that workers' organizations were committing the sin of putting class before nation. The Austro-Prussian War of 1866 had killed the hopes of many German radicals for a revolution in Germany, and some of them began to inject a revolutionary note into the American labor movement. Early in 1868 German groups in New York formed the Social party, which within a year had been reconstituted as Section 1 of the International Workingmen's Association in the United States. For the first time American workers were being recruited into a revolutionary organization led from abroad. One consequence of the Paris Commune was to draw attention to the International, which had played its part in those momentous events. If Radical solicitude for labor had been weakened by industrial disputes and the workers' use of class rhetoric in the late 1860s, the destruction and bloodshed in the French capital further eroded it.

Public abhorrence of these events tarnished the appeal of Radical Reconstruction. The metropolitan press in the United States, reflecting the sensibilities of the urban middle and upper classes, reviled the Commune as a "revolution of pillage." Much was made of the expropriation of property, the repudiation of debt, the condemnation of landlords, and the murder of churchmen. "The short career of the Communists has been dreadful for its proscription and savagery," sighed a San Francisco paper as the Commune was suppressed. Leading journals like the *Nation* and the *New York Times* saw the Commune as a product of conflict between capital and labor and warned that the working classes of the American cities might similarly be incited to a revolt against property and individualism. The *New York Times* spoke of "the deep explosive forces which underlie all modern society" and of the specter "of a toiling ignorant and impoverished multitude, demanding an equal share in the wealth of the rich." Leading Protestant and Catholic clerics lamented the destructive consequences of atheism. Such middle-class apprehensions were not quieted by the enthusiastic support that several labor papers gave to the Commune, or by the meetings and demonstrations held in the larger cities to commemorate it. An official of the International in the United States wrote to London that "the ruling classes had the Commune on the brain."

Henceforth the idea of revolution, at least in the minds of the large numbers of propertied Americans, was associated less with the growth of liberty among an oppressed people and more with the selfish demands of labor. The ideal of republicanism itself, with its concern for the whole community, could be imperiled by revolution—that is, an insurrection of the lower orders. The violent potential of American urban workers had already been demonstrated by the New York "draft riots" of 1863, and the Paris Commune provided a truly terrifying model. The American sections of the International had barely been noticed before the Commune, but now they were invested with an aura of menace. When one Internationalist in 1872 publicly called for the use of arson in an eight-hour-day dispute in New York—also the occasion of an apparent murder attempt—the apparition of violence doomed the movement and enabled the employers' association to see "the outline of the spirit of communism." Even labor reformers began to distance themselves from the International, and the leading labor paper, the *Workingman's Advocate*, which had published Marx's defense of the Commune, by the end of 1872 was urging American workingmen to repudiate the "Anti-American element." As both the middle classes and working-class moderates turned against the International, its image as a violent, subversive, and alien organization began to approach conventional wisdom. When the International was dissolved in 1876, various radical groups formed the Working-Man's party of the United States (WPUS), becoming a year later the Socialist Labor party, which was similarly distrusted and isolated.

The fears of the respectable classes were kept vividly alive through the 1870s, which were punctuated by violent industrial disputes and urban disorders, particularly during the five harrowing years of depression beginning in 1873. On each occasion memories of the Paris Commune were invoked. Red scare tactics began to be used regularly to further the power of employers, to break trade unions, and to frustrate demands for public works. They were also deployed against those agrarian movements that sought to regulate private enterprise, notably against the state Granger laws, which attempted to put controls on railroads. The largest mine operator in Ohio's Hocking Valley refused to recognize a newly formed union branch in 1873–74 on the grounds that the concession would lead to "anarchy and bloodshed that would approach, if not equal, the Communism of Paris." A parade of the unemployed in Chicago was said to mark the destructive appearance of "La Commune," and when similar demonstrations in New York culminated in the so-called Tompkins Square Riot of 1874, when the red flag of the Commune precipitated the violent clash between police and workers, the police proferred evidence blaming the disturbances on Parisian "Communists," "heavily armed German revolutionaries," "atheists," and "drunkards." The "Molly Maguire Riots" in the Pennsylvania coalfields in the mid-1870s, as mine officials became the victims of murders and arson attacks imputed to a secret miners' order, greatly enhanced the public impression that unionists were drawn disproportionately from the violent, criminal, and foreign elements in the population.

The bitter industrial disputes of the depression came to a climax with the great railway strike of 1877, when for the first time in American history something like a national strike occurred, as distressed railroad workers across the country, reacting against successive wage cuts and blacklistings, withdrew their labor. The strike reached into seventeen states and won more supporters than any industrial dispute of the nineteenth century, a vivid signal that a new and unpredictable economic order was transforming the United States. As the disturbances mounted, local police and vigilante forces, the state militias, and even federal troops were mobilized against the strikers, and in the accompanying violence much railroad property and dozens of lives were destroyed. The respectable classes were thoroughly frightened by this near-simultaneous eruption of strikes on several railroads, as they were too by the resistance of whole communities to the railroad companies and the constituted authorities and by the fraternizing of local militias with the workers. The *New York Times* feared a general communist uprising and at one point headlined the message that Chicago was "in Possession of Communists." Much of Chicago was in fact brought to a standstill as workers in several industries joined the strike, which the mayor blamed on the "ragged Commune Wretches." In Terre Haute, Indiana, Richard W. Thompson, then secretary of the navy, spoke for the local business community when he called the strike "nothing more or less than French Communism . . . entirely at war with the spirit of our institutions."

What limited middle-class sympathy there had once been for the labor movement, as articulated by some Radical Republicans, did not survive the fearsome encounters of the 1870s. The Radical Republicans themselves were in retreat by the early 1870s, many of them abandoning their belief in state action and embracing the laissez-faire doctrines of the Liberals, ready to see any kind of socialism as un-American, an affront to the American tradition of individualism. The intensification of class conflict was producing an intellectual and ideological reaction that agreed the essence of American republicanism lay in equality of individual rights and opportunities in an unfettered world. The labor movement itself was disturbed by the violent and un-American characteristics imputed to it, and some elements sought to demonstrate their compatibility with American traditions. Early in 1874 a union local in New York denounced the "Communists, Internationalists, and other social disturbers" who were bent on "social anarchy," and later in the year the Industrial Congress, an annual gathering of trade unions and other labor bodies, declared itself "a purely American institution . . . neither having nor seeking an entangling alliance with foreign organizations or institutions." Samuel Gompers later claimed it was his own presence at the Tompkins Square "Riot" that showed him "how professions of radicalism and sensationalism concentrated all the forces of organized society against a labor movement," and by the late 1870s Gompers and others were beginning to pioneer that "pure and simple" unionism that gave greater priority to the immediate needs of members than to the reconstruction of society.

The economic and social formations that enabled socialism to be identified both with foreigners and with violent change were already greatly limiting its appeal, allowing middle-class liberals and also many labor reformers to be marshaled against it. This repudiation by both liberal intellectuals and labor spokesmen was to be repeated many times in American history, rendering socialist groups exceedingly vulnerable. In the 1870s, as later, the charges against social protest contained a tiny grain of truth. The International or WPUS members or other radicals usually were present somewhere in these outbursts of labor and urban discontent, and it was easy for employers and the ruling classes to raise the cry of red revolution indiscriminately. As John F. Bray, an old British

Chartist living in Pontiac, observed, "If the word had been in use among us a few years since, every anti-slavery man would have been denounced as a 'Communist.' "

Anticommunism was being developed as a weapon to isolate labor organizations and control the untamed urban masses. Invoking republican values, it legitimated the use of strong-arm tactics and the expansion of police powers, and it mobilized public opinion behind the business community. The anticommunist animus in the years following the Paris Commune stemmed largely from the employers, elected officials, police authorities, and newspaper editors of the large cities, though the big operators of mines and railroads were equally prepared to use red scare tactics against both labor and agrarian radicals. In the smaller towns, as the great railway strike illustrated, local officials and editors often sympathized with the workers, extending their protection to the vulnerable members of their own communities as they were menaced by outside forces such as strikebreakers or militia units sent in by the corporations or the state authorities. In the larger cities, however, there was greater hostility toward workers. That the Paris Commune had erupted in a metropolis was itself a fearful warning of the dangerous character of the urban lower classes. More significant, the ruthless commercial ethic of the bustling industrial city sanctified profit as the primary objective. Increasing residential segregation made the poor a distinct and suspect class in the eyes of respectable citizens, not neighbors but untrustworthy strangers whose alien nature was underlined by the increasing proportion of immigrants among them. Economic expansion both increased the distance between the classes and forged stronger links of identity within the business community, whose influence became extensive as it cultivated government officials and patronized civic institutions and the leading churches.

Although they were in the ascendancy, however, the business interests never acquired complete control over the urban environment, where machine politicians mobilized immigrants and labor groups had some political presence, and it was their relative insecurity that drove them to wage class war. A British visitor observed in 1877 that rich Americans were "pervaded by an uneasy feeling that they were living over a mine of social and industrial discontent with which the power of the government . . . was wholly inadequate to deal." So beleaguered were they that they attempted to turn the American republican heritage against the forces that threatened them.

The antilabor and antisocialist predilections of the upper and middle classes were upheld by the conventional wisdom of the day. Orthodox academic economists spelled out the virtues of laissez-faire. State action "should be permitted only when there is an absolute necessity," explained Professor J. Laurence Laughlin of Harvard University, "and even then it should be undertaken with hesitation." Such theorists insisted that workers benefited from the free enterprise of the capitalist, that trade unions were potential monopolies that disrupted the free market, and that labor actions like strikes were offenses against society and violated "the inalienable right of every individual to dispose of his industry and his property as he pleases." These academic doctrines were popularized by such stable journals as E. L. Godkin's the *Nation*, which described attempts to legislate on wages and hours as "communistic."

Like industrialists, academics and elite journalists tended to be recruited from the Anglo-Saxon and generally Protestant middle classes. The imperatives of religion, race, and even gender reinforced those of class. The Protestant clergy were preaching the message of self-help with more conviction than ever, and Roman Catholic priests too were elaborating on papal encyclicals depicting socialism as a threat to private property and social order. The laws of supply and demand, according to the leading church periodical the *Independent* in 1872, were as "immutable as those of gravitation or magnetism." In a sermon following the great railway strike of 1877, the popular Reverend Henry Ward Beecher deplored the importation of "the communistic and like European notions," thought "un-American" the idea that government should provide for the welfare of its citizens, described collectivist theories as destructive of that "individuality of the person" that alone preserved liberty, and unabashedly insisted that "God has intended the great to be great and the little to be little."

Patrician New Englanders, hankering perhaps for a day when they were accorded greater respect, also retreated into this kind of conservatism against the growing urban mob. In Boston the Reverend Joseph Cook held out the church as "the chief barrier against communistic and socialistic inroads from the howling sea of an ignorant and unprincipled population." Traditional moral values were also deployed in the war against communism, as when the activities of the feminists Victoria Woodhull and Tennessee Claflin in the International, with their reported championship of "free love" and sexual freedom, enabled it to be presented as a threat to the family as well as to private property. Such an image, Friedrich Sorge believed, prevented the International from establishing its influence among Irish Catholic immigrants.

The unstable nature of the urban population became more apparent to old-stock Americans as immigration continued to surge. In the 1870s the yearly number of immigrants averaged a little over a quarter of a million, but in the 1880s over half a million on average arrived each year. The numbers eased somewhat in the depression years of the 1890s, but by that time another characteristic of this immigration was becoming evident, the growing numbers from central, southern, and eastern Europe. As significant numbers of poor and apparently unskilled and illiterate Slavs and Italians appeared in the cities, the middle classes doubted whether such aliens could be successfully assimilated and American workmen became uneasy about their jobs. Such tensions eventually fueled a nativist movement that sought to restrict immigration. What gave nativism a particular potency was the fear of imported revolution. Racial and ethnic fears were reinforcing class fears of insurrection.

Foreigners had been accused of introducing radicalism as early as the 1790s, and the charge had been revived after the arrival of the German Forty-eighters and during the urban and coalfield riots and railroad strikes of the 1870s. In 1881 Harvard senior Curtis Field spoke for many of his class when he saw modern civilization threatened by "the ignorant mob misled by crafty demagogues, . . . Irish Molly Maguires, German socialists, French Communists, and Russian Nihilists." A few years later Andrew Carnegie restated an old theory when he described a Socialist procession as "a parcel of foreign cranks whose communistic ideas are the natural growth of the unjust laws of their native land, which deny these men the privilege of equal citizenship, and hold them down as inferiors from their birth." Conservative property owners worried that such perverse foreign radicals might put a flame to the tinderboxes of the cities. With the Haymarket Affair of 1886, such citizens saw their nightmare acted out before their eyes—or rather, in their imaginations.

The Haymarket Affair

No major city had grown faster and more uncontrollably than Chicago, and none had proved more attractive to European radicals. Where a small town stood before midcentury, midwestern and western expansion and industrial growth had thrown up a mighty urban colossus on the edge of the prairies. Chicago's population had reached 100,000 even before the Civil War, and it soared to over a million by 1890, German immigrants constituting the largest single ethnic group. Chicago, indeed, became something of a wonder of the world, much visited by foreign travelers, such as Rudyard Kipling, who called it a "real city"— adding that, having seen it, "I urgently desire never to see it again." Thronging Chicago's busy streets were country boys displaced from the farms and thousands of European immigrants, among them the Germans, some of whom had been captivated by the liberating promise of Marxism and anarchism.

The equation that native Americans often made between radicalism and the foreign-born carried a certain plausibility because it had a factual basis. Though the great majority of immigrants possessed conservative political and social temperaments, the various labor political groups did tend to be composed of foreigners, however few in number. The Socialist Labor party, which could trace its pedigree after a fashion to the First International via the WPUS, contained adherents of the ideas of both Karl Marx and his fellow German Ferdinand Lassalle. Whatever discord these competing socialist theories created for the Socialist Labor party, they were unmistakably of European origin, and after a poor showing in the 1880 elections, the party's membership of under fifteen hundred remained 90 percent foreign-born. In Europe the Marxists and Lassalleans were also competing with the communist anarchism associated with the Russian Mikhail Bakunin, and in 1881 various anarchist groups attempted to reconstitute the First International, forming what became known as the International Working Peoples' Association or, more notoriously, the Black International. Later that year revolutionary members of the Socialist Labor party in Chicago, New York, Philadelphia, and other cities, most of them Germans who had become disillusioned with the ballot box, created the Revolutionary Socialist party as a branch of the Black International in the United States. These anarchists firmly repudiated conventional political action; they believed in arming the workingmen so they could protect their rights and insisted that the workers had "but one recourse—FORCE." They gained members during the depression beginning in 1883, particularly in Chicago, where they probably had a membership of nearly a thousand, including supporters in the larger unions.

In 1886 Chicago became the center of labor agitation for an eight-hour day, and on 1 May some forty thousand workers laid down their tools, while a parade of eighty thousand followed the principal anarchist leader, Albert R. Parsons, through the city center. When police violence occurred three days later at the McCormick Harvester plant where hired Pinkerton guards and pickets had been clashing daily, local anarchists called a protest meeting in Haymarket Square, which was addressed by August Spies and other members of the Black International. The police arrived, a bomb was thrown at them and they opened fire on the crowd, a few members of which may have responded in kind. At the end of this bloody encounter one policeman lay dead, six more were dying, as was a similar number of civilians, and dozens were injured. The number of deaths was not as great as in the railway strike of 1877, but the deliberate throwing of a bomb at police officers seemed to presage an era of anarchy. Ever since the Paris Commune there had been fears about the insurrectionary potential of urban workers, and in Chicago the anarchists had been preaching revolution for years. The bomb vindicated the fearful prediction. The *New York Tribune*, speaking from a distance that allowed it to see what it had been waiting for, reported that "the mob appeared crazed with a frantic desire for blood, and, holding its ground, poured volley after volley into the midst of the officers."

Chicago was gripped with panic. Newspapers, businessmen, and churchmen demanded the immediate suppression of the "red ruffians." The International had been frightening Chicago merchants, industrialists, and dignitaries with its parades and demonstrations of popular support since 1884, and anarchists and police had clashed regularly and bitterly. The presence of the reformer Carter Harrison in the mayoralty and of socialists on the city council had done little to reassure the business community. After the bombing scores of radicals were rounded up, and the Chicago jails were soon filled with people who, according to one newspaper, "looked like communists." A zealous police squad regularly announced the discovery of dynamite or weapons, conveying the image of a widespread conspiracy to overthrow the city. Ten local anarchists, including Albert Parsons and August Spies, were indicted for murder, and eight—six of them foreign-born—were subsequently brought to trial. These men were central figures in Chicago's anarchist movement, which had prophesied revolution and extolled the use of dynamite, but the bomb thrower was never identified. The judge nonetheless ruled that if "by print or speech" the defendants had "encouraged" the commission of murder, even without designating time or place, then "all of such conspirators are guilty." Anarchist rhetoric was laced with violence, and the defendants were duly convicted, for their beliefs if not for their actions.

Across the country there were fears that the dynamite that exploded in Haymarket Square would signal risings in other cities, precipitating police raids and vigilante attacks on radicals and labor groups. Newspapers, clergymen, politicians, and labor leaders generally reacted to the bombing with horror and ascribed it to the vicious doctrines of communism and anarchism. To the Saint Louis *Globe-Democrat* there were "no good anarchists except dead anarchists," and the *Washington Post* voiced a widespread view in identifying anarchists with a "horde of foreigners, representing almost the lowest stratum found in humanity's formation."

The Chicago anarchists were the victims of America's first major red scare. Radical trade unionists had often enough lost their jobs, and some had died in the violent encounters between workers and police in the 1870s, but never before had the full machinery of the law been mobilized in the cause of anticommunism. A worried mayor, an insecure business community, a zealous police captain, an unscrupulous prosecution with access to business funds, juries composed largely of white-collar workers and businessmen, and a high-handed and biased judge, translated the general public conviction of an anarchist conspiracy into a legal verdict.

Seven of the accused were sentenced to death, and the eighth was given a prison term. The announcement was greeted with relief. The "people will breathe freer," sighed a New Orleans newspaper, and a Louisville editor agreed that "there is everywhere a feeling of greater security."

As the clamor for revenge died down, a modest measure of sympathy emerged for the condemned men. The unfairness of the trial, the behavior of the judge, and the harshness of the sentences disturbed such prominent figures as William Dean Howells and Henry George, and though their views remained those of a minority, a vigorous protest movement was launched. Labor groups of varying political persuasions held demonstrations in many cities, and anarchist theories enjoyed an airing they had never previously known. The Haymarket "martyrs" became a cause cèlébre, and pleas for clemency were made from all parts of the United States and Europe. Protest meetings were held even in Australia. In any event, one of the convicted men committed suicide and two had their sentences commuted to life imprisonment, but four died on the scaffold. For anarchists and labor activists throughout the world, they were the heroic victims of an implacable American capitalism.

The destruction of the anarchist leaders made possible by the Haymarket Affair reflected the apprehensions of the urban propertied classes, of the bankers, manufacturers, railroad barons, newspaper proprietors, of their allies in the legislative chambers, courts, universities, and churches, and of their sympathizers among upright citizens of all ranks. Long fearful that the exploding industrial city was a breeding ground for insurrection, they had sent a stark message to alien conspirators and the urban mob. The message was also directed at organized labor, which had been agitating for the eight-hour day. Radicalism had been growing in the depression, not only the social-revolutionary variety associated with the scattering of German anarchist groups, but also in the trade unions. A relatively new order, the Knights of Labor, had been particularly successful in enrolling unskilled workers who had never before been unionized, and they alarmed conservatives by calling for an end to "wage slavery" and for the establishment of producers' cooperatives. As labor disputes erupted during the hard times of the mid-1880s, employers' associations were formed in several cities, a mark both of the greater cohesion within each business community and of the growing chasm between the classes. The Haymarket victims were not hanged until November 1887, and through 1886–87 every labor disturbance was represented as a step toward anarchy.

In this intensified class war, employers used conspiracy charges, lockouts, blacklists, and Pinkerton detectives in fierce antiunion campaigns. Illinois, responding to the alarums of its beleaguered metropolis, enacted the first state criminal syndicalism law. In part because of the assaults on labor, local labor parties appeared in several cities, to the further distress of businessmen. The most celebrated was formed in New York behind the advocate of the single tax, Henry George, who won nearly a third of the vote in the mayoral election of 1886, despite being labeled an "apostle of anarchy and destruction." George's strong showing was another sign of the uncertain control of the urban upper classes. Charges of communism and anarchism were leveled indiscriminately at trade unions and labor parties, alien and violent characteristics being imputed to them in order to marginalize and destroy them. This offensive enjoyed considerable success, since the labor movement generally suffered from the sustained outrage aroused by the Haymarket Affair. In the late 1880s there were sharp drops in strike activity and in the membership of the Knights of Labor (which had begun to meet reverses before the bombing).

Many trade unionists concluded that their cause would best be served by dissociating themselves from radicalism and violence, and the Knights of Labor themselves bitterly condemned "the red flag of anarchy." At the end of 1886 the American Federation of Labor (AFL) was formed, committed to Samuel Gompers's gradualist philosophy of "pure and simple" unionism, and this organization of craftsmen soon won preeminence in the labor movement. Haymarket and its aftermath had played a part in directing American labor on its nonsocialist and even antisocialist course. The Haymarket Affair also left an indelible image on the native mind of foreigners as radical revolutionaries. In 1888 Congressman George E. Adams of Chicago introduced a bill "to provide for the removal of dangerous aliens from the territory of the United States." Given the prevailing definition of the red menace, this was a logical response.

Antiradical Responses

The proposal to deport aliens proved premature, but the scares of the 1870s and 1880s were prompting citizens to take defensive measures. Their responses were conditioned by a governmental framework characterized by Stephen Skowronek as one of "courts and parties," that is, a strong judicial system and active party competition, but not much in the way of government supervision or bureaucratic agencies. Frustratingly limited in their access to coercive power, the propertied classes reached for the language of republicanism to outlaw their enemies. Their responses were also informed by their perceptions of the mutualistic ethic of labor as dangerously obstructive of the acquisitive individualism of the employer, of the industrial city as exploding out of control, and of anticapitalist doctrines riding in on the backs of immigrants.

The business interests adhered fiercely to a laissez-faire ideology in part so that their own activities would not be regulated in the interests of farmers and laborers, but their insistence on limited government left them with inadequate forms of social control. Municipal government in particular seemed barely to be functioning, at least in the larger cities. The railway strike exposed the weakness of the local police forces, which, according to a police historian, in many cities were "unable to protect corporate property from mobs of rebellious workers." Over the following decade considerable resources were devoted to expanding, training, and professionalizing city police forces, which won a legitimacy in the eyes of honest citizens that they had not previously been accorded. The Haymarket Affair added to the incentive to complete the transformation of the police into disciplined and effective agents of law and order. In the 1880s the number of police per capita in Chicago almost doubled, and similar increases were effected in several other large cities. Merchants, bankers, and manufacturers were among the leading champions of these reforms. In Chicago, following the Haymarket Affair, leading business men raised perhaps $100,000 each year for the use of the police.

More in keeping with American traditions of government was the militia, with its reliance on citizen soldiers to protect the republic. This too was overhauled, particularly after the 1877 strikes revealed flaws in the system, for some militiamen had joined the strikers and others proved trigger-happy. In the urban-industrial states in particular appropriations were increased, riot training was emphasized, greater central control was introduced, and armories were established near major cities. The militia's voluntary nature permitted some scope for businessmen to increase their influence over it; they made financial contributions, and its officer class came to reflect industrial and merchant interests. From the 1880s, when the militia became generally known as the National Guard, it became a principal instrument for attacking the labor movement, and many unions prohibited their members from joining. The heirs of the citizen soldiers who had repulsed British tyranny were being invited once more to defend republican liberty. "The volcano of Communism burns angrily beneath the thin crust of civil law which holds it in subjection," wrote one National Guardsman, and "it falls to the lot of the young men of the country to stand as a bulwark in times of emergency in defense of liberty and the preservation of law and order."

In much the same spirit, businessmen and other citizens harnessed the vigilante tradition to the purposes of industrial and urban order, turning to citizens' associations, "law and order" leagues, and private detective agencies like the Pinkertons. In Saint Louis in 1877 the rich formed a "citizens' militia" to suppress a strike that was being represented as a "commune." A citizens' association in Chicago declared that its object was "to fight Communists," and in 1878 it presented the city with two Gatling guns. The detective and security forces employed by corporations not only coerced strikers and others but also claimed power to arrest them and on occasion exercised direction over the police. The American militia and vigilante traditions, themselves in part a product of the distrust of strong government, blurred the distinction between public and private responsibilities and allowed business and propertied interests a considerable role in law enforcement. To justify their resort to quasi-military forces, they had to insist that not only were their own businesses in peril, but so was the republic itself. The red menace became an ally of the urban propertied elites in their quest for social control.

But in the polity of "courts and parties" there was a limit to how far merchants and industrialists could effect changes in the law. State legislatures were arenas for party competition rather than sustained policymaking, and their sensitivity to rural and even labor and reform interests did not make them compliant creatures of the corporations unless large sums of money were spent on them. In any case, the prevailing laissez-faire doctrines did not encourage positive state action. In the absence of legislation businessmen turned for protection to the courts, which had already begun to exercise an extensive supervision of economic affairs. In an era of conservative politics, corporation lawyers were often appointed to the bench. The courts were not immune to the conservative ideological currents of the day and increasingly adopted the perspective of management, agreeing that property was essential to social order. A railroad attorney argued before the Supreme Court that the Granger laws represented "the beginning of the operation of the commune in the legislation of this country." Old conspiracy laws were revived and employed against unions. Federal and state courts became more prepared to issue injunctions against strikers and union boycotts, no longer confining injunctions to cases of immediate danger to physical property. The Massachusetts Supreme Court on one occasion upheld an injunction against a two-man picket line. Collective action by workers was being treated as a species of criminal conspiracy, a technique that was also to be deployed against the Communist party in the twentieth century.

Reinforcing the conservative instinct to protect the existing distribution of property was a nativist instinct to protect the standing of old-stock Americans and their religious values. The republican tradition of an active citizenry was invoked not only by the vigilante "law and order" leagues but also by the host of patriotic societies that sought to defend the republic from alien and subversive influences. These groups extended considerably beyond the urban business elites, but they helped to mobilize public opinion behind the objective of taming the foreign mob. In California in the wake of the Haymarket Affair a railroad attorney founded the American party to combat "the restless revolutionary horde of foreigners who are now seeking our shores from every part of the world." That party did not survive long, but a number of other organizations emerged to harness the patriotic instinct that immigrants were awakening in native-born Americans. Well-established families, no longer enjoying the influence that had once been theirs, formed hereditary societies like the Sons of the Revolution, the Daughters of the American Revolution, and the Order of Founders and Patriots. The well-to-do gentlemen and gentlewomen and the prosperous business and professional men who composed those societies tended to be hostile to both immigrants and radicals. These societies were soon sponsoring patriotic history textbooks and prize essays in schools, launching a tradition of the patriotic surveillance of public education. Farther down the social scale secret fraternal organizations were reinvigorated, among them the Patriotic Order Sons of America and the Order of United American Mechanics, which denounced revolutionary agitators who came from abroad "to terrorize the community and to exalt the red flag of the commune above the Stars and Stripes!"

Several such groups in effect merged with the American Protective Association, formed in 1886 to resist the growing influence of Catholics in politics, schools, and the labor movement. The suggestion that much industrial unrest was the product of a papist plot made Protestant unease at Catholic immigration serve an antiradical purpose. Some of the patriotic, veteran, and nativist organizations became influential interest groups in their own right, not only shaping public opinion but also lobbying school authorities and city and state governments. Among the antisubversive products of such activity were state laws of the 1890s requiring that the American flag be displayed and that American history and civics be taught in public schools.

The antiradical strategies fashioned in response to labor and urban unrest, the railroad strike, and the Haymarket Affair faced their most challenging tasks in the 1890s. The intense class and sectional conflict of that decade called into question the urban-industrial order that was emerging, but the ruling classes, however alarmed they may have been, were now well equipped to defend their citadel. Further, the course of American economic development was bringing employers new allies. Major industrial corporations now transcended city and even state boundaries, as did the much weaker union bodies that sought to combat them. Industrial conflict was no longer primarily fought out within particular urban communities, and state governments were more regularly drawn into the task of controlling radicalism, as on occasion was the federal government. In this rapidly changing polity, it became more important to businessmen to know they had friends in the governors' mansions and in the White House.

The urban-industrial elites also entered the 1890s having successfully designated socialism and communism as un-American, as not only of alien inspiration but also possessed of perverse religious and moral values. They had used the ideology of Christian republicanism to discredit them. Radicals sought to avoid being tagged with socialist labels. An important socialistic movement of the day was inspired by Edward Bellamy's prophetic novel *Looking Backward* (1888), but Bellamy used the word "nationalism" to describe his utopian philosophy, and his movement was conducted through a chain of "nationalist" clubs. Such vocabulary was more consistent with the patriotic spirit of these years than the suspect language of socialism. As Bellamy himself observed, "the words socialist and communist fall unpleasantly on American ears, being generally taken as implying atheistic or superstitious beliefs and practices." In 1891 a district court judge in Texas denied the citizenship petition of a German socialist on the grounds that the principles of socialism were "un-American" and "antagonistic to the principles of the constitution of the United States."

The ideological, legal, and military weapons that the manufacturing and commercial classes had been developing in response to the threats of urban insurrection enabled them to survive the great sectional and class confrontations of the closing years of the century. Their indiscriminate use of red-baiting tactics was illustrated by their response to farm anger. For years long-term economic forces had been destroying the livelihoods of many staple farmers in the cotton and tobacco states of the South and in the wheat states of the trans-Mississippi West, and in the hard times of the 1890s agricultural discontent erupted in the Populist movement. This assault on the business community in the name of the people, accompanied as it was by demands for the free coinage of silver, public ownership, and progressive taxation, was easily represented as a socialistic threat to the propertied and respectable classes everywhere. When the Democrats in 1896 accommodated themselves to Populist passions by adopting William Jennings Bryan as presidential candidate and including a free-silver plank, the *Philadelphia Press* charged that "this riotous platform rests upon the four cornerstones of organized repudiation, deliberate confiscation, chartered communism, and enthroned anarchy." The Whigs back in the 1830s had sometimes accused the Democrats of a crazed leveling agrarianism, but 1896 was perhaps the first occasion in American presidential politics when a major political party was explicitly smeared with "communism." Recognizing the challenge to the urban-industrial system, many employers instructed their workers to vote for the Republican candidate, William McKinley, whose election they greeted with considerable relief. "By defeating Mr. Bryan," said *Harper's Weekly*, "the country has escaped an actual experiment in Socialism."

Socialist and revolutionary intentions were also espied behind the labor protests of the 1890s. Acts of collective resistance by workers were almost routinely condemned as forms of insurrection, variants on the Haymarket Riot—that is, as assaults on the law, private property, and social order. The widespread identification of labor activists with foreigners encouraged the perception of their behavior as illicit. When "workmen were all American," recalled charity workers in Boston, "strikes and contests were unknown." During a spate of strikes in 1892 the governors of several states obligingly sent in the National Guard and sometimes allowed it to be used to destroy unions. They had accepted the business community's view of organized labor as inherently subversive, as incompatible with that fraternal republican tradition that insisted on the indivisibility of the common weal.

The most celebrated confrontation occurred at Andrew Carnegie's Homestead mills, then directed by Henry Clay Frick, who fired all union workers and surrounded the town with Pinkerton detectives. After violence broke out the governor sent in the militia, and the state prosecuted union leaders under an 1860 treason law. The Pennsylvania chief justice spoke for the new urban-industrial order when he equated the strikers' attempt to retain some control over their workplace with "insurrection and rebellion." No convictions were secured, but the strike and the union had been destroyed by the process of branding the workers as subversive. "Pennsylvania can hardly appreciate the actual communism of these people," said the National Guard commander. "They believe the works are theirs quite as much as Carnegie's." The presentation of the dispute as an assault on the republic was abetted by an assassination attempt on Frick by a foreign-born anarchist.

The need to defend republican order also drew the federal government into combating labor subversion. The city of Chicago had remained a cauldron of class and nativist hatreds, and in 1893, when the country was plunged into a devastating economic depression, the business-oriented city fathers prohibited the holding of a national convention of anarchists. The governor of the state, however, the pro-labor John Peter Altgeld, could not be relied on to behave with such circumspection, and in the same year he alarmed conservatives throughout the country by pardoning the surviving Haymarket anarchists. Altgeld's reliability became an issue during the mighty Pullman strike of 1894, when Eugene V. Debs's fast-growing American Railway Union decided to boycott Pullman cars. Soon some twenty thousand railroad employees were on strike in and around the country's most crucial railroad center. The strike commanded national attention, the *New York Tribune* speaking of "the greatest battle between labor and capital that has ever been inaugurated in the United States." Conservatives bitterly complained that the public was being made to suffer as well as the Pullman company. When Altgeld proved reluctant to move against the workers, the federal government decided to intervene: the attorney general designated the boycott a "conspiracy in restraint of trade" and secured a court injunction ordering an end to it. Federal troops were sent into Chicago, where for several nights there were burnings in the rail yards, and several deaths occurred. What the governor of Illinois was able to view as a labor dispute the federal government viewed as something approaching an insurrection. Even twenty years after the event William Howard Taft recalled the action of the railwaymen as an attempt to "terrorize a community" and to "take the country by the throat." Debs was indicted for conspiracy and sent to prison for contempt for refusing to obey the court order, his fate thus demonstrating the efficacy of "government by injunction." Unionists, it seemed, were now the enemy within, subversive and lawless conspirators who should be put behind bars.

The legal and military suppression of labor and other protests in the 1890s was the more ruthless because the propertied classes did feel besieged. A considerable part of the nation was arrayed against them, particularly during the devastating depression of 1893–97. Displaced tenant farmers, hunger marchers, and brutalized strikers were capable of evoking public sympathy, and radical doctrines did gain ground in labor circles. At its national convention of 1893 the American Federation of Labor endorsed a socialist program including "the collective ownership by the people of all means of production and distribution." Businessmen were not altogether mistaken in perceiving the red menace in labor activities, at least if the menace were defined in terms of the public appropriation of some forms of property. But the power and influence of the established classes prevailed, and the radical tide ebbed. In the Pullman dispute the authorities demonstrated the raw power they could wield, while labor emerged from it once more implicated in acts of violence. The AFL determined to avoid a direct confrontation with capital and distanced itself from the strike, and after it the AFL national convention declined to endorse the socialistic program approved the previous year. These craft unions also repudiated sympathy strikes, further distancing themselves from the growing numbers of unskilled industrial workers. The number of strikes dropped after 1894, a mark, at least in small part, of the success of business interests in imputing to them unAmerican, subversive, and criminal characteristics. In 1894 too a reinvigorated Republican party won control of Congress, and with the victory of McKinley in 1896 and the return of prosperity in 1897 the urban-industrial elites could feel secure in their ascendancy.

.

During the last three decades of the nineteenth century a strong anticommunist persuasion had emerged in American political culture. The scattered attacks on labor radicals in antebellum America had been succeeded by influential campaigns to identify the mutualist ethic of the workers with alien and revolutionary doctrines. The right to revolution that Americans had once claimed was not conceded to those who were held to be advancing class at the expense of common interests. Republican liberty was indivisible, and an active citizenry needed to be aroused to protect it. The equal-rights ideologies proclaimed earlier by such groups as the Jacksonian Democrats and Radical Republicans had given ground to a pervasive definition of the American promise of equality as one of opportunity, a right by individuals to pursue their own destinies without the guiding hand of government. As this belief found expression in economic, sociological, and political theory, the collectivist and statist ideas of socialism took on an increasingly subversive cast. Since most socialists and labor leaders were European immigrants, their ideas were reviled as the class-inspired products of the hopelessly class-ridden Old World, not only unnecessary but positively dangerous when introduced into the egalitarian but fragile American republic. By the close of the century demands were being made to withhold the traditional privilege of refuge from foreign radicals.

It was the rise of industrial and urban America, serviced by a growing immigrant work force, that was effecting these changes in political attitudes. The inexorable growth of the new order masked the insecurity of individual businessmen, whose capacity to make a profit was threatened by the collectivist actions of their workers, and of the urban middle classes, who watched their cities expand beyond the capacities of the archaic municipal governments. It was in their struggles to control the workplace and the city that employers and the propertied classes developed the ideology of anticommunism, couched in the values of the imperiled republican community. Their fears were real enough, for they had long since been taught that the republic was easily subverted, and insurrection seemed only too possible in the strange and troubled world of the industrial city. But anticommunism was also used as a weapon, a means of damaging or removing political enemies. And it was also a tool, an instrument that allowed the business classes to increase their influence over government and to expand the resources at the command of the urban-industrial order.

American religious and racial values were also pressed into the antiradical cause. Protestant and Catholic churchmen alike darkly viewed socialist rationalism as atheistic and amoral, even though many American socialists did embrace the ethics of Christianity. Old-stock Americans feared for their own status and the good order of society as the cities filled up with eastern and southern European immigrants, a form of subversion that was readily associated with a political intent. Patriotic Americans sprang to the defense of their Anglo-Saxon republic, bequeathing a host of patriotic societies that would long remain vigilant sentinels on the ramparts of liberty.

The patriotic crusade enjoyed considerable success. The professional and middle classes and many American intellectuals aligned themselves with the emerging urban-industrial order, leaving the radicals with little protection. Even the American labor movement, at least that part of it represented by the craft-oriented AFL, for a variety of reasons was set on a firmly nonsocialist course, and in time it would become a major component of the anticommunist cause. By the turn of the century American businessmen were even acquiring a degree of control over the urban environment, although they were turning to municipal reform to enhance their ascendancy. Yet by locating the red menace in foreign-born radicals, patriots were marginalizing rather than terminating the threat. Foreign workers, after all, were needed. Despite the hangings in Chicago, aliens continued to invade the land.

The Haymarket executions may have disrupted the anarchist movement in Chicago, but these martyrdoms stirred interest and sympathy elsewhere. For Emma Goldman "the Chicago tragedy was the awakening of my social consciousness." Similarly inspired was Alexander Berkman, who made the attempt on the life of Frick. Berkman was Russian-born, and his example reinforced the image of anarchism as an alien monster, as did the murders of a French president, a Spanish prime minister, and an Austrian empress by anarchist assassins in the 1890s. When the king of Italy met a like fate in 1900, Chicago anarchists celebrated the event. Nonetheless, attempts to prohibit anarchist immigration, supported mainly by the urban-industrial communities in the North and East, failed to command majorities in Congress. The proponents of restriction received vindication of a kind when the personification of urban-industrial America, President McKinley, was assassinated in September 1901 by Leon F. Czolgosz, a self-proclaimed anarchist. The European terror, it seemed, had come to America.

3

THE ANTIANARCHIST
OFFENSIVE
(1900–1918)

•

THE ASSASSINATION of President McKinley, as it happened, did not trigger an intensive red scare. Anarchists certainly received unwelcome attention, but for the moment the hostility toward radicals and aliens was largely confined to particular areas and interest groups. A Progressive spirit was already invading American public life, as the confidence created by the renewed prosperity, combined with uneasy memories of the recent class violence, fostered a popular mood broadly sympathetic to proposals for economic, social, and political reform.

In many cities members of the middle classes, who not long since had been reviling the seething hordes around them, found some attraction in Progressive solutions, which promised to end class conflict by removing the most conspicuous evils of urban life, promoting greater economic equality, and subordinating vested and individual interests to "the general welfare." Insofar as Progressivism responded to the tensions of industrialization by advancing reform as an alternative to either repression or revolution, it was able to recruit supporters from a variety of classes and constituencies and to promote greater accord between them. Middle-class Progressives looked with some sympathy on workers and their causes, and the more radical Progressives found occasional good words even for the more militant of labor organizations. This commitment to a "cooperative commonwealth" among many of the men and women in public life in Progressive America afforded a measure of protection to the groups that had been tormented by the nativist and antiradical impulses of the late nineteenth century.

The Progressive spirit was strong in the major cities, where fears of urban insurrection had somewhat abated. But an accommodationist mood did not suffuse the entire society, and many businessmen continued to use red scare tactics against "union tyranny." The resilience of class conflict was demonstrated by the formation of employers' associations, particularly in the Midwest, West, and Southwest. Before the twentieth century the South and especially the West had been relatively free of active and organized antiradicalism, and nativism too had been slow to reach these areas, not making much headway until the depression of 1893. During the Progressive Era propertied interests frequently envisioned communists and anarchists in these developing regions. The geographical sources of antiradicalism were being redistributed somewhat, in response to the course of economic development, although the principal target remained the same. It was the foreign anarchist who was identified as the most serious threat to American society, and insecure local businessmen and state politicians administered their own remedies until the outbreak of the First World War afforded them the opportunity to entangle the federal government in their cause.

The growth of government as well as of the economy was influencing antiradical strategies. To a considerable degree, by the 1900s the focus of class conflict had shifted from city to state, as in the West in particular the resources of state governments were frequently mobilized against strikers and labor organizations. But the definition of the red menace as the foreign anarchist limited the states' ability to act, for immigration was a federal responsibility, and by the 1910s considerable pressure was being placed on Washington for greater curbs on radical aliens. Progressive reform was tending to enhance the authority of the federal government, but Progressives and especially Democrats were reluctant to join an antilabor crusade. It was the First World War that escalated the western drive against alleged anarchists and other radicals into a national campaign. As the Wilson administration mobilized patriotic emotions and vigilante energies in the war effort, Progressive sensibilities weakened and new weapons were forged to prosecute the antianarchist offensive.

The Progressive Mood

For many Americans in the 1900s reform offered a more constructive response to the threat of radicalism than outright repression. The dread example of the Paris Commune was more than a generation in the past, and the ambiance of affluence soothed some of the old tensions. Muckraking journalists drew attention to the ills within American society, pungently providing evidence that some of the most powerful institutions themselves, such as political machines and the major corporations, were at fault.

Progressive reform was being advanced particularly as the answer to the social problems of the cities. Businessmen were themselves often eager to support municipal reform, seeing it as a means of creating urban environments where business might thrive. For some, Progressive reform was an antidote to socialism. "We have no extreme Bolsheviks, and we have no extreme radicals in the City of St. Louis," a spokesman for that city was to boast at the end of the reform era, "because we have a department of public welfare here that has been functioning for the last ten years." The profusion of immigrants and the presence of anarchists and socialists in the labor movement continued to cause unease, but the Progressive mood encouraged accommodationist responses. Many Progressives did see good reasons to restrict immigration, but there was also substantial support for programs to "Americanize" the immigrants. Social workers in the city settlements had been trying to find ways of integrating immigrants into American society for some years, and patriotic societies like the Daughters of the American Revolution sponsored lectures and classes to teach newcomers the principles of American citizenship. It was the assassination of McKinley that propelled the Sons of the American Revolution into such programs. In New York in the Progressive years Frances Kellor led campaigns to secure better education and protective welfare legislation for immigrants. In 1914 she and others formed the Committee for Immigrants in America, and the outbreak of the First World War gave considerable impetus to the Americanization movement.

Some employers were also taking a more tolerant attitude toward labor. In 1900 the National Civic Federation (NCF) was formed, composed of representatives of business, labor, and the public, with the object of promoting industrial peace through an acceptance of trade unionism and the use of conciliation and arbitration. Some of the country's biggest businessmen identified themselves with the NCF. For this group trade unionism was "consonant with American institutions" and an "antidote for the socialistic propaganda." Other employers remained skeptical and continued to deploy republican values against labor organizations. The National Association of Manufacturers, which tended to represent small businessmen, was fiercely antiunion and strongly endorsed the "open shop" crusade to ban union influence in industrial plants. Employers of this persuasion organized employers' associations in many midwestern cities and encouraged local businessmen, professional men, and other stable elements to form citizens' alliances to resist union demands. And in 1903 a national Citizens' Industrial Association was created to uphold "free institutions," repudiate labor violence, and combat "legislation of a socialistic nature." Nonetheless the arbitration procedures and welfare schemes of the NCF, however fitfully implemented, represented an alternative to repression. For many businessmen the question whether to support the conciliation or the open shop option was one of tactics.

The accommodationist mood of Progressivism helped to avert a serious red scare following the assassination of McKinley, although a lone assassin's bullet could not inspire the same fear of the mob as an anarchist's bomb. Nonetheless, the killing briefly revived antiradical sentiments, and the official response to it anticipated the later thrust of government policy with respect to controlling the menace of red revolution. In Chicago and elsewhere a number of anarchists were arrested, including Emma Goldman, but there was no evidence that they had been conspiring with Czolgosz, and they had to be released. Less fortunate was Johann Most, who as it happened had reprinted in his journal *Freiheit* some old revolutionary writing championing tyrannicide hours before the assassination, and he went to prison for a year for advocating murder. Around the country settlements of philosophical anarchists, who did not believe in the propaganda of the deed, were harassed and sometimes attacked by mobs. Even apologists for anarchism, argued the new president Theodore Roosevelt, who had once hanged the Haymarket anarchists in effigy, were "morally accessible to murder before the fact," and he called for legislation to bar anarchists from entering the country and to deport alien anarchists who advocated assassination.

Congress, for the first time in American history, finally concluded that it was legitimate to turn people away from the United States because of their political beliefs. The Immigration Act of 1903 provided for the exclusion of defined categories of anarchists and prevented anarchist aliens who were already in the country from becoming naturalized. Federal laws were at last tentatively being fashioned for use against radicalism, and this precedent would be enlarged in later red scares. The irony in these proceedings was that Czolgosz was not foreign-born, but Congress had been unable to agree on legislation to control domestic anarchists. The federal government's limited powers meant there was little it could do to police the social order. This was a state responsibility, and three states, New York, New Jersey, and Wisconsin, illustrating the government activism of the Progressive Era, did enact criminal anarchy laws, seeking to prohibit advocating the forcible overthrow of the government and the assassination of public officials to that end.

Before the First World War, when reform was offered as the cure for social discontent, the federal and state antianarchist laws were not often invoked, although there was a minor furor in 1903–4, when the English anarchist John Turner was barred and a Free Speech League was formed to fight his case, asking the question, "Shall the Federal Government be a Judge of beliefs and disbeliefs?" The Supreme Court apparently thought it could be, for it upheld the new law. Anarchism was being officially defined as un-American. Thereafter the control of anarchism largely reverted to individual employers and the states, until continued class conflict in the West eventually intersected with the First World War to recruit a strengthened federal government to an intensified antiradical drive.

The relatively benign attitudes toward immigrants and workers that could be discerned in Progressive America seem in significant part to have been associated with the urban-industrial centers of the North and East, with the corporation leaders and professional men who constituted a substantial part of their elites, and with middle-class reformers anxious to promote social harmony. There were important exceptions to these accommodationist tendencies throughout the United States, but some of the most unrestrained assaults on radicalism were to be found in the Southwest, Midwest, and West. As the nation's older cities were learning to live after a fashion with their radicals and aliens, antiradicalism was emerging as a potent force in these other rapidly developing regions.

The War on Wobblies

When the most conspicuous locus of class conflict shifted from the metropolitan areas to the western mines, lumber camps, and large-scale agricultural enterprises, it came to center on economic activities that were not contained within traditional city boundaries. The responsibility for policing the conflict, that is, rested not so much with the municipal authorities as with the state governments. Although there was pressure on city governments, as in Seattle, to curb radicalism, increasingly the business and press barons expected the state to act. The Progressive ethos was enjoining the greater use of government powers to regulate industrial society, and conservative interests sometimes attempted to turn the strengthened spring of state government to their own account. The control of aliens and of migratory labor, however, was beyond the power even of the states, and by the 1910s several western states were appealing to the federal government to take action against radical labor movements. Rather as Progressivism is said to have moved from city to state to federal levels, so did antiradicalism.

Economic growth in the first two decades of the twentieth century was still transforming large parts of the United States and generating social tensions. The expansion of the western economies was dependent in part on the section's exploitation of its mineral, lumber, and petroleum resources, and these industries expanded under the guidance of increasingly powerful corporations. In both the Southwest and the West agriculture revived after the hard times of the mid-1890s, along with agricultural industries like canning. In some areas these processes were associated with changing patterns of landownership as small farms were swallowed up by large ones, and with the emergence of large-scale commercial farms or—as they would later be called—"agribusinesses" as large landowners came to direct what was almost a form of industrial enterprise. The large landowners often developed substantial investments in the commerce, banking, and industry of their region, links with the press, and considerable influence in local and state politics. Uncertainly riding the economic boom, however, they sought allies in the difficult task of disciplining their workers.

In the traditional South, economic elites still constituted the political rulers, albeit shaken by the recent Populist fury, and the planters in the Black Belt and the bankers in the towns were joined by industrialists eager to use cheap labor to exploit the region's natural resources of coal, lumber, and oil. If the poll taxes and literary tests of these years were mainly the products of the racism and insecurity of white southern leaders, they also represented a resurgence of their traditional antiradicalism, for poor whites as well as blacks lost votes in the process. In the 1890s congressional support for legislation against alien radicals had tended to come from the industrial cities of the North and East; the strongest support for bills requiring a literacy test for immigrants in the 1910s—which often contained clauses barring revolutionaries—came from the South and the Far West.

Through the Progressive Era, then, class violence continued to flicker in the mines, lumber camps, canneries, orchards, and tenant farms of the West and Southwest. Several of the features that had characterized the major cities in the late nineteenth century and had been conducive to a red scare atmosphere—a concentration of capital, an insecure ruling class, even a growing immigrant labor force tinged with radicalism— were appearing in the western economies. When the tenants of one absentee farm owner in Coleman County, Texas, struck for better conditions in 1908, the owner mobilized the local merchants and sheriff against them and declared the battle part of the nationwide struggle against "red agitation." In parts of the Southwest independent farmers were being turned into tenants at a prodigious rate—in Oklahoma fewer than 1 percent had been tenants in 1890, but 54 percent were by 1910— and the Socialist party, which had been formed in 1901 from the moderate wing of the Socialist Labor party and various Marxist and trade union groups, made rapid advances.

More threatening than the Socialist party to the employers of the West, however, was the emergence of labor militancy. The mining communities of the mountain states, where the Knights of Labor had once had a presence, were not new to industrial conflict, which had been intense in the 1890s when the Western Federation of Miners (WFM) had appeared. Conflict between the WFM and the employers' associations in the frontier mine towns sometimes degenerated into local civil wars. In 1904 the Mine Owners' Association and local citizens' alliances brutally crushed a strike at Cripple Creek, Colorado, and the wounded WFM turned to a search for allies. Eugene Debs of the Socialist party and Daniel De Leon of the Socialist Labor party, among others, responded to these overtures, and the result was the creation in 1905 of the Industrial Workers of the World.

The early years of the IWW or Wobblies were confused ones, as the Socialist party members and even the WFM left the new body again, but it survived under the leadership of former miners William S. ("Big Bill") Haywood and Vincent St. John. In many ways the Wobblies were an authentically American movement, unskilled and migratory workers reacting against brutal conditions and the self-serving craft unionism of the AFL, but it suited their enemies to exaggerate the presence of immigrants among their leaders, and the IWW did become associated with a version of French anarcho-syndicalism. This emphasized complete control by the workers, organized by industry, and the use of the general strike, sabotage, and other forms of direct action to effect this end. The Wobblies used evocative and inflammatory prose, rejected religion, adopted the red flag, and distributed the "Red Card" and the "Little Red Song Book" to members. Their aim was to unite American workers into "one big union" with which to fulfill their historic mission "to do away with capitalism," and they attracted recruits particularly among the footloose lumber, farm, and waterfront workers and other migratory laborers of the West.

Employers dependent on seasonal workers came to hate the appearance of the IWW—a strike at harvest time could ruin a fruit farmer. The Wobblies' defiant poses, their ready resort to strike action, and their mobilization of the disaffected seemed tantamount to insurrection to many hard-pressed businessmen, municipal and county governments, and even local federal officials, who turned their power against them. Local federal officials in the Pacific Northwest used the Immigration Act of 1903 and the Naturalization Act of 1906 to obstruct the naturalization of alien Wobblies, who were held to profess disbelief in organized government. Law officers broke up their meetings and sometimes arrested the speakers. From 1909 the Wobblies struck back with the "free speech" movement, thronging into towns where they had been denied a platform and getting themselves arrested until the overcrowding of the jails forced their release. Such confrontations gave Wobblies a reputation for violence and lawlessness. In 1912 they moved east, winning a stunning strike victory for the immigrant textile workers of Lawrence, Massachusetts, and transfixing the entire country.

The Lawrence strike popularized the ideas of syndicalism and intensified conservative fears of anarchy and revolution, particularly as Wobbly leaders publicly expounded the doctrine of sabotage. The return of hard times in 1913 brought a rash of strikes, one at Wheatland, California, dissolving into a bloody riot and prompting Governor Hiram Johnson to send in the National Guard to protect the fruit growers, who themselves formed the Farmers' Protective Association. This organization employed its own gunmen and detectives against labor rebels, invoking republican values and the vigilante tradition in the name of law and order. Under pressure from the growers, the governors of four western states urged the Wilson administration to investigate the IWW, but lobbying activity focused on Congress when the Justice Department was unable to find any violation of federal law. Congressmen like the fiercely antiradical Albert Johnson of Washington sought more restrictive immigration legislation, hoping thereby to secure some federal regulation of a work force composed increasingly of foreigners. Bills of 1913 and 1915 that sought both to introduce a literacy test and to provide for the deportation of aliens "advocating or teaching the unlawful destruction of property" were passed by Congress but vetoed by President Wilson.

For the moment the official war on the Wobblies remained a matter for state governments; some deployed the National Guard, and in 1913 and 1914 three states enacted laws prohibiting the raising of red flags. IWW activity was being treated in these areas as a species of revolution. The outbreak of war in Europe then worked to the Wobblies' advantage, for the resultant economic boom in the United States enabled them to expand. As midwestern farmers increased production to meet European demands, they found their wheatfields invaded by IWW organizers eager to sign up agricultural laborers. The IWW also launched organizing campaigns in the copper mines of Arizona and Montana and in the lumber industry. By 1917 the IWW was reaching toward 100,000 members, over five times as many as in 1912, but powerful forces were already mobilizing xenophobic sentiments against the movement, particulary since it had adopted a fierce antiwar stance. Woodrow Wilson had insisted on "a strict and impartial neutrality" when war broke out in Europe, but by 1915 he was urging the need for defensive military preparation, and in 1916 military expenditures were increased. The IWW enthusiasm for strikes and sabotage in this context seemed positively harmful to national security, and the number of strikes was spiraling to record levels, though most were not led by the IWW. There was "disloyalty active in the United States," warned Wilson during the 1916 presidential campaign, summoning the fraternal spirit of republicanism and pointing the finger at those "born under foreign flags." The nativist fever of the winter of 1916–17 finally enabled Congress to override a presidential veto on immigration legislation, and the Literacy Test Act of 1917 both imposed a literacy test on immigrants and provided that aliens could be deported for advocating the unlawful destruction of property, anarchy, or the violent overthrow of the government. This was aimed largely at the IWW, and in effect it placed aliens on permanent probation. Also directed at the IWW were state criminal-syndicalism laws, Idaho leading the way in March 1917 by prohibiting the advocacy of "crime, sabotage, violence, or other unlawful methods of terrorism as a means of accomplishing industrial or political ends." Even before the American entry into the war the legislative assault on Wobblies and other radicals had begun.

Workers in many trades resorted to direct action in the 1910s, sometimes led by Socialist party or Socialist Labor party spokesmen, but it was the IWW that became most prominently identified with militancy. Its advocacy of sabotage and its bloody confrontations with the police, the militia, and company guards in the West gave it a reputation for violence. Although the flamboyant belligerence of the IWW undoubtedly appealed to many footloose workers, it also deepened divisions within the American labor movement. Those groups working for change within constitutional channels veered away from the IWW and its image of lawlessness. There had never been any love lost between the IWW and the AFL, but the latter stepped up its denunciation of radicalism, particularly after two of its own members admitted in 1912 that they had been responsible for dynamiting the *Los Angeles Times*. The Socialist party, increasingly emphasizing political and parliamentary action, in the same year purged the Wobbly Big Bill Haywood from its leadership and disavowed "sabotage" and "violence" at its annual convention. As always a reputation for violence, whether deserved or not, was isolating the militants, who were denounced almost as much by other labor spokesmen as by the propertied classes.

The renunciation of radicalism and violence by American workers was also being actively encouraged by the churches. Evangelical ministers and trade unionists cooperated in the Labor and Religion Forward movement, which won the approval of the AFL convention in 1912. Moderate labor leaders sometimes encouraged Protestant clergymen to promote revivals in the hope of outflanking their socialist rivals. Employers themselves on occasion sponsored evangelists like Billy Sunday to remind workers to be "faithful to their duties." Perhaps more important by this period was the influence of the Catholic church in fostering the antisocialist tendencies of American labor. Catholic antiradicalism had its roots in papal encyclicals condemning communism as atheistic and socialism as hostile to private property, and American church leaders such as Cardinal William O'Connell of Boston insisted that "there cannot be a Catholic socialist." The large Irish and German elements in the AFL meant that many of its leaders were Roman Catholic and were prepared to work with churchmen like Father Peter E. Dietz and such organizations as the American Federation of Catholic Societies, which by 1917 could speak for three million Catholics. It promoted Roman Catholic values among trade unionists and others and pledged "unceasing opposition to the . . . destructive propaganda of Socialism." The antireligious sentiments of some Wobbly leaders and their apparent disregard for property and the law made them favorite targets of both Catholic and Protestant spokesmen. By the time the United States went to war in 1917 the kind of labor militancy symbolized by the IWW had become dangerously exposed. The IWW was well placed to be perceived as that enemy within that Americans had long been schooled to look for.

World War

Woodrow Wilson knew that to lead his country into war could only divide American society. Since 1914 public opinion had been generally against American entry, and when Wilson did call for intervention he was faced with extensive and vexatious opposition. The Socialist party and the IWW were only the most outspoken critics of intervention, their antiwar stance being shared by many Progressives who feared that war would undo the cause of reform. The homelands of millions of Americans lay within the territory of the Central Powers, for the most part workers who regarded the war with dismay. Irish constituencies frequently were fervently anti-British, and many Germans retained an affection for their old country. Further, socialist immigrant craftsmen were important in industries that would play key roles in any war effort. Yet the federal government, still a flimsy edifice by European standards, lacked even a police force to guard against possible sabotage.

The weakness of the federal government, its commitment to total war against a major industrial power, and the prospect of a considerable and paralyzing antiwar opposition, with which the beleaguered president had little patience, were to have fateful consequences for American radicals, not only during the war but also after it. The administration had to rely on the uncertain techniques of persuasion to create a new consensus. The government did extend its controls where it could, and repressive legislation was enacted, but perhaps more important, it embarked on a mammoth propaganda campaign to harness public opinion to the war, and it also in effect licensed vigilantes to keep the home front under surveillance. Patriotism, however, was to prove an ill-controlled emotion.

The principal responsibility for mobilizing public opinion was vested in the Committee on Public Informaton (CPI). Chaired by George Creel, who brought to his task a Progressive faith in democracy and harmony, the CPI disseminated torrents of information that became increasingly indistinguishable from patriotic propaganda. It distributed pamphlets and films, sponsored seventy-five thousand public speakers, and organized exhibitions, parades, and rallies. The CPI also furthered the Americanization movement, which had been given a new stimulus by the war, by organizing "loyalty leagues" among the ethnic communities. Creel later explained that the CPI's objective had been to create "a passionate belief in the justice of America's cause that should weld the people . . . into one white-hot mass of instinct." For the CPI, Creel, President Wilson himself, and not a few Progressives, the war became a holy mission. "Woe be to the man," said Wilson, "that seeks to stand in our way." Creel and Wilson disapproved of loyal citizens' taking the law into their own hands, but their own crusading zeal and willingness to equate dissent with disloyalty tended to encourage popular outbursts of patriotism.

The administration also turned to volunteers to police the home front, relying on the vigilante tradition that American attitudes to government and citizenship had long encouraged. It sponsored the American Protective League (APL), a private body formed quietly in 1917 under the auspices of the understaffed Justice Department, which hoped to use local volunteers to look for spies and undertake loyalty investigations of those applying for wartime jobs. (In World War II an expanded FBI would assume these functions.) The semisecret APL units recruited from the business, professional, and local governmental classes and often reflected the values of the propertied elements in their communities. In Chicago the Commonwealth Edison Company provided offices for the APL; in Philadelphia members of the Chamber of Commerce helped cover running expenses. Some APL members behaved responsibly, but many did not, and their patriotic zeal spilled into excesses like breaking up Socialist meetings, burglarizing offices, rounding up draft evaders or "slackers," and forcing those held to be disloyal to kiss the flag or suffer a beating. By 1918 there were some 250,000 leaguers, "the largest company of detectives the world ever saw," according to an admirer. As one APL chief in Kansas wrote, the league had "a great Moral Effect on the community by the people knowing that Uncle Sam was among them at all times and they not knowing who was keeping tabs on them." Paralleling the APL at state level, and often overlapping with it in personnel and functions, were the councils of defense, nominally under the direction of a Council of National Defense. They were augmented by private vigilante groups like the Knights of Liberty and by two larger patriotic associations that had been preaching preparedness and "one hundred percent Americanism" since 1914—the National Security League and the American Defense Society.

The republican tradition of an active citizenry was thus being invoked in the name of freedom, but at the cost of the civil liberties of many individuals. The vigilante excesses of both the quasi-official and private bodies disturbed the president, but he did little to restrain Attorney General Thomas W. Gregory, who savored the novel experience of having hundreds of thousands of unpaid agents reporting to his department's Bureau of Investigation. The APL volunteers were meant to monitor the activities of the agents of foreign governments and of unfriendly alien residents, but Americans of German origin were frequent victims, as were pacifists and radicals of all kinds. The APL networks and the state and local councils of defense offered patriots an opportunity to serve their country in time of war, to act as citizen soldiers like the Minutemen of the Revolution, and also to be initiated into the arts of surveillance. When peace returned many were loath to abandon these gratifying activities.

Disquiet over the extent of antiwar feeling in the United States fueled not only the government's propaganda crusade but also demands for protective and repressive legislation. The states' rights tradition had left the federal authorities with few legal controls over American citizens, but the war emergency made possible some fitful extension of their powers. Senator George E. Chamberlain, reflecting the interests of Oregon conservatives, proposed that the entire country be put under martial law. Wilson was able to resist this, but he did press for other forcible security measures, such as the Espionage Act of June 1917, which, while designed to curb treason, made it a crime to obstruct enlistment or to interfere with military operations or industrial production. But even this flexible statute seemed inadequate to those who felt threatened by antiwar or pacifist speakers or writers, and sensitive to charges of laxity, the administration agreed to the Sedition Act of May 1918, which prohibited language disloyal to the American form of government and the Constitution or intended to promote the cause of the enemies of the United States. Any disrespect toward the flag or any disloyal statement could be punished by twenty years in jail. This punitive and potentially totalitarian law, which could be used—or misused—to silence political opponents of almost any stripe, was at least to be confined to the duration of the war emergency. Much of the pressure for such laws came from local and state levels, where vigilantes often took matters into their own hands, and the far-reaching Sedition Act at least gave dissidents the possibility of being dealt with by the courts rather than by the mob. Yet once empowered by federal legislation, local federal officials, with their links to the power structure in their communities, often proved all too willing to act. In these communities federal attorneys interpreted the law in their own way, and across the land critics of the war were hauled before the courts. Prosecutions under the Espionage and Sedition acts were most common in the western states, notably those with a strong IWW presence.

The government use of legislation to dispel opposition to the war, then, was encouraged by local economic and political elites long hostile to the labor and socialist movements. The recruitment of federal officials to the campaign against the Socialist party greatly damaged the party, which early condemned the American declaration of war as "a crime against the people of the United States" and emerged as the most important political force opposed to it. The party's antiwar stance rendered it vulnerable to both mob action and legal prosecution, and its relative political strength invited attack. Its presidential candidate had won 6 percent of the popular vote in 1912, and though less successful in the 1916 election, the party was well established in several cities, some of which had Socialist mayors. Federal agents raided its national headquarters in Chicago in September 1917, but the Socialists made dramatic gains in local elections in November, suggesting that their depiction of the war as a device of the "American plutocracy" to make money was striking a chord with some workers.

In the same month the Bolshevik Revolution in Russia underlined to conservatives whither attacks on the plutocracy could lead. The indictments of Socialist leaders increased, and the party's first congressman, Victor L. Berger of Milwaukee, and its general secretary Charles T. Schenck, were successfully prosecuted under the Espionage Act. In June 1918 the party's preeminent leader, Eugene V. Debs, was arrested after making an antiwar speech in which he promised that his party would soon win power and destroy "capitalistic institutions." He was sentenced to a stunning ten years in prison for these (intentionally provocative) remarks. His words, Justice Oliver Wendell Holmes, Jr., later affirmed, had created "a clear and present danger" of impairing the war effort. The Socialist movement was also hurt by the censorship provisions of the Espionage and Sedition acts, which enabled a zealous postmaster general to ban from the mails many socialist and other radical newspapers, and since these often depended on cheap mail privileges for distribution, several collapsed completely. Even the Socialist party's leading daily paper, the *New York Call*, had difficulty surviving. By the end of the United States' brief participation in the First World War, several Socialist leaders were in prison and the greater part of the socialist press was effectively suppressed.

The use of wartime legislation against a party that had been legally contesting elections for years bothered a few federal officials, but their sympathy rarely extended to the IWW. Western mine and lumber operators and midwestern farmers had been alarmed by the successful IWW union drives during the economic expansion of 1914–17; now the war gave them an opportunity to destroy their enemy. Their ambitions interacted with government anxieties about IWW subversion. To the IWW the war was a capitalist plot, and it saw no reason to refrain from strikes during mobilization, an attitude that patriots could not easily distinguish from treason. Employers in the summer of 1917 represented a strike in the lumber industry as an assault on the war effort, which needed wood for the construction of weapons—not least airplanes, which were then expected to win the war for the allies. The owners refused to bargain with the IWW, formed the Lumbermen's Protective Association, and called in the government. The army was authorized to suppress acts "committed with seditious intent," and troops were used to break timber and mine strikes in the summer of 1917, though they also contrived to raid IWW halls and to detain strikers and demonstrators.

The official harassment of the IWW served to encourage vigilante action, as in Bisbee, Arizona, in July 1917, when nearly twelve hundred Wobblies and others were rounded up by local businessmen and mine officials, shipped out of town in boxcars, and dumped in the desert. Soon afterward IWW organizer Frank Little was lynched in Butte, Montana. The Wobblies responded to such atrocities with strike threats, and the governors of eight western states demanded that all Wobblies be placed in concentration camps because they were obstructing war work. This demand the Wilson administration refused, but it did agree to investigate the IWW, and Justice Department agents and APL members energetically gathered what information they could. This suited the interests of local businessmen. One APL captain later recalled that his men's most important work had been "breaking up the activities of labor agitators and anarchists."

The federal government had ample reasons of its own for wanting to stop strikes during wartime, and it was occurring to Justice Department officials that the arrest of IWW leaders might accomplish this end. In September 1917 federal agents raided local IWW headquarters across the country, looking for evidence of reasonable or criminal activity. There followed the arrests of 166 IWW members, including Big Bill Haywood, on charges of criminal conspiracy to violate the espionage act and obstruct the war effort. The principal mass trial was held in Chicago, where over ninety individuals were in effect convicted for being Wobblies and given prison sentences of up to twenty years and fines totaling $2,300,000. As the federal authorities locked away the IWW leaders, local officials brought indictments against many of their followers. The official branding of the IWW as treasonable encouraged vigilantes and mobs to lay rough hands on IWW members and sympathizers, particularly in the western states, where the self-styled patriots were spurred on by the press. The *Tulsa World* told its readers that the first step in defeating Germany was the death of the Wobblies: "Don't scotch 'em; kill 'em! . . . It is no time to waste money on trials." The old American urge to locate an enemy within was being strengthened and directed by the tensions of foreign war.

The ferocity of the demands emanating from the employers and their allies in the statehouses and the press sometimes horrified Washington administrators, as did the violence in the western copper mines, lumber districts, and shipyards. The president appointed a Mediation Commission to visit the troubled areas, and it was appalled by the miserable living conditions provided for migratory workers and attributed much of the tension to the "bitter attitude of the operators toward any organization among their employees." From such circumstances there arose a unique body, the Loyal Legion of Loggers and Lumbermen, a kind of government union supervised and subsidized by the army, which recruited workers by offering them jobs and better living and working conditions in return for their loyalty. IWW members were not welcome unless they convincingly demonstrated their "loyalty." Conservative employers accused the 4-L of "groveling" to labor agitators, while labor officials complained that it was an antiunion device, but its paternalistic surveillance system suffused the lumber camps with the rhetoric of patriotism, improved physical conditions and brought a measure of order. As the IWW leaders were going to prison, their potential followers were succumbing to this suffocating patriotic embrace.

The government co-optation of the lumber workers tended to marginalize the IWW and other radicals, as did its attempts to co-opt the labor movement generally to the war effort. The Wilson administration was anxious to maximize war production and to avoid unnecessarily offending workers during a period of labor shortage, and it was able to reach an accord at least with the craft unions of the AFL. With government blessing, the AFL secured substantially better wages, and the old demand for an eight-hour day was widely achieved. The AFL for its part eventually agreed to a no-strike policy during the war, even if it stopped short of a pledge. The AFL leader Samuel Gompers, seeing an opportunity to make gains at the expense of capital, emphasized the patriotism, reliability, and moderation of his members. He wrote to Woodrow Wilson in August 1917 that unless government and employers dealt with the AFL they would have "the alternative of being forced to take the consequences of the so-called IWW with all that implies." Gompers's hostility to the IWW and the Socialists was the more intense because the antiwar stance of those groups threatened his hold on his own rank and file, and he flayed the radicals as vigorously as any government spokesman. Gompers and the government furthered their joint campaign through the American Alliance for Labor and Democracy, established by the Committee on Public Information in August 1917, which directed patriotic propaganda at workers and branded the antiwar groups "disloyal." The leading representatives of organized labor were themselves actively disavowing Socialists and Wobblies, impugning their patriotism, furthering their isolation, and thus rendering them even more vulnerable to government and vigilante repression.

Such radicals were also being left stranded by the course of events abroad. The Bolshevik withdrawal of Russia from the war was widely resented as a betrayal of allied liberal ideals; it fostered the myth that the Bolsheviks were German agents, opened the way for Allied military intervention against them, and rendered even more suspect their supposed sympathizers in the United States. As the war ended, the un-American and antirepublican qualities imputed to the Wobblies expedited the final assault upon them. If it had occurred to some officials that the wartime obstructionism of the IWW might be ended by jailing its leaders, it had also occurred to them that the IWW might be finally destroyed by banishing its organizers from the country. Many IWW activists were immigrants, and for years local courts in the West had been using the acts of 1903 and 1906 to refuse to naturalize alien members of the IWW. The massive immigration preceding the First World War, when radical industrial workers were leaving Russia, Finland, and Poland for the United States, swelled the numbers of aliens attracted to the IWW and other radical organizations. Local and federal officials pondered ways of excluding the supposed troublemakers among them from the United States.

One of the most disturbed communities was Seattle, which experienced an annual invasion of workers each winter as they left the lumber camps, orchards, and fields. Troubled by the Wobbly growth earlier in 1917 and by the Bolshevik Revolution in November, city officials and local vigilantes viewed the influx of workers in the winter of 1917–18 as a Wobbly plot to seize the city, and in their panic they intensified their own lawless actions. Federal officials in Seattle, anxious to preserve a modicum of order, proposed to Washington that one solution would be to deport those Wobblies who were not American citizens. The secretary of labor responded that IWW membership of itself could not be grounds for deportation, but the Bureau for Immigration began to examine more closely the feasibility of stripping radical aliens of their remaining rights. The Espionage and Sedition acts would expire with the war, and some officials wanted a more permanent weapon to turn against radicalism. Make aliens more readily deportable, it was reasoned, and radicalism would be crippled. One advantage of this technique was that aliens could not normally claim the rights afforded to citizens by the Constitution, and deportation was regarded as an administrative rather than a judicial operation, a summary procedure in which legal protection was at a minimum.

From assumptions of this kind the Immigration Act of October 1918 was formulated, providing not only for the exclusion of anarchists and those believing in the violent overthrow of the government, but also for the deportation of aliens who were subsequently found to hold such ideas. Henceforth obstreperous aliens could simply be shipped out of the United States and this law was to be the basis for the celebrated Palmer raids of 1919–20. Native-born Americans, it seemed, could legally be anarchists and communists, but not the newcomers who were held responsible for the red menace. This legislation represented the culmination of a long campaign against anarchists, particularly the anarcho-syndicalist Wobblies, and it was the product both of pressures from western employers and state politicians and of the fears and suspicions of certain federal officials. The law reflected not only the old assumption that subversion was invariably foreign inspired and the undoubted fact that many Wobbly and Socialist leaders were immigrants, but also the limited nature of the police power that the federal government possessed over its own citizens. American republicanism had always implied an absence of official coercion. The government could not easily and constitutionally legislate against dissent as such during peacetime; but immigration policy was its responsibility, and the immigration laws were now to be used for political control. The offensive against anarchists of all stripes had all but compelled the authorities to identify radicalism as a foreign import.

.

The assassination of President McKinley had prompted the first piece of federal legislation that could be used against communists, albeit only those who were both aliens and of the anarchist persuasion. The Progressive temper of the 1900s had averted a ferocious scare, but the red menace continued to be sighted, particularly in those areas of the country where the class struggle was intensifying. The reputed violence of the Wobblies distanced them from middle-class sympathies, and the rationalist doctrines of some socialist groups rendered them suspect in a determinedly Christian republic. While Progressivism emerged as an alternative and as a counter to reaction, the antianarchist offensive was gradually assuming regional and eventually national form, as first the western states and later the federal government were recruited to the cause. Continued industrialization was disseminating class conflict throughout the United States, and pressure groups of various kinds were progressively shifting their attention from local to state to national governments. Insecure antiradical interests followed the same trajectory.

The outbreak of war in Europe greatly increased the pressures buffeting the federal government, as did its decision to enter that war. Committed to a total war, yet lacking much in the way of regulatory powers and faced with extensive antiwar opposition, the Wilson administration resorted to the techniques of persuasion, notably a massive propaganda campaign and a reliance on volunteer police forces. Employers had earlier bent the American vigilante tradition to their own antilabor purposes; during the war the government intensively exploited the tradition in the national interest. It similarly enlisted the AFL. The federal government also resorted to the techniques of repression, its campaigns against the antiwar elements aligning it with those business interests and state governments that had long been fighting socialists of various kinds, especially the IWW. The application of the wartime espionage and sedition laws severely savaged the Socialist party and the Wobblies as they were cast as enemies of the republic. More lasting were the controls that were being extended over aliens, the one group in the population that was subject to federal regulation. The government strategies of persuasion and coercion left ominous legacies, notably popular patriotic activity that was assuming a vigorous life of its own and a fledgling bureaucracy anxious to root out un-American elements. These two features did not sit easily together. One reason for the extension of federal regulation was the need to contain the vigilante excesses being reported in local communities. But the interaction of popular pressures and bureaucratic impulses had at last fashioned a logical response to that form of communism that had allegedly menaced the republic for over three decades. Anarchism had always been defined as being of foreign pedigree; henceforth it would be possible to eject the foreigners held responsible for it from the United States.

4

THE
BIG RED SCARE
(1918–1920)

•

THE CELEBRATED "Big Red Scare" of American history was a relatively short-lived affair. It might be said to have begun in the spring of 1919 with the discovery in the mails of several bombs addressed to distinguished persons and to have ended with the failure of revolutionary activity to materialize as predicted on May Day 1920. In the intervening year the home of the attorney general of the United States was dynamited, a committee of a state legislature raided an agency of the Russian government, a Socialist congressman was denied his seat in the House of Representatives, four members of the American Legion and one Wobbly died as a result of the "Centralia Massacre" in Washington State, some 249 "dangerous reds" were bundled onto a transport ship destined for Russia, perhaps 6,000 suspected radicals were arrested in raids directed by the Justice Department, and five members of the law-abiding Socialist party were expelled from the New York legislature. Across the country, too, in countless official and vigilante actions, strikers were beaten and sometimes killed, socialist meetings were broken up, radical newspapers were suppressed, allegedly unpatriotic teachers were fired, and men and women suspected of disloyalty were assaulted, arrested, or forced to kiss the flag. In 1919 alone twenty-six states enacted laws prohibiting the display of the red flag. A West Virginia businessman expressed the perceptions of many when he wrote in October of that year that "there is hardly a respectable citizen of my acquaintance who does not believe that we are on the verge of armed conflict in this country."

But the fears and outrages of 1919 – 20 were not without ample precedent. The Big Red Scare had long been gathering momentum, spurred by the responses of American society and government to the First World War. American society had been divided by the war, with substantial ethnic and political groups being hostile to the American commitment to the Allied cause. The Wilson administration had embarked on total war against a major industrial power conscious that it needed the full mobilization of American industrial resources and conscious too that the country was not united behind it. Lacking coercive powers, the administration turned to engaging public opinion to the war effort, employing massive propaganda campaigns and secret armies of volunteers to ferret out subversives and slackers. Where it could extend its legal controls it did, as over aliens, and in due course the war emergency enabled it to subject much of American industry to regulation. The First World War did not of itself produce the Big Red Scare, but an active citizenry had been awakened to guard the republic, while bureaucratic tools had been forged in the defense of national security.

Events in the outside and postwar world interacted with this wartime heritage to detonate an intensive scare. The revolution in Russia of March 1917 had been generally welcomed by Americans as a herald of democracy, and the United States was the first nation to recognize the new regime, but the Bolshevik Revolution in November introduced the disturbing specter of anarchy to the propertied classes everywhere. Bolshevism's identification not only with common ownership but also with irreligion and free love deeply offended the Victorian values many Americans were attached to. Yet the Russian Revolution also exhilarated American radicals, and Communist risings in eastern and central Europe in 1918 and 1919 immeasurably strengthened both radical hopes and conservative fears that the appeal of revolutionary communism knew no national boundaries. When in 1919 bombs exploded in several American cities and major steel and coal strikes wrenched at the very core of America's industrial capitalism, many were ready to believe that Bolsheviks were abroad in the land.

This intensification of class conflict itself was largely a consequence of the war. Major industrial corporations had emerged more prosperous than ever, while the AFL and organized labor had also grown in size and respectability, and both businessmen and workers took the Armistice as a signal to turn on one another with their war-acquired muscles. As they did so the Progressives and the middle classes grew disenchanted with labor and reform. Many Progressives had initially embraced the war for the opportunities it would afford for promoting social justice, but the war effort left little room for reform while showering huge profits on many corporations. The fading of Progressivism and the deepening fissures of class and ethnicity promoted a growing polarization in American politics. If the insistent signs of fundamental social conflict prodded many respectable citizens to veer to the right, the glowing light of the Russian Revolution drew many socialists and a few liberals to the left, and new Communist parties were established in the United States. Within the federal government machinery that had been erected primarily to combat the IWW was soon being mobilized against this latest alien invasion, driven by the convictions and ambitions of a few prominent men. As the vigilante spirit flickered over the land, and as the Russian Revolution and the deepening class warfare displaced the accommodationist politics of Progressivism with starker alternatives, the scene was set for the most pervasive red scare thus far mounted by American political culture.

The Bolshevik Apparition

Well before the Russian Revolution sent new shivers of apprehension through the respectable classes, an intense class conflict had characterized American industrial relations. Despite the cooperative attitude of the AFL during the war, the 1910s had witnessed an unprecedented degree of direct action by workers, often in response to the "scientific management" thrusts of the employers. The ending of the war promised even greater convulsions. With the passing of the urgent need for labor cooperation in the defense industries, the federal and state governments had less reason to befriend trade unionists or to mediate between labor and capital. The labor movement, eager to protect wartime gains and to win compensation for galloping inflation, adopted a more belligerent posture, which employers were not slow to impute to Bolshevist influence. Many businessmen were itching to throw off wartime constraints and assert their managerial prerogatives. In the western states in particular the war had enabled employers to win greater support from state and federal governments in their anti-Wobbly drive, and after the war business leaders in the urban-industrial states generally made fuller use of red scare tactics in their efforts to beat back labor advances. As the war ended, the old conflicts between employers and workmen again commanded public attention.

The opening salvos of the Big Red Scare were fired in the West, where the long-standing class strife reached an explosive intensity as economic dislocations brought new hardships. During the war, pressure from the authorities in Seattle in particular had persuaded the Bureau of Immigration that deporting aliens would decapitate the IWW, the Immigration Act of 1918 being designed to effect this, and the Armistice did nothing to deflect these plans. Early in 1919 the Seattle office of the Bureau of Immigration was ready to dispatch forth Wobblies to Ellis Island for deportation.

Meanwhile tensions were spiraling in the city, where wartime shipbuilding projects had exacerbated a housing shortage, raised prices, and strengthened the unions, whose bargaining position was abruptly impaired by the ending of the war. When a wage demand was refused, the shipyard workers withdrew their labor in January 1919, supported by the Seattle Central Labor Council, a body representing the city's unions, which called a general strike. Leading members of the council were known to be sympathetic to the IWW, Soviet Russia, and the nationalization of key industries. Some sixty thousand workers responded to the strike call, and economic activity in Seattle ceased on 6 February as much of the local press discerned the origins of red revolution. Mayor Ole Hanson, a sometime Progressive, described the general strike as the work of men who "want to take possession of our American Government and try to duplicate the anarchy of Russia"; he represented its IWW leaders as Soviet inspired and called in federal troops to help him resist Bolshevism. The press throughout the country echoed his warnings, and worried national AFL leaders counseled the local unions to abandon the strike, which collapsed after four days. Ole Hanson emerged as the hero of the hour, and he resigned his mayoralty to tour the country giving lectures on the need to fight the red menace. "Our terms," he said, are "Deportation, Incarceration, Annihilation!" Even a moderate like Wilson's secretary of labor agreed that the Seattle strike and others aimed at a revolution to "establish a Soviet form of government in the United States."

This view had some credibility because conservatives had for decades been representing labor militancy as incompatible with republican traditions, because Wobblies and other anarcho-syndicalists had promoted the idea of the general strike as a revolutionary weapon, and because some Seattle radicals evidently sympathized with the Soviet experiment. Further, Americans had long been accustomed to think of government as rather a fragile and limited construction, less able than a European despotism to withstand a determined assault. Disturbed by the portents in Seattle, the middle classes and many Progressives became even more hostile to the demands of organized labor and suspicious that industrial action could be a prelude to revolution.

Unconvinced that the Wilson administration would take adequate meaures against radicals, the western states—where Wobblies were still being harassed and arrested—made their own preparations. Washington, Oregon, Idaho, and California enacted criminal syndicalism laws in the early months of 1919, each fearful of being invaded by Wobblies fleeing from neighboring states. In Idaho the governor persuaded the legislature to establish a state constabulary, which gathered information on the IWW and compiled a "red list." The bomb scare that disturbed the country generally in the spring of 1919 began when a bomb was discovered in the mail of Seattle's patriotic hero Ole Hanson and was intensified in June by the bombing of the house of no less a figure than the country's attorney general. As A. Mitchell Palmer prodded his department to antiradical action, governments and vigilante groups in the Northwest pressed home their advantage. At Centralia in Washington State, the lumbermen's Citizens Protective League encouraged members of the American Legion assembled for an Armistice Day parade to run the local Wobblies out of town once more, and when legionnaires attacked the IWW hall four of them were shot dead. Several Wobblies were arrested, and one was sadistically lynched. The deaths of the patriotic legionnaires ignited an orgy of anti-Wobbly sentiment throughout the West. "Ordinarily I do not believe in mob law," observed a Washington lumberman, "but the action taken by the citizens of Centralia in hanging the leaders of 'Reds' was the only right and proper thing." The destruction of IWW halls and the hounding of Wobblies escalated and continued into 1920, by which time over a thousand had been arrested. The once-flourishing IWW was finally being eliminated as an effective labor organization.

The long years of class warfare in the western states merged imperceptibly into the Big Red Scare. The accommodationist mood of the Progressives was being dispelled in the aftermath of the Great War by unnerving events both abroad and at home, and the growing conservatism of most Americans was defied by a new revolutionary impulse among a few. The number of real communist revolutionaries in the United States was never large, but there were enough to frighten some citizens, and it suited business, press, vigilante, and government interests, dependent on public opinion in a democratic polity, to magnify their presence. That they were enemies of the republic seemed to be confirmed by the continued deployment of American troops to save Russia from the Bolsheviks. The bomb scare in the spring of 1919 and a series of major strikes in the fall gave some credence to conservative warnings. It had been a Wobbly boast that "every strike is a small revolution and a dress rehearsal for the big one," and the eruption of industrial conflict, violence, and political radicalism in 1919 suggested to many that the revolution was at hand. Business prepared for an assault on labor, patriotic citizens readied themselves to defend the republic, and government resumed the attempt to curb radicalism by expelling aliens.

Respectable citizens who pondered the significance of such events as the Seattle general strike and the Centralia "massacre" had good reason to believe that revolutionary communism was on the march. They may have shrugged off the Bolshevik Revolution's promise in November 1917 of the dissolution of capitalism throughout the world, but the prophecy seemed to acquire disquieting substance in 1918 with revolutions in Hungary, Austria, and Bulgaria and in 1919 when soviet regimes appeared in Finland, Hungary, and Bavaria. In March 1919 the Third

International was created expressly to further world revolution. According to the *Washington Post*, groups in the United States were indeed working to bring about "bloody revolution and the establishment of a Bolshevik Republic." American radicals for their part thrilled to the signs of the coming age of socialism. As Wobblies were being clubbed in the West, the American Socialist party itself was growing rapidly, from about 80,000 members in 1917 to almost 110,000 by 1919, and its left wing in particular identified with the Bolsheviks. Immigrant workers, aroused by the antilabor and scientific management initiatives of employers, contemptuous of the conservatism of the AFL, and impatient with the anti-institutional temperament of the Wobblies, flooded into the foreign-language federations of the Socialist party.

But the radicalizing influence of the Russian Revolution also divided the Socialists, and in September 1919 two new parties were formed—the Communist party, retaining the bulk of the foreign-language federations, and the Communist Labor party, led by John Reed and other native-born radicals. These revolutionary stirrings were made overt by the proliferation of communist and anarchist newspapers, which often underlined the alien origins of the new movements by being in foreign languages. American communism was not a figment of a fevered reactionary imagination; communists themselves by 1919 were insisting that "the United States seems to be on the verge of a revolutionary crisis," and there were perhaps seventy thousand of them loose in the land. Such evidence of a revitalized radicalism all but extinguished such middle-class sympathy as there had once been for reform and labor, a hardening of attitude already reflected in the success of the Republican party in winning control of both houses of Congress in November 1918. These ominous Republican victories encouraged the Democratic administration to show greater sensitivity to business demands and less to labor. The polarization of American society and politics left radical minorities perilously exposed.

Democrats and Republicans alike were moving to the right, and the Progressives among them were losing their faith. Ole Hanson and the United States attorney general, A. Mitchell Palmer, were but two examples of men who had once supported liberal causes but now regarded every strike as a prelude to revolution. Progressives of greater intellectual weight abandoned the cause of reform. Albert J. Beveridge had denounced the 1916 Adamson Act setting an eight-hour day for railroad employees as a surrender by government to the "threat of force by special interest," and in 1919 he complained that constitutional government was being usurped by "predatory groups." Like the Radical Republicans before them, Progressives were dismayed when class was put before commonwealth. The disintegration of their fraternal vision freed patriots, businessmen, and other conservatives to intensify their assaults on their enemies.

The middle-class reaction against radicalism tended to be reinforced by the churches. Roman Catholic distaste for communism was vindicated and intensified by the Bolsheviks' attack on the Catholic church in Russia as well as on organized religion in general. Most Protestant denominations embarked on membership drives in the postwar period and offered religion as an antidote to communism. A leading Episcopalian, the Reverend G. A. Carstensen, observed that "Reds" were "creatures to whom the world owed nothing but sufficient voltage to rid the earth of them," and the popular evangelist Billy Sunday more moderately hoped to "fill the jails" with so many of them "that their feet would stick out of the windows." Although there were exceptions, Protestant church spokesmen were generally unsympathetic to radicals, unions, and strikers, and saw religion as a force for social order in the troubled years after 1918.

Also disturbed by the growing signs of radicalism were those patriotic societies spawned by the First World War, eager to find new uses for the republican tradition of an active citizenry. The patriotic organizations that had manned the home front during mobilization were reluctant to disband. The government decreed that the American Protective League (APL) should cease to function from February 1919, but APL locals lingered on, and individual APL members put themselves at the disposal of the various military, civil, and legislative agencies investigating radicals. Private societies like the National Security League and the American Defense Society remained on parade, as did the National Civic Federation, with powerful support and financial aid from major corporations and businessmen. These bodies furnished the country with patriotic speakers and pamphlets, preaching the message that "when you hear a man tryin' to discredit Uncle Sam, that's Bolshevism." Many of those who had fought on the foreign front were as anxious to protect the nation's patriotic honor as the home guard. Vigilante attacks on radicals were not infrequently led by former servicemen resentful of "slackers."

In May 1919 World War I veterans created the American Legion, which announced its aim to support the Constitution and "to foster and perpetuate a one hundred per cent Americanism." Many veterans felt betrayed by the Bolsheviks' sudden withdrawal of Russia from the Allied cause during the war. The Legion grew with remarkable rapidity, passing one million by the end of 1919 and becoming an influential lobby for antiradical measures, an early cause being its campaign to deport alien "slackers." In some states, such as Washington and Idaho, legionnaires were recruited by the authorities into the anti-Wobbly drive, and elsewhere they sometimes took the law into their own hands. Picket lines were sometimes broken and strikers beaten; in Astoria, Oregon, the editor of an allegedly communist newspaper was run out of town. Also espousing One Hundred Percent Americanism was the Ku Klux Klan, formed in 1915 but growing significantly during the Big Red Scare of 1919–20. Blacks, foreigners, Jews, and Catholics were the Klan's primary targets, but it often espied radicals among them.

While the patriotic groups searched for enemies to give themselves a raison d'être, businessmen grasped the chance to discredit government regulations and to break the hold of labor. During the war various experiments in economic planning had been introduced, perhaps best exemplified by the War Industries Board. "Legislation is aimed and boastfully aimed against business and [for] the destruction of values," complained J. P. Morgan of these Progressive-inspired measures. The government had taken over the railroads, and in the first days of peace there was talk of persisting with the arrangement. Some liberal newspapers saw merit in the railroad brotherhoods' Plumb Plan for nationalization of the railroads, and a version was introduced into Congress. But enthusiasm for the survival of a government presence in industry did not long survive outside labor circles, and the new Republican Congress had no taste for regulation. It returned the railroads to private owners and put ships built by the government into private hands. The eagerness of business to return to laissez-faire was matched by its eagerness to repulse the wartime labor gains. Bodies like the National Association of Manufacturers and the National Metal Trades Association worked with the patriotic societies in propagating open shop ideas, insisting that unionism "ranked with Bolshevism."

Organized labor was also in a combative mood, determined to preserve and improve on its recent gains and chafing under the spiraling inflation of 1919, described by the *Washington Post* in August as "the burning domestic issue." Early in the year several strikes were won, and by the end of it the number of workers involved in stoppages exceeded that of 1917, many of the disputes revolving around workers' right to organize. The phrase "workers' control" became popular on the shop floor. Employers pointed to the growing menace of Bolshevism, aided by the general strike in Seattle in February and another in May in the Canadian city of Winnipeg, which was reported to have been taken over by a "soviet" directed by American radicals. Some labor groups called for a general strike on 4 July on behalf of Tom Mooney, the celebrated California radical in prison for his alleged part in a fatal bombing, and though it did not materialize, policemen and soldiers throughout the country were placed on alert. Conservatives inspected every labor incident for signs that the Bolshevism that appeared to be spreading across Europe had reached the United States. Samuel Gompers felt obliged to organize an "All-American" committee of labor leaders to repudiate "bolshevism, IWWism and red flagism in general."

The increasing suspicion that the labor movement had been penetrated by revolutionaries aiming to overthrow capitalism was strengthened in the autumn of 1919 with the outbreak of major strikes in critical areas of American life. After the very foundations of social order were laid bare by a police strike, the industrial might of the United States was challenged by strikes in the steel and coal industries. More to the point, these conflicts enabled conservatives to discern the fell influence of Bolshevism, to rally law-abiding citizens to their cause, and to poise the government against the labor movement. The consummation of the Big Red Scare would not be long delayed.

The police strike occurred in Boston in September, after the suspension of a number of officers who had wanted to affiliate with the AFL. "Lenin and Trotsky are on their way" was the verdict of the *Wall Street Journal*, and Woodrow Wilson himself denounced the strike as "a crime against civilization." (A similar police strike in London in August 1918 was later described by Prime Minister Lloyd George as bringing Britain "nearer to Bolshevism . . . than at any time since.") Governor Calvin Coolidge of Massachusetts became a national celebrity with the publication of his pungent telegram: "There is no right to strike against the public safety by anybody, anywhere, any time." The strike collapsed, but not before rowdyism and rioting in underpoliced Boston had apparently caused a few fatalities and given upstanding Americans an unnerving glimpse of anarchy.

If unionism was unthinkable in the police force, it was still being successfully resisted in the steel industry, which had maintained the open shop through the First World War and a twelve-hour day for over half its workers. The wartime strengthening of the AFL had rekindled its ambition to unionize the iron and steel industry, and in 1918 AFL leaders in Chicago, prominent among them the former Wobbly William Z. Foster, began a drive in the steel plants, with some success. But the chairman of U. S. Steel, Elbert H. Gary, in August 1919 peremptorily refused even to meet with the "representatives of a labor union," and other business leaders, seeing steel as a test case, supported his open shop stand. On 22 September some quarter-million steel workers laid down their tools. The companies responded with strikebreakers and in Pennsylvania swore in special "deputies," while rioting in Gary, Indiana, brought in federal troops.

Some twenty people died in these incidents, eighteen of them workers. But the companies' main weapon was propaganda. William Z. Foster's earlier anticapitalist writings were resurrected and selectively quoted, and advertisements in the press represented the strikers as red agitators. A Senate committee investigated the strike and agreed that it was supported by "a considerable element of IWW's, anarchists and revolutionists and Russian Soviets"; radicals were said to be seeking power by penetrating organized labor. The strike collapsed, and U. S. Steel emerged as the conqueror of Bolshevism—and of collective bargaining. During the strike public opinion had seemed to move significantly against labor.

Soon after Bolshevism was being discovered in the steel plants it was also sighted down the mine shafts. When miners sought wage increases to combat steeply rising prices, the operators clung to the technical point that the Armistice had ended only hostilities, not the war itself, and that wartime agreements to restrict wages still stood. With winter approaching, even moderate opinion viewed with dismay the call for a strike unless miners' demands for a 60 percent wage increase and a twenty-hour week were met, and the conservative press gorged itself on red scare stories. There were radicals among the miners who favored public ownership, and communist pamphlets were located calling for a general strike against "industrial slavery." The *New York Tribune* claimed that thousands of miners, "red-soaked in the doctrines of Bolshevism, clamor for the strike as a means of syndicalizing the coal mines . . . and even as starting a general revolution in America."

The administration itself, demonstrating its increasing coolness towards labor, agreed with the owners that wartime constraints still applied and that to breach them was "unlawful," and it secured an injunction forbidding United Mine Workers (UMW) leaders from taking any part in a strike. Labor leaders like Gompers, who thought they had established an accord with government during the war, felt betrayed. When nearly 400,000 miners nonetheless walked out on 1 November without the direction of UMW officials, the press concluded that Bolshevists were secretly controlling them. The government's antiunion stand, which owed more to Attorney General Palmer than to the sick Woodrow Wilson, nonetheless eventually ended the strike. Bureau of Investigation agents riddled the coalfields, alien labor activists were arrested, and UMW officials were cited for contempt of court. Influential members of the administration and many erstwhile Progressives outside it, even if they discounted warnings of a Bolshevist plot, came to regard the conflict as between the commonwealth and an interest group prepared to use force, and they concluded that they had to align themselves with the conservative champions of the former.

Saving the Republic

Even before the government lost patience with labor, it was taking action against radicals. Its legislation of 1917 and 1918 had rendered resident aliens vulnerable to deportation, and the secretary of labor had been attempting to deport some western Wobblies since the beginning of 1919. The wartime censorship of revolutionary publications remained in force. That revolutionaries were abroad in the land had been confirmed for many by the bomb scare of spring 1919, for not only had the attorney general's house been dynamited, but so had the homes of other officials and businessmen, and three dozen bombs had been found in the mail addressed to prominent persons. The source of the bombs has never been determined, although there was some evidence that the Palmer bomber, who had died in the explosion, was not only an anarchist but also an alien. While the newspapers were publicizing the first bombing incidents on May Day, socialists and other radicals in the major cities staged meetings and red flag parades, which in some cases police and vigilante action, often involving service veterans, turned into riots. For years there had been labor disturbances in Europe on May Day, and now it seemed that alien influences were invading the United States. After the bombing of his home in June, A. Mitchell Palmer secured $500,000 from Congress to pursue radicals, appointed the former head of the Secret Service, William J. Flynn, as chief of the Bureau of Investigation, and in August created the General Intelligence (or Radical) Division under the young law-school graduate J. Edgar Hoover.

Radicals could expect little protection from the courts. In 1919 the Supreme Court on several occasions upheld convictions that had been secured under the repressive wartime legislation. In the *Schenck* case in the spring Justice Oliver Wendell Holmes dismayed his liberal admirers by holding that the defendant's seditious utterances had represented a "clear and present danger" to the war effort. In the fall Justice John H. Clarke, one of those Progressives whose commitment to civil liberties had receded before the prospect of social disruption, framed the Court's decision in the *Abrams* case, confirming the conviction of a group of Bolshevik sympathizers who had attacked the American military intervention in Russia. Such court decisions did nothing to inhibit the mounting government campaign against radicalism.

Legislative pressure for an assault on radicals had been growing for some time. The Seattle general strike and a radical meeting in Washington had prompted an investigation by the Senate's Overman subcommittee, which had heard a parade of witnesses telling horror stories of Bolshevik rule in Russia and reported that aliens had created a serious Bolshevik menace in the United States. Even more spectacular were the investigations of the Lusk committee, set up by the New York legislature under pressure from local patriots and conservatives. The Lusk committee secured the cooperation of the Justice Department and the state police in a June raid on the Russian Soviet Bureau, a Russian government agency in New York, from which it removed cartloads of Russian propaganda. State Senator Lusk claimed this material showed that a Bolshevik revolution was being plotted in the United States, and to secure further evidence for this charge he authorized further raids on the Rand School, a socialist college, on the headquarters of the Socialist party, and on the IWW. The committee claimed that documents taken from the Rand School showed it was collaborating with the Russian Bureau and hatching revolution.

As radicalism was once again being defined as a foreign importation, government bureaucracies fumbled for ways of controlling aliens. The strikes of fall 1919 seemed to reinforce the need for some kind of administrative action. The Bureau of Immigration (in the Department of Labor) had lengthy experience of tagging Wobblies, and it now began to cooperate with the new General Intelligence Division (in the Department of Justice) in the task of identifying alien radicals, focusing particularly on the Union of Russian Workers (URW), whose constitution spoke of "forcible social revolution," and on the two Communist parties. Attorney General Palmer, prodded in October by an impatient Senate, settled on deportation as his most usable weapon, for the earlier war against the Wobblies meant that the legal machinery for ejecting subversive aliens was already largely in place, an administrative procedure that would avoid the inconvenience of proving crimes in courtrooms. Early in November he authorized raids on the offices of the URW in a dozen cities, and several hundred persons were arrested. Local officials were emboldened to follow suit, not least in New York, where the Lusk committee supervised police raids that netted about 500 suspected radicals, some of whom, including Benjamin Gitlow, were charged under the state's criminal anarchy laws. Although many had to be released after these various raids, 246 aliens were eventually detained for deportation. Palmer reported to the Senate on the widespread radical activity he believed he had found in the United States and asked for a peacetime sedition law so that citizens as well as aliens could be rounded up. A red scare would thus enable a flimsy federal government to extend its internal controls.

Several members of the cabinet were hostile to the trend of administration measures, particularly to the coal strike injunctions and the URW raids, but President Wilson had recently suffered a stroke, and A. Mitchell Palmer and presidential secretary Joseph Tumulty, both firmly antiradical, were effectively conducting domestic policy. They were sustained by a public alarmed by the unnerving events of the fall of 1919, notably the police, steel, and coal strikes and the Centralia massacre, and by the evidence of bomb and revolutionary activity apparently uncovered by the raids. A hesitant Labor Department finally yielded to the pressure from other parts of the government for deportation, and on 21 December some 249 aliens left New York harbor on an army transport ship destined for Soviet Russia. Aboard the "Soviet Ark" were about 200 members of the URW arrested in the November raids and a number of anarchists, among them Emma Goldman. The protracted campaign to behead radicalism by banishing its presumed leaders was finally producing results.

Attorney General Palmer now believed he had perfected the techniques for protecting the republic from its enemies. He would conduct raids on radical organizations, arrest those found, and deport the aliens among them with a minimum of judicial procedure. On 2 January 1920 Palmer unleashed hundreds of agents in over thirty cities in twenty-three states across the country, aided by former APL members and other volunteers, the targets now being the two Communist parties. Over six thousand arrests or detentions were effected, many of them without warrant, in an operation that scooped up most local Communist leaders as well as others who happened to stray into the net. The aliens among them were to be detained for deportation; radical citizens were to be prosecuted under the state criminal syndicalist laws. Smaller raids followed. Although the scope of the raids, and the unpleasant conditions in which the detainees were kept, provoked some criticism even from conservatives, A. Mitchell Palmer emerged as the nation's patriotic savior, confidently announcing that he had halted "the advance of 'red radicalism' in the United States."

The January raids were the high point of the Big Red Scare. The enormous publicity they generated briefly buoyed up antiradical elements across the nation. Congress excluded the Milwaukee Socialist Victor Berger from his seat for a second time, because of his conviction under the Espionage Act, although his constituents had recently insisted on returning him again in a special election. In New York five Socialist members of the legislature were expelled in April, though they had sustained no criminal convictions, the Speaker of the assembly claiming that their party represented a conspiracy to overthrow the government by force. Elsewhere local officials took it on themselves to arrest suspected radicals, to break up strikes, and to wreak revenge on Wobblies for the Centralia deaths. In April the Justice Department arrested the leaders of a railroad strike, alleging Wobbly and Communist influence.

The attorney general also attempted to use the prevailing temper to secure stronger antiradical legislation, and Congress turned to the formulation of its first peacetime sedition law since 1798. But Palmer's bid to enlarge the federal police power was frustrated, for the Senate and the House passed different bills, and agreement had not been reached when the Big Red Scare began to subside. But if citizens thus retained their constitutional rights, aliens remained vulnerable, and an Immigration Act of June 1920 provided for the deportation of aliens associated with organizations deemed subversive by the 1918 act and of those convicted under wartime legislation and certified by the secretary of labor as "undesirable residents of the United States." Nativist sentiment for restricting immigration was mounting, and this continued to be one area where the administration could augment its antiradical apparatus.

The states too decided to strengthen their legislation. Indeed, many states regarded federal antiradical legislation as inadequate, since it had for the most part been framed for the war emergency and had already expired or was in the course of doing so. Although A. Mitchell Palmer was an attested patriot, other members of the cabinet, such as Secretary of Labor William Wilson, were regarded as unreliable on this issue, and by February 1920 Congress itself was having difficulty in framing an acceptable peacetime sedition law. The prosecution of radicals—as opposed to aliens—thus fell to the states. Several western states had enacted criminal syndicalist laws during the wartime assault on the IWW, and in 1919–20 most other states adopted similar measures, prohibiting the advocacy of the violent or unlawful overthrow of government. Sedition laws were also passed, punishing abusive criticism of public officials. By 1921 there were sedition or criminal syndicalist laws, or both, in thirty-five of the forty-eight states, and laws prohibiting displays of the red flag were similarly widespread. Such legislation made it possible for state and local officials to strike at radicals within their communities. By the end of 1919 they were doing so, and perhaps three hundred of the many arrested under state laws during the Big Red Scare were ultimately sentenced to prison.

In New York, where the Lusk committee had raided Communist party headquarters, charges of criminal anarchy were pressed against Communist leaders, most notably Benjamin Gitlow, who was convicted in February 1920. "A few more convictions like this," commented the *New York Times*, "may cool the ferocity of the thousands of Communists now in the United States." New York had found an apparently acceptable way of removing radical leaders from public life, and other convictions followed. Leading members of the Communist party and the Communist Labor party in Illinois, where Chicago remained a center of radicalism, and California, where state prosecutions ran into the hundreds, were also given prison sentences. As the attorney general attempted to round up aliens, those states conscious of housing significant numbers of Communists sought to put them behind bars.

But the Big Red Scare did not long survive the January raids. A. Mitchell Palmer had never enjoyed the firm backing of his government colleagues, and some stiffened their resistance when they saw the indiscriminate nature of the raids and their failure to uncover evidence of revolutionary conspiracy. At the end of January they were encouraged by a ruling of Justice Oliver Wendell Holmes that evidence seized illegally could not be used in a criminal prosecution. Secretary of Labor Wilson, who had been ill at the time of the Palmer raids, restored an earlier rule strengthening an alien's right to counsel during deportation proceedings. The assistant secretary, Louis F. Post, was even less enamored of Palmer's actions, and since he was formally in charge of deportation proceedings he insisted that such rights as aliens possessed by respected. He soon began releasing large numbers of those hauled in by Palmer, insisting that in most cases there was no firm and legal evidence that they were anything other than law-abiding and industrious men. Palmer suggested that Post was "a Bolshevik himself," and impeachment proceedings against him were initiated in Congress, but in an appearance before a House committee Post impressively detailed the abuses suffered by the detainees, pointed out that the only evidence of revolution discovered in the raids was a meager three pistols, and reproved committee members for slighting the Bill of Rights. His critics began to concede that even aliens were entitled to some protection against arbitrary treatment. The Department of Labor maintained its stance, and by the summer of 1920 departmental and court rulings had asserted that mere membership in the two Communist parties was not grounds for deportation. About six hundred aliens of those arrested in 1919–20 were eventually deported, but not the thousands Palmer anticipated. The long-standing bureaucratic ambition to save America from radicalism by expelling its alien sponsors was in large measure ultimately frustrated.

The Department of Labor's success in its contest of wills with the Justice Department was aided by a changing public mood. The publicity given to Justice Department abuses by the Post hearing and other inquiries had given pause even to many conservatives. The arrests of law-abiding citizens, the illegal detentions, and the occasional deaths in custody served to discredit the attorney general's operation. In May twelve distinguished legal authorities published their pungently titled

THE BIG RED SCARE

Report upon the Illegal Practices of the United States Department of Justice. In June the respected and conservative *Christian Science Monitor* concluded that an apparent excess of radicalism "was certainly met with something like an excess of suppression."

The ousting of the five Socialists from the New York Assembly occasioned an even greater outcry than the Palmer raids. The Socialist party, after all, had been contesting elections since the beginning of the century, federal legislation had never been aimed at it, and four of the Socialists had served in the assembly before. The Republican party's presidential candidate of 1916, Charles Evans Hughes, himself protested strongly against the expulsions, as did Theodore Roosevelt, Jr., and such stalwart conservatives as Senator Warren G. Harding. They registered dismay at the arbitrary disfranchisement of sixty thousand voters of New York City. So did the voters, who reelected the five Socialists in special elections held in September, and when the assembly again barred three of them the press widely condemned the act as "a worse blunder than the first." The rule of law and the principle of representative government possessed sufficient vigor in the United States to truncate the Big Red Scare.

Greater sensitivity to civil liberties was made possible by the apparent ebbing of the red tide. The foreign threat was demonstrably lower. Although Soviet Russia had withstood the attention of the Allies, the Bolshevik revolutionaries elsewhere in Europe had been repulsed. The Communist International was failing. Within the United States the series of sensational strikes had ended, and though smaller stoppages continued they were less often concerned with the issue of collective bargaining. The bombings of May and June 1919 had ceased, and by the time another bomb exploded on Wall Street in September 1920 public tensions had eased. The economy itself was thriving by early 1920, prosperity lasting long enough for fears of labor disorder to subside. Further, the Big Red Scare had largely succeeded in cutting down radicalism. The labor movement had become less aggressive, and the AFL was cooperating in denouncing what radicals remained in its ranks. The IWW had been virtually destroyed, and the Socialist party had been weakened by the defections of its left-wing members to the new Communist parties. The two Communist parties themselves had totaled about seventy thousand members on their formation in the late summer of 1919, but a year later they had been reduced to perhaps ten thousand, and by then they had both gone underground. As both the enemy without and the enemy within shriveled, press and government increasingly shrugged off the red scare warnings of the patriotic societies.

The collapse of the Big Red Scare was hastened by the unspectacular events of May Day 1920. The attorney general, anxious for vindication, continued to insist on the possibility of revolution, and as 1 May approached he admonished the nation to expect a repetition of the disturbances of the 1919 May Day. J. Edgar Hoover's Radical Division, eager to guarantee its survival, searched for evidence and warned of a revolutionary plot to assassinate government officials and blow up government buildings. In many areas the police and militia were duly placed on alert, but May Day passed without a single disruptive incident.

Palmer's influence waned rapidly, and so little enthusiasm was displayed for his nomination for president at the Democratic national convention in June that he was obliged to withdraw it. Calvin Coolidge fared better; his celebrated handling of the Boston police strike secured for him the Republican vice-presidential nomination. But the presidential campaign of 1920 demonstrated that the Big Red Scare was over, for even the horrific Wall Street bombing that inflicted twenty-nine immediate deaths failed to precipitate a panic. The Democratic candidates loyally sought to make the League of Nations the central issue, while Warren G. Harding for the Republicans delivered himself of good-natured banalities and promised a comforting return to "normalcy." He also observed that "too much has been said about Bolshevism in America." The amiable Harding won with 61 percent of the popular vote, and A. Mitchell Palmer's responsibility for American justice was at an end.

Yet the red scare had left its mark. Another presidential candidate was Eugene V. Debs, who with 3.5 percent of the vote polled better than he had in 1904 and 1908, if not 1912. This time, however, Debs was fighting the election from the Atlanta penitentiary.

From one perspective the Big Red Scare marked the climax to a half-century of tension. Ever since the Paris Commune, as American society was being brutally wrenched into new shape by the processes of industrialization, urbanization, and immigration, the propertied classes had feared a popular insurrection fomented or controlled by foreign revolutionaries. Such fears had waxed and waned with commercial prosperity and social discontent, but they had never entirely disappeared and they erratically thrust their way up the polity with the emergence of a national economy and the growing authority of state and federal governments. The first major red scare, the Haymarket Affair, had centered on a city; the second, consummated by the Palmer raids, was national in scope and was largely the work of federal authorities, and between the two many state governments had vigorously used red scare tactics. The bursts of antiradical activity signaled the trajectory taken by class conflict through the growing layers of government responsibility during the long process characterized by Robert Wiebe as "the search for order." They also signaled the weakness of republican government, as labor protests were regularly magnified into revolutionary conspiracies in order to mobilize public opinion, vigilantes, and police machinery against them. Even the federal government was unequal to the challenge, for it resorted to the Palmer raids only because it lacked other counterrevolutionary weapons, and one of Palmer's objectives was to increase government power with a sedition law when the raids had uncovered sufficient evidence to justify one. The long-felt insecurity of respectable citizens was paralleled by the insecurity of the administration. In the event, the federal authorities had to surrender the peacetime control of sedition to the states, which had already been extending their own antisubversion measures because of their doubts about the capability of the national government.

Nonetheless the Big Red Scare had for the first time brought the authority of the federal government into the anticommunist cause. Federal agents were liaising with employers, as well as with patriotic societies and local police officials, in the political surveillance of foreign-born residents. The administration, of course, had been drawn into the offensive against the Wobblies during World War I, and the deportation procedures it had fashioned then, as well as the propaganda and vigilante activities it had unleashed in its efforts to unite the population against the Kaiser, were among the ingredients that had made possible the excesses over which A. Mitchell Palmer presided. The federal government was not solely responsible for the scare, but its wartime strategy had contributed to it.

It would be perverse, however, to root the Big Red Scare solely in long-term or even wartime trends. As it happened, industrial conflict in the United States was reaching its peak at about the same time as news was arriving of the revolution in Russia and the subsequent communist successes in other parts of Europe. The modest protection that Progressive sensibilities had afforded to radicals could not withstand this ominous eruption of class warfare at home and abroad. American political culture had long nurtured suspicions of enemies both without and within, bent on wrecking delicate republican forms, and for some the Bolshevik apparition fulfilled an old prophecy. The uncertain democratic politics of the United States encouraged them to trumpet its dangers in alarmist tones. Their warnings seemed to have some credibility because a small minority did excitedly respond to the promise of the Russian Revolution, a minority largely composed of those aliens whom Americans had long been taught to distrust. The scare subsided as the Communist International faltered both abroad and at home, but it left behind it an abiding suspicion of the Soviet model of government, a cluster of patriotic organizations ever vigilant for signs of subversion, and a body of federal and state laws and a bureaucratic apparatus ready to be mobilized in the defense of the republic. In the 1920s it would be possible to put into place the final barriers against that form of revolution imported by foreigners.

5

ONE HUNDRED PERCENT AMERICANISM (1920–1929)

•

In November 1921 the ratifications for the German peace treaty were exchanged, thus ending such justifications as there were for retaining the measures adopted during the war emergency. One consequence of the nation's now-confirmed peacetime status was the release from the Atlanta penitentiary on Christmas Eve of Eugene V. Debs, for as the president said, "I want him to eat his Christmas dinner with his wife." As it happened, Debs did not dine with his wife on Christmas Day, for he accepted an invitation to call at the White House during his journey home, after which he told reporters, "Mr. Harding appears to me to be a kind gentleman, one whom I believe possesses humane impulses." This exchange of pleasantries was an expression of the mood heralded by Warren G. Harding in his promise to return "serenity" to American life, or, as he less elegantly put it, to restore "normalcy." Warren G. Harding was as conservative a political figure as any, but his was a conservatism married to civility, which offered a shred of protection to America's surviving radicals.

The normality ushered in by the Harding administration, however, was no golden age of political liberty. With the federal government again denying that it had much of a regulatory role in American life, social tensions that had been exacerbated by the strains of war could no longer be contained. Deprived of the tenuous glue of Progressivism and the self-sacrificing ethic of wartime patriotism, American society fragmented into its querulous parts. For half a century the great transforming processes of industrialization, urbanization, and immigration had been multiplying the number of competing economic, cultural, and ethnic forces in the United States, and the recent war had heightened consciousness of race and class. Many of these interests had acquired an institutional substance, and the major parties that had for so long ordered American political life were themselves subject to competition from pressure groups like the National Association of Manufacturers and the Anti-Saloon League.

As the need to unite against a common enemy receded, Americans were more prepared to indulge their mutual hostilities. Prominent agnostics affronted those who passionately upheld literal-minded Christianity, the "drys" virtuously defended the Prohibition experiment against the "wets," nativists forthrightly demanded the exclusion of immigrants from the country, labor unions fought against a new employers' offensive. For much of their history Americans had been united after a fashion by the common political values of republicanism, but these no longer seemed to bind this discordant society. Those groups who identified with the old-stock communities of the past responded by transmuting republican principles into the strident values of One Hundred Percent Americanism. This impulse for cultural homogeneity went with a rejection of all foreign influences. As isolationism once more became the guiding principle in foreign policy, conservative economic, racial, and religious interests converged in demanding the preservation of a God-fearing Anglo-Saxon America in which property was sacrosanct. Whatever radicals were loose in this society would not gain much comfort from the presence of "humane impulses" in the White House, and those who were linked to a foreign power would certainly find themselves without friends.

Harding's geniality, and the forbearance of his gloomier successors, were in any case as much the product of calculation as of temperament. Many businessmen and politicians as opposed to radicalism as A. Mitchell Palmer recognized that the attorney general had overplayed his hand. The twin interests of property and order might be better served by a more relaxed conservatism. Further, the passing of the wartime crisis reduced the legitimate functions of the federal government. If it saw little reason to harass radicals, it saw just as little reason actively to defend them, and state and local authorities, reactionary businessmen, small-town fundamentalist Protestants, and vigilante groups were able to prey on dissidents with relative impunity. World War I and the Big Red Scare had left a fistful of patriotic organizations strewn across the land, convinced that the republic remained in danger and that its survival rested on an active citizenry. The dissolution of republican harmony, after all, was witness to an ideological as well as a physical invasion, and the exclusion of aliens had to be accompanied by rejection of their ideas. For much of the 1920s patriotic impulses would prevail over humane impulses.

Patriotic Impulses

Harding's pardon of Debs did not mark the return of comity to American public life. For one thing, it was prompted not so much by kindness as by the administration's desire to maintain control over more dangerous radicals. A campaign for amnesty for *all* political prisoners had been mounting, and the new attorney general, Harry M. Daugherty, hoped that the Christmas freeing of Debs and twenty-four others would arrest the general amnesty drive before it had "gone too far." They were enough to satisfy the AFL, which withdrew from the amnesty crusade. Many Wobblies and others that the Justice Department feared would reanimate American radicalism remained in prison, at least for the time being, although most had been freed by the end of 1923. Further, the cautious conservatism of the Harding and Coolidge administrations did little to curb the patriotic passions that were searing the country. Although A. Mitchell Palmer's deportation drive had been frustrated, the tensions the Big Red Scare had fed on remained formidable and in some respects were exacerbated by the collapse of Wilsonian idealism and the consequent abhorrence of involvement with Europe. The isolationist impulse deepened the repudiation of foreign influences, and if immigrants for the moment aroused greater fears than radicals, the two could never be entirely separated. The rejection of the European world and all it stood for unleashed an ideological crusade that demanded adherence to the values of One Hundred Percent Americanism.

The xenophobic patriotism of the 1920s owed a great deal to heightened sensitivity to issues of class, race, and religion, which mocked that old American impulse to find union in political ideology. In this divided and troubled society conservative economic and ethnocultural interests, particularly those feeling threatened by the cosmopolitan culture emerging in the cities, cleaved fiercely to traditional values. The demand for One Hundred Percent Americanism held some appeal for a variety of disparate if sometimes overlapping constituencies, whether antilabor businessmen, fundamentalist clergymen, old-stock midwesterners, southern racists, or World War I veterans. The powerful republican tradition of active citizenship proved well suited to a polity in which parties as mass organizations had contracted and in which interest groups, with their enthusiastic members, lobbyists, and well-directed propaganda, were playing larger roles. Several interest groups lent their money and muscles to the ideal of Americanism and kept up the pressure for cultural uniformity throughout the decade.

Among the leaders in this intensified ideological warfare were the patriotic societies. Older bodies like the Daughters of the American

Revolution continued to prowl the republic, but the quintessential examples of patriotism in action were the veterans' groups, composed of men who had fought for their country or at least had served it. Having risked their lives for "the last, best hope of earth," many of them cherished an idealized image of the republic in which there was no more room for socialism than for other foreign influences. The American Legion in particular was becoming a respected institution, and it promoted a version of patriotism that differed little from that of conservative businessmen. At its 1921 annual convention it defined a "radical" as anyone who attempted "to change our form of government through revolution"; it opposed the distribution of left-wing literature and urged its members to keep a "watchful eye" on radical propagandists. Veterans, it seemed, were appointing themselves the guardians of civic virtue, an increasingly institutionalized form of vigilance that was part of the growing bureaucratization of modern life. Reports of violence by overzealous legionnaires hastened the establishment of the Legion's National Americanism Commission, which was destined to play a major role in combating subversion. The commission's goal was to realize in the United States "the basic ideal of . . . one hundred per cent Americanism through the planning, establishment, and conduct of a continuous, constructive, educational establishment," to which end it urged English and civics courses for immigrants, encouraged patriotic rituals in schools, distributed patriotic literature, organized essay contests, and sponsored junior baseball teams. The Veterans of Foreign Wars (VFW) also pioneered an "Americanization" program in the 1920s. More elitist was the Military Order of the World War, which was disturbed by the American Civil Liberties Union's belief in "rampant free speech" and by the presence at a women's pacifist meeting of Bertrand Russell, "the effeminate, pacifist representative of the 'Pink Intelligentsia' of England."

Among the earliest to enlist in the patriotic cause were business corporations. They marched under the flag of the "American Plan," a new designation given to the open shop to emphasize the alien nature of unionism. Anxious to put an end to the incessant strike and union activity that had characterized the 1910s, and emboldened by the crushing of organized labor in the great steel strike of 1919, many employers were determined to win greater control over their work forces. In the aftermath of the Big Red Scare it was an easy matter to represent unionism, or at least the closed shop, as unpatriotic. "You can hardly conceive of a more un-American, a more anti-American institution than the closed shop," insisted a member of the National Association of Manufacturers in 1920. "It is really very remarkable that it is allowed to exist . . . under the American flag." The American answer to this alien growth was to be the open shop, where unionists and nonunionists alike in theory received equal treatment (though in practice unionists were not often tolerated), and employers across the country formed local open shop associations. Such organizations as the Detroit Employers Association and the Los Angeles Merchants and Manufacturers Association championed the open shop in their own communities.

In January 1921 several state associations met in Chicago to coordinate their activities and formally endorsed what they called the "American Plan." Influential national bodies like the National Association of Manufacturers and the National Founders' Association aggressively promoted the Plan as more compatible with traditional American ideals than collective bargaining. "Every man to work out his own salvation," said the Plan, "and not to be bound by the shackles of organization to his own detriment." In many areas union organizations suffered serious reverses, particularly during the depression of 1921–22. Employers supplemented the American Plan campaign with blacklists, labor spies, and "yellow dog" contracts disavowing union membership. This patriotic offensive, designed to deepen the un-American coloring of class-conscious unionism, was not pressed by all employers, but even those who preferred to experiment with welfare capitalism, such as company-sponsored pension and insurance plans, as Stuart Brandes has noted, were largely motivated by the fear of Bolshevism.

The American Plan groups and employers' associations shaded into ostensibly patriotic societies dominated by the business ethic. In a country where a president could avow that "the chief business of the American people is business," the distinction between patriotic and business activities was unclear. Old organizations like the American Defense Society and the National Civic Federation continued to flourish, the latter still trying to promote peace between employers and workers and encouraging Sam Gompers's antiradical activities in the labor movement. There were new and more intemperate groups too, such as the Better America Federation, founded by California businessmen to champion the open shop and warn against red revolution, and the Minute Men of the Constitution, organized by the Illinois banker (and future vice president) Charles G. Dawes with similar objectives. These bodies distributed literature, provided speakers, mobilized voters, and lobbied governments in the interests of One Hundred Percent Americansm, keeping alive the language of the Big Red Scare.

The economic conservatism of the 1920s was powerfully reinforced by a vibrant racism that also veiled itself in patriotic imagery. If white workers remained indifferent or hostile to employers' assaults on labor, they might respond to calls to preserve Anglo-Saxon purity. A part of the support for immigration restriction stemmed from labor's fears for jobs.

THE RED MENACE IN INDUSTRIAL AMERICA

The organization that most successfully harnessed the nativist fears and patriotic impulses of blue-collar workers, clerks, policemen, and many small farmers, as well as a few professional men, was the Ku Klux Klan. Many Klansmen were rural migrants to the growing cities, rootless and insecure individuals seeking refuge in traditional values from the strains of modern life. Between 1920 and 1926 the Klan enrolled over two million members and became a political force in several midwestern and southern states. Although it was primarily anti-Catholic, its superpatriotism was displayed in such publications as the *Texas 100 Per Cent American*, and it stridently perpetuated the old equation between the alien and the radical. In Kansas, for example, the Klan avowed a policy of preventing "unwarranted strikes by foreign labor agitators," as if American-born labor agitators were unheard of. Klansmen sometimes indulged in vigilante action, as in San Pedro, California, where employers incited Klansmen to prey on Wobblies in 1923–24.

The strength of the Klan in the Midwest and West testifies to the strength of nativism in those regions, but it was also sustained by the more traditional racism of the South, which took on an increasingly reactionary coloring in these years. With the fading of southern Populism and Progressivism, the South was restored to a conservative hegemony. The poll taxes, literacy tests, and low electoral turnouts of this one-party section left almost complete political power in the hands of the local economic elites, such as Black Belt planters and low-wage industrialists, who were generally ill disposed toward welfare and other legislation, which they branded as socialistic. Such southern Democrats looked with unease at the urban politics of Al Smith. Senator Nathaniel B. Dial of South Carolina complained in 1925 that the Democrats were falling prey to "a small alien faction. . . . the Democratic Party must declare whether it will serve high, straight, outspoken American Democracy or some kind of shambling, bastard, shame-faced mixture of so-called Democracy and alien-conceived bolshevism or socialism or hell broth of both." The parochial self-interest and racism of the ruling groups in the South shaped a political culture that was conservative to the point of reaction and instinctively antipathetic to any kind of radicalism. The powerful bond of race linked these elites to the small farmers and blue-collar workers who donned the robes of the Klan.

If the imperatives of class and race made their contributions to the patriotic atmosphere of the 1920s, so did those of religion. Intertwined with the traditionalism of small-town and rural America was the preservative and even fundamentalist thrust of American Protestantism. The perfectionist impulses of Christianity were capable of sending its believers on some highly radical odysseys, and there were a few American churchmen who thrilled to the promise of the Russian Revolution, but in the 1920s the Protestant denominations for the most part reflected and reinforced the conservatism of the larger society. Although attendance declined in the second half of the decade, more Americans were church members than ever before, in part because material success was widely believed to be a reward for rectitude, and a best-seller of the era was Bruce Barton's *The Man Nobody Knows,* which presented Christ as an enterprising young executive. During the Big Red Scare some churchmen had offered religion as an antidote to radicalism. "If American life is to have a tone, this tone must come not from the cities with their varied and heterogeneous racial groups, but from the villages and country districts," argued one religious journal. "It is the task of the churches to see that this tone continues one of Godliness and patriotism, high ideals and clean living." Such articles in the religious press as "Socialism is Un-American" were presumably intended to strengthen this tone.

If the mainstream churches seemed to be succumbing to business values, the evangelicals and fundamentalists more fervently struck back at the moral degeneration and irreligion they discerned in the Jazz Age. The powerful cause of Prohibition did little to foster respect for civil liberties. The fundamentalists often enough lost their battles with the modernists, but they spoke for many Americans who hankered after an oldtime religion and the strict inerrancy of the Bible. Protestant fundamentalism was central to the beliefs of the Ku Klux Klan, which recruited many clergymen in the early 1920s for its version of "practical patriotism."

The patriotic offensive of the 1920s was an assault on ideas and customs as well as persons. It was not only foreigners themselves but foreign influences that were occasioning disquiet. Fears of an urban revolt or of violent industrial conflict may have declined, but the xenophobic sentiments of isolationist America deepened apprehensions of a more insidious subversion of American ideals, whether by free-thinking Darwinian evolutionists, Jewish intellectuals, or even American radicals aided and abetted by Moscow. In this perspective, America's ills were proof of the erosion of that Christian republican ideology that had united a diverse people in the past. If the traditional values of white Anglo-Saxon America were to be preserved, it was reasoned, alien influences had to be kept out of those institutions that molded opinion, most notably the schools. The American Legion, the Klan, and the patriotic societies, as well as the Hearst press and other newspapers, supported immigration restriction and antisedition laws, but they were also determined to use the education system to promote the goal of One Hundred Percent Americanism.

"It is notorious," said the Klan, "that our public school system, which is the strongest bulwark of Americanism, is being attacked from within and without by papists and anti-Christian Jews of the bolshevik Socialist stripe." More reputable lobbies like the bar associations were also worried about impressionable young minds and called for "patriotic instruction," loyalty oaths for teachers, and the scrutiny of textbooks. Two states had adopted oaths (of loyalty to national and state constitutions) during the heightened wartime and postwar fervor, and seven others followed suit in the 1920s. In California the Better America Federation managed to have the "radical" periodicals the *Nation* and *New Republic* banned in schools. The American Legion in 1921 formed an accord with the National Education Association, an organization of school superintendents and teachers, to promote their mutual interests in the teaching of American history and the Americanization of immigrants.

In 1922 the Legion commissioned the preparation of an American history text that would "preach on every page a vivid love of America," and the VFW's National Americanization Committee devoted its energies to the "elimination of un-American textbooks." Public utility corporations, frightened of municipal ownership, sponsored with some success the writing of "Americanized" texts. As a result of such pressures, in some states school boards threw out history textbooks that were deemed insufficiently patriotic. If the offense of some books was to give a kindly view of the British during the American Revolution, supposedly subversive influences were also being chased out of the schools, and a tradition had been further developed subjecting education to the demanding scrutiny of patriotic societies, businessmen, and politicians. Future red scares would bring a resurgence of these pressures.

The ideological warriors of the 1920s did not always win their battles; much of their intensity, after all, stemmed from the recognition that the values of white Anglo-Saxon Protestant America had already been seriously eroded. A new urban political culture was emerging that would be strong enough to make Al Smith, Roman Catholic son of immigrants, the Democratic candidate for the presidency in 1928. But the attempts to drive foreign tendencies from American life served for the moment to strengthen the hands of those who wanted to place additional curbs on communism.

Containing Communism

The popular campaigns against foreign influence made it possible to strengthen the country's defenses against red revolution. Although fears of a Bolshevik uprising were not what they had been in 1919–20, they did not disappear, and the Soviet Union's support for the Communist International (Comintern) meant that American officials at least had to consider the possibility that revolution might be exported to the United States. The State Department carefully monitored the extent of Comintern activity abroad, and in 1923 it uncovered Comintern instructions to the American Communist party anticipating the day "in the not too distant future" when it would "raise the red flag over the White House." For the most part government officials avoided the overreaction of A. Mitchell Palmer, but national and state governments availed themselves of whatever opportunities occurred to constrain radical movements.

Within the Justice Department there survived bureaucrats who had never quite shaken off the fear of insurrection, and Attorney General Daugherty himself inherited some of the perspectives of his predecessor. In 1922 disruption of the railroads was threatened when the rail shopmen went on strike, and although President Harding looked to a peaceable solution, Daugherty regarded the strike as "civil war" and began talking of "Reds" and "bolshevism." The strikers, he insisted, were prompted by "Red Agents of the Soviet Government." He secured an injunction against the unions that ended the strike, but it was so far reaching, seeming even to deny free speech to the strikers, that it attracted widespread criticism. When Senator Burton K. Wheeler attacked the injunction, Daugherty called him "the Communist leader in the Senate."

In fact Daugherty was almost alone in seeing the rail strike as inspired by Moscow, but his action reflected both the old tendency of American conservatives to equate strikes with rebellion and their new fear that revolution was being plotted by the Soviet Union. Some of Daugherty's information came from his department's Bureau of Investigation, headed by William J. Burns, formerly the chief of a detective agency known for its antiradical activities, and from its General Intelligence Division (GID), under J. Edgar Hoover. These agencies were developing a kind of bureaucratic vested interest in radicalism, against which they were charged with protecting the country. The GID employed undercover informers to report on Communists and other radicals, and Hoover set his agents to investigate the sundry critics of Palmer's raids. With the lapsing of the wartime espionage and sedition laws, the GID cooperated with state officials in having radicals prosecuted under the state criminal syndicalism laws. When Daugherty was replaced as attorney general in 1924 by Harlan F. Stone, who had disapproved of the bureau's red-baiting and other improprieties, Stone demanded Burns's resignation and ordered the termination of the antiradical activities. Nonetheless J. Edgar Hoover, who became director of the subsequently

reconstituted Federal Bureau of Investigation (FBI), maintained a surreptitious surveillance of liberal, radical, and labor organizations.

By the time federal agencies were relaxing their watch on Socialists,
Wobblies, and Communists, a body of legislation had come into existence to control the movements they represented. In a sense the antiradical campaigns that had been launched in the 1870s and 1880s were
finally consummated in the early 1920s, when the last barriers to a possible workers' insurrection were erected. The federal government assumed
responsibility for protecting the country from an alien invasion; the
state governments guarded against internal disruption.

The widely accepted premise that almost all dangerous radicals were
foreigners meant that the threat of subversion would in theory eventually be eliminated if immigration was ended. During and after World
War I various pieces of legislation had sought to ensure that aliens, particularly radicals, remained American residents only on sufferance.
When the drive to make radical aliens instantly deportable fell into dis-
repute following the Palmer raids, a logical alternative was to stop
aliens from entering the United States at all. The more ardent nativists
did call for total exclusion. Business leaders shrank from this solution,
because immigrants had always provided a supply of cheap and mostly
docile labor, but the nativist crusade was reaching its peak, determined
to save the United States from being overwhelmed by the supposedly
inferior races of eastern and southern Europe. It was the Anglo-Saxon
racism of both patrician elites and struggling poor whites, rather than
economic conservatism as such, that thus provided the final answer to
the invading red menace. The immigration acts of 1921 and 1924 for the
first time put a ceiling, a low one, on the number of foreigners from
outside the Western Hemisphere annually settling in the United States
and assigned to each nationality a quota reflecting its overall contribution to the existing American population. Thus only those countries
that had been sending immigrants for generations, like Britain and
Germany, could expect significant quotas. The system was designed to
perpetuate the ethnic composition of American society as it existed in
1920. As it happened, it would also keep out those Italian anarchists and
Russian Bolsheviks who had recently been suspected of plotting revolution in the United States.

By 1924, then, isolationist America had barricaded itself against an
alien and radical invasion. Formidable barriers had also been con-
structed against internal subversion, though with the demise of wartime
legislation the responsibility for sedition laws had returned to the states.
The western states had been using criminal syndicalism laws against the
Wobblies during the war, and in the red scare atmosphere after it sedition laws had been more generally adopted. By the time of the Harding

administration about three-quarters of the states possessed some legislation of this kind. A few attempted more ambitious antiradical measures. In New York the Lusk committee had proposed a raft of legislation, including laws to outlaw the Socialist party and to require loyalty oaths from teachers, which eventually passed in May 1921 when a Republican had replaced Al Smith as governor. But Smith soon won the governorship again on a Democratic platform hostile to the Lusk laws, and they were repealed in 1923. The Big Red Scare flickered on too in California, where criminal syndicalism laws were pressed against Wobblies and other radicals and where Upton Sinclair was arrested in 1923 for attempting to read the preamble of the American Constitution to a meeting of strikers. In Idaho the criminal syndicalism law was broadened in 1925 to increase the types of deeds defined as sabotage. The sedition and criminal syndicalism laws were generally upheld by the state courts, and together with a revitalized National Guard they complemented the fence built around the country against the alien hordes. They also provided some kind of legitimacy for the "red squads" established by many city police forces to harry communists and labor activists. The governing authorities had never been better equipped to resist revolution.

The political and bureaucratic guardians of property and order were powerfully buttressed by the Supreme Court. William Howard Taft became chief justice in 1921, and through the rest of the decade he presided over a court that generally protected the privileges of private property and corporate enterprise and that was prepared to curb the liberty to assault the status quo. Taft's objective, he told his brother toward the end of his reign, was "to prevent the bolsheviki from getting control." When the constitutionality of state antisubversion laws was challenged, the Court normally upheld them, as it did in the case of Gitlow v. New York in 1925, when it sustained the state's conviction of the Communist leader Benjamin Gitlow, and in 1927 in the case of Charlotte Anita Whitney, who had been convicted under a California law for her part in organizing the Communist Labor party. In the former case, in fact, the court had theoretically conceded some constitutional protection for personal liberties against state action, but it had left Gitlow in prison, and his rescue by a pardon from Governor Al Smith only illustrated the uncertain fates of radicals at the hands of local and state officials.

By the mid-1920s Americans had in principle gone a long way toward exorcising the specter of communism, at least in its classic shape as a lower-class uprising led by foreigners. The Big Red Scare had shattered the left-wing movements, and the federal immigration laws and state sedition laws militated against their resurrection. Labor militancy had also declined, business interests for the most part having won the mighty confrontations between labor and capital after the war. Those conservative fears that focused on the machinations of radical aliens and labor agitators did indeed begin to abate, but only very slowly, for Comintern meant that revolution could now be plotted from afar.

The Retreat from Reform

Active repression was all but superfluous when the pervasive conservative ethos of the 1920s—and the relative prosperity of many citizens—denied radicals a popular following and confined them to a few scattered retreats. The two Communist parties of 1919 had united after a fashion into the Communist party of the USA (CP) by 1923, when it emerged from underground with at most 15,000 members, but they continued to melt away, and in 1929 there were only 9,300 members paying dues, most of them foreign-born. The CP's bold forays into presidential elections told a similar withering story; its modest 24,000 votes in 1924 ebbed to a mere 21,000 in 1928. The Socialist party, for its part, had reached an impressive 109,000 members by 1919, but after the secessions to the Communist movement—and the Big Red Scare—its membership was massively down to 40,000 in 1920 and to a mere 8,477 by 1926. Further, these fragmentary parties expended some of their energies in assailing one another. The socialist moment had clearly gone. With the Wobblies also moribund, it is little wonder that conservatives of the stripe of Warren Harding and Herbert Hoover saw little in the way of a red menace.

Contributing to the flimsiness and isolation of the radical groups was the continued retreat of many liberals and Progressives from the cause of reform. The popular revulsion against foreign influences, together with the CP's evidently close ties to Moscow, encouraged men and women in the traditionally reformist sectors of public life to distance themselves from the suspect Communist movement. Settlement houses, for example, found that the taint of "radicalism" made fund-raising difficult, and a proposed constitutional amendment to protect child labor was obstructed by charges that it was inspired by Moscow. Settlement leader Vera Scudder was to recall that in the wake of the Big Red Scare even "social workers . . . carefully avoided any identification with the phraseology of social reform."

The cause of reform was also losing its appeal to politicians. The Big Red Scare had completed the disenchantment of many Progressives with the prospect of a benign state serving the interests of all. Government power, rather than being used for social reconstruction, had been used to suppress America's cherished liberties. Rather as some Radical Republicans had become disillusioned with the notion of government as an agent of reform after the Civil War, when corruption and labor activism had driven them instead to become champions of laissez-faire, so the misuse of government authority after World War I impelled erstwhile Progressives to rediscover the virtues of classical liberalism. Many liberals did remain true intellectually to the Progressive tradition, but there was little to be said for seeking to enlarge government at a time when it was in the hands of conservatives, with its regulatory commissions increasingly staffed by businessmen. Some liberals and intellectuals opted out of public and political life, and a few found their faith in democracy wavering. In any case, the old Progressive constituencies were themselves now often prepared to settle for "normalcy," the consumer boom of the 1920s perhaps serving to assuage their old yearnings for social improvement. Middle-class citizens who might once have been aroused by the reforming fervor of Theodore Roosevelt or Woodrow Wilson now delighted in the iconoclastic darts of H. L. Mencken, with their coating of contempt for both government and people. The chastened liberalism of the Progressives—the "tired radicals," in Walter Weyl's phrase—meant that such socialists and communists as survived enjoyed few well-placed allies and that the reigning conservatives could feel unusually secure.

Those Progressives who did continue the struggle found they were forced to make their own accommodation to the temper of the 1920s. There were liberals in both major parties who were deeply distressed by the conservatism of their colleagues and of the Republican administrations, but an effective reformist strategy eluded them. For the 1924 presidential election a sprinkling of Progressive, farm, labor, and socialist groups attempted to offer an alternative to reaction by launching a separate Progressive ticket. Robert M. La Follette headed it, linked to an antimonopoly platform calling for the public ownership of railroads and water power, but he successfully excluded Communists from the proceedings, insisting that they were acting under "orders from the Communist International in Moscow" and that their aims were "absolutely repugnant to democratic ideals and to all American aspirations." The rebuffed CP for the first time ran its own candidate for president, but as later anticommunist liberals also were to discover, La Follette's stance did not protect him from red baiting. It was La Follette rather than the CP candidate who drew the fire of the major parties, not least for his alleged Bolshevism. President Coolidge himself declared that the question was "whether America will allow itself to be degraded into a communistic or socialistic state or whether it will remain American." The subsequent Coolidge landslide, greatly aided by economic prosperity, spelled the end of the inchoate Progressive party. It also disheartened

those liberals who had remained within the established parties and persuaded the Democrats in Congress to assume a yet more conservative
stance.

The American Federation of Labor was no less anxious to dispel any
suspicions that it dallied with radicalism. Indeed, one of the most enduring and influential legacies of the 1920s was the bitter anticommunism
of much of the American labor movement. Samuel Gompers and like-
minded AFL leaders, of course, had long repudiated political action and
inveighed against socialists, but the struggling CP's attempts through
much of the 1920s to advance its cause by "boring from within" the existing unions were greatly resented by the AFL leadership. Union membership fell by 25 percent between 1920 and 1923, and Gompers was not
willing to incur further unpopularity. At the 1923 AFL convention a
Communist trade unionist was expelled by an overwhelming vote, the
first time an accredited delegate had been cast out of the broad church of
the AFL for his political views. The same convention opposed both
industrial unionism and the recognition of Soviet Russia on the grounds
that they were Communist issues.

The anticommunist and anti-Soviet sentiments in the AFL were
encouraged by the Roman Catholic church, to which many trade unionists belonged. Deeply distressed by the repression of Catholics in Soviet
Russia, which included the execution in 1923 of the vicar-general of the
church, Catholic priests were vehemently condemning the communists'
"atheistic" war on religion and leading their city congregations in regular prayers for the "conversion of Russia." The identification of the
American CP with Moscow severely limited its appeal among a large
proportion of American workers and drew the wrath of a patriotic AFL
leadership rendered exceedingly insecure by "the fall of the house of
labor."

When William Green succeeded Gompers as president in 1924, the
AFL became, if anything, even more conservative, eager to present itself
as a partner of business and an adversary of communism. The Communists hoped to appeal to disaffected workers, but the modest gains
they made in a few unions only made the AFL leaders even more hostile
to them. "It is no secret that the American Federation of Labor is the first
object of attack by the Communist movement," said one AFL official:
"Consequently the American Federation of Labor is the first line of
defense." In 1928 the AFL withdrew its support from the Brookwood
Labor College, a workers' school that was held to have become dangerously communistic in its teaching.

The beleaguered AFL repudiated the CP as much for its apparent foreign parentage as for its revolutionary ideology. The American CP may
not have been the knee-jerk agent of Moscow, but its connections with

Russia were intimate, in part because of the very hostility of the American environment. In the One Hundred Percent American atmosphere of the tribal twenties the AFL could ill afford such questionable associations. Its anticommunist stance, however, did not end the "threat" to organized labor represented by the Communist movement. The CP in the late 1920s abandoned the strategy of "boring from within," but its decision to create separate unions was no more welcome to the AFL.

The unorganized and demoralized state of much of American labor afforded the new policy some plausibility. That Communists might win recruits among American-born workers was illustrated by the Gastonia strike of 1929, where the despairing millworkers of this depressed North Carolina textile town clutched at the aid offered them by Communist union organizers. The Communist presence was visible and brought a predictable reaction. "Red Russianism Lifts Its Gory Hands Right Here in Gastonia," blazed a local newspaper advertisement, and a Department of Labor conciliator condemned the strike as "communistic." The violence that accompanied it took the lives of the local police chief and a woman strike leader. The national and local press had no difficulty discerning the bloody fangs of Bolshevism in these incidents, and the crushing of the strike was followed by the conviction of its apparent instigators for conspiracy leading to murder. The identification of these leaders in the public mind with "Red Russianism" was completed when they took refuge in the Soviet Union while out on bail. Anarchism and revolutionary communism had always been seen as alien creations, but the CP's evident closeness to a major and disturbing foreign power reinforced its un-American image. The patriotic AFL distanced itself from industrial disputes in which Communists were seen to be involved. It condemned the Gastonia strike and prohibited its members from having anything to do with it. The AFL hierarchy was never willing to accept Communists as allies, and the emergence of Communists as rivals for working-class support only intensified its antipathy.

The hostility shown by the Progressives and by organized labor completed the Communists' sense of isolation. Condemned by public opinion, hemmed in by the law, and hounded by police "red squads," by employers' hired detectives, and by patriotic vigilantes, not only Communists but countless Wobblies, labor organizers, civil liberties lawyers, and aliens suffered beatings and arrests in the 1920s. The vulnerability of radicals was most vividly exemplified by the Sacco-Vanzetti case. Arrested in 1920 for the murder of a factory paymaster in South Braintree, Massachusetts, Nicola Sacco and Bartolomeo Vanzetti were Italian-born anarchists whose guilt was readily inferred from their foreign origin and radical beliefs. Called "those anarchist bastards" by the judge who tried them, their conviction in 1921 was based on evidence and procedures that were so questionable as to fuel a protracted campaign for a new trial. Prominent civil libertarians took up their cause, which enlisted the energies and passion of liberals throughout the United States and of distinguished persons abroad. Like the Haymarket Affair four decades earlier, the Sacco-Vanzetti case reverberated around the world. The campaign was unsuccessful, except in polarizing emotion, and as the day of the executions approached the authorities prepared for disorder. On 6 August 1927 six bombs exploded in three different American cities, and later demonstrations were broken up by the police. The electrocution of Sacco and Vanzetti served to confirm the radicals' conviction that American capitalism was prepared to murder its critics and effected the final disillusionment of many liberals with American civilization. The case displayed to the world the antialien prejudices of popular patriotism, the primacy of business values, the conservatism of the courts, and the cynical acquiescence of federal and state governments in a process that victimized men for their political beliefs.

·

In the 1920s Industrial America finished fashioning its protracted response to the threat of a violent insurrection inspired by the foreign-born. That species of red menace that had haunted the propertied classes since the Paris Commune was finally being routed. On the eve of the Great Crash American anticommunism was a more formidable force than it had been even in the days of the Big Red Scare. Under A. Mitchell Palmer's direction it had been discredited by its very zeal. Indeed, Progressive and labor-endorsed candidates had done relatively well in the midterm elections of 1922, and the CP had more members in 1923 than it did in 1929. By the end of the decade many more aliens were being quietly deported than had been dispatched by Attorney General Palmer, in large part because of the tightening of the immigration laws. The antiforeign sentiments meant that the popular identification of a radical as an alien was stronger than ever, and it was given considerable legitimacy as American Communists affirmed their faith in the Russian experiment and appeared to accept direction from Moscow. The barbed-wire fence of the new immigration laws, however, ensured that this alien body would not be significantly replenished from foreign sources, and the network of antisubversion laws across the states was upheld by a Supreme Court sensitive to the needs of property and order. The Republican administrations did not actively harass radicals, but J. Edgar Hoover's FBI and the State Department kept a surreptitious eye on them, supplemented by the vigilantes and patriots who roamed the land and by pressure groups like the American Legion and the Ku Klux Klan who were discovering their political clout. A Protestant, widely Prohibitionist, and in parts fundamentalist countryside, particularly in the Midwest and South, sought a new ideological harmony in the values of One Hundred Percent Americanism.

Radicals in the past had sometimes reached a protective accord with influential middle-class reform or working-class labor movements, but Progressivism had lost its self-confidence in the 1920s and organized labor was fast losing members, and so both defensively arrayed themselves against the Communists. The propertied classes no longer felt particularly insecure, but the labor movement did. The growing bitterness within the trade union movement toward the Communist party was to remain an important ingredient of American anticommunism, comparable to the suspicion and hostility found in business and certain church circles. American capital for its part was gaining self-confidence from its repeated victories over labor and its profits from the consumer boom, and its very success was serving as its triumphant vindication. In 1928 Americans elected as their president a man who assured them that "no one can rightly deny the fundamental correctness of our economic system." When he took the oath of office the resilient strands of American anticommunism were woven together as tightly as they were ever likely to be.

PART TWO

THE RED MENACE
IN GLOBAL AMERICA

•

In the aftermath of the Russian Revolution and the ending of large-scale immigration, American perceptions of the communist threat gradually changed. Communism had ceased to be a free-floating European "ism" that might excite the "dangerous classes" and had become identified with the implacable regime in Russia, whence revolutions directed at capitalist states could henceforth be plotted. The class war was being replaced by a global struggle. Further, the new immigration laws largely removed the danger posed by the radical alien. For a red revolution to succeed now in the United States, American institutions would have to be penetrated and American citizens themselves recruited to the cause. The threat lay not so much in a lower-class insurrection as in a conspiracy, which through infiltration, manipulation, and ideological seduction could reach into every corner of American society and implicate perhaps even the highest in the land. This image of the red menace underlined the need for systems of surveillance, which patriotic groups and government agencies sought in different ways to provide.

The primary sources of the anticommunist drive were also changing. As the specter of communism assumed less the aspect of a class revolt and more that of subversion by a foreign power, the issue became one of national security and hence of compelling concern to those guardians of the state, party politicians and bureaucrats. The politicization of anti-communism at the national level was promoted by the evolution of the American polity. When the New Deal extended government responsibilities and aligned itself with the labor movement, red scare tactics were directed for the first time at those in power. Class conflict and party conflict were intersecting, as all the old charges against labor came to be leveled against its formidable allies in the Democratic party.

The convulsions of World War and Cold War furthered the growth of the national security state and deepened the perception of American Communists as the disciplined agents of a revitalized Soviet Union, and politicians of almost all persuasions felt compelled to avow their patriotism by repudiating the Left. The dynamics of party politics now became the chief motive force of anticommunism. In the modern American state politicians and bureaucrats had vested interests and a degree of autonomy of their own. While politicians used the communist issue against one another, bureaucrats obligingly expanded the techniques of surveillance, displacing the lawless vigilantes of an earlier day. Internal security measures were a logical response to the definition of the red menace as a Soviet conspiracy, although as the Cold War deepened into a limitless ideological confrontation it was no less logical to fear the most insidious forms of subversion, notably those aimed at institutions that molded opinion. By the 1950s there was less reason to fear social disorder than at almost any time in American history, yet the anticommunist crusade was at its fiercest. It had been unleashed by merciless political and party rivalry for control of an enlarged national state strained by Cold War. But the perception of the red menace as a form of ideological subversion also made possible a fateful convergence between governmental and popular pressures. Loyal citizens as well as government agencies could mount surveillance against such a danger. Patriotic, class, racial, and religious impulses were being mediated by a host of interest groups, many of which enthusiastically engaged with the bureaucratic and political classes in fastening an anticommunist consensus on the land.

6

THE
RED MENACE
REACHES
WASHINGTON
(1929–1938)

•

THE STOCK MARKET crash of 1929 abruptly called into question the viability of the capitalist free enterprise system that Americans proudly claimed for their own. As thousands joined the breadlines and millions searched for work, the American economic system stood, if not altogether discredited, at least seriously compromised. In a decade when the world's prime model of a capitalist economy patently failed to function adequately, alternative economic theories gained some credibility. In the past one of the most effective constraints on the growth of communism in the United States had been the success of American capitalism. With that constraint removed, the cause of communism gained adherents among Americans. In 1931 the Communist party claimed a paid membership of little more than 9,000, but by 1934 the figure was 26,000 and by January 1938 a noteworthy 75,000. Although this expanded total was negligible compared with the big battalions of the major political parties, it probably exceeded the combined membership of the two parental Communist parties at their inception in 1919, and it was over ten times that of the eviscerated Socialist party. Further, since the turnover in CP membership could be as much as 50 percent a year, the figure vastly underestimates the number of Americans who at some stage were touched by the appeal of communism. If American communism had a heyday it was in the 1930s, and if Americans ever had reason to fear its influence it was then, for by the end of the decade Communists were cultivating links not only with Moscow but also with office holders in the United States.

If the growth of the Communist party provided America's anticommunists with a tangible enemy, the rise of fascism in Europe provided them with an alternative political model of their own, should they want it. Yet despite provocation at home and encouragement abroad, the anticommunist cause failed to reach the momentum of 1919 or of the early 1950s. The depression itself sapped the strength and morale of the old anticommunist interests, and those patriots who had so long reviled Bolshevism could not easily embrace another foreign ideology. The success of European fascism did precipitate a number of American imitators, but their militarist and alien image severely limited their appeal, and torn between fealty to the United States and admiration for Mussolini or Hitler, they could not even cohere among themselves. Nonetheless, as the decade progressed the anticommunist persuasion gathered some force, partly because of the growth and political strategy of the Communist party, but mainly because a new menace was detected at the very heart of the republic. In the eyes of some Americans, at any rate, liberals in government were abandoning the nation's distinctive individualist tradition in favor of a collectivism savoring of Europe. Not all the New Deal's critics believed it was communistic, but some of them did and others affected to do so. Apart from a few peevish business swipes at the powers assumed by the Wilson administration during World War I, the federal government itself had never previously been a serious target of the antiradical forces. For the first time, American anticommunism was being mobilized not only against labor activists and political dissidents, but against those in command of the White House. And it was also taking lasting institutional form, for towards the end of the decade the House Un-American Activities Committee made its admonitory appearance.

In the past class conflict had been the principal motive force of antiradicalism, particularly when allied to fears aroused by insurrection abroad. In the future, in the 1940s, political and party competition would overshadow class conflict in the generation of red scare emotions. The New Deal linked the two, because it aligned the administration with the working class and thus permitted the communist issue to become one of party politics. The absence of a serious foreign crisis before the late 1930s, however, limited its utility.

The Slump

In 1929 the gross national product of the United States surged to a new historical high, reaching over $104 billion; as the stock market crash felled the economy GNP dropped to $95 billion in 1930 and to a devastated $74 billion in 1933. The unemployment figures told a similar dispiriting story; in 1929 official records showed unemployment to be barely over 3 percent, in 1930 it was nearly 9 percent, and by 1933 about a quarter of the work force was without employment. As misery spread across the land hungry men and women simmered with anger, and there was sporadic talk of revolution. The reporter Lorena Hickok wrote in 1932 that "I still feel that most members of the unemployed in Pennsylvania are 'right on the edge,' so to speak—that it wouldn't take much to make Communists out of them." Communists and other radicals did make some modest headway among the unemployed, and among vulnerable groups of employed workers too. In 1928 the CP presidential candidate, William Z. Foster, had won a feeble 21,000 votes; in 1932 he polled nearly 103,000. This heightened Communist activity did trigger the widespread use of red scare tactics, but a deep and intensive red scare comparable to those of 1886 and 1919 failed to take hold.

In part this was because the economic and political philosophy of the Republican administrations of the 1920s was perpetuated by the Hoover presidency. Its failure to do much about the depression was paralleled by its reluctance—and inability—to take steps against radicalism. As before, dissidents had more to fear from state and local officials and from private bodies than from the federal government. Their fate therefore depended very much on the balance of political forces in particular communities. In some, governments were reasonably sympathetic to the protests of the unemployed; in others they saw the hand of Bolshevism.

In many areas local authorities and employers responded savagely to signs of discontent. In the early 1930s the American Civil Liberties Union was complaining of the greatest suppression of civil liberties since the Big Red Scare. Several states deployed their antisubversion laws once more. These statutes were often used to break up demonstrations, if not necessarily to press for convictions. The CP organized Unemployed Councils, which agitated for jobs. Activity of this kind in Portland, Oregon, produced a police raid on the local CP headquarters in 1930 and prosecutions under the state's criminal syndicalism law of 1919. In California, apparently at the prompting of the Better America Federation, the authorities arrested the Communist leader of a children's summer camp where the Soviet flag was displayed, and she was given a prison sentence under the state's red flag law. In Atlanta the Communist organizers of an integrated meeting in 1930 were arrested for insurrection, as was the black Communist Angelo Herndon in 1932. The early 1930s also witnessed Communist-led demonstrations throughout the country on behalf of the Scottsboro boys, a group of black youths facing a "legal lynching" on a rape charge, meetings that were often broken up by police. In 1930 Comintern called for demonstrations on "International Unemployment Day," and on 6 March large meetings were held in Washington, New York, Detroit, Chicago, Milwaukee, and elsewhere. In New York, where the estimated number of demonstrators varied from

35,000 to 110,000, the police resisted a march on city hall with clubs and fists, injuring over a hundred people. Two years later the city's mayor promised to "preserve the metropolis from the Red Army."

But as usual the main thrust of red scare tactics was directed at the labor movement. The strategy of welfare capitalism crumbled with the onset of the depression, and in many areas employers made greater use of strike breakers, labor spies, and charges of Communist agitation in attempts to weaken their work forces. The most celebrated confrontations occurred in California and the South, where Communists were attempting to organize impoverished and abused workers largely unreached by the AFL unions. In the early 1930s migratory farm workers in southern California's Imperial Valley began to resist wage reductions, and when Communist union organizers arrived to help them, the growers and the local authorities literally struck back. On one occasion the strike leaders were flogged and red enamel was poured over their shaved heads. Captain William Hynes of Los Angeles's notorious police "Red Squad" lent his services to this antilabor drive, which resulted in several prosecutions under the state's criminal syndicalism law.

In the South the pattern was not dissimilar. Serious violence broke out in 1931 in Kentucky's Harlan County, where coal miners were resisting a series of wage cuts. Attempts by Communists to organize a union provoked raids by coal guards and police, the seizure of property, beatings, and the arrest of strike leaders. One local newspaper proposed that "Harlan agitators . . . would be much safer in a pine box six feet under ground," and a Communist organizer was murdered by a deputy sheriff. A local judge, in refusing a court order sought by the ACLU to protect its officials, said that the county had the right to be "protected from free speech." In such communities employers and local authorities equated unionism with communism, not altogether incorrectly, and they discovered that they could still resort to illegal and brutal methods to destroy labor organizations if they donned the patriotic guise of resisting red subversion.

A few national politicians endorsed the charge of radical subversion. Hoover himself for some years resisted pressures for an anticommunist assault, although his secretary of labor William N. Doak did launch a deportation campaign against illegal aliens, claiming that many of them were "Reds." Alien radicals were shipped out of the country in greater numbers than ever. Some congressmen, apparently believing that Communists were somehow responsible for the depression, introduced antialien and antiradical bills. The conspicuous presence of Communists in demonstrations, notably those of "International Unemployment Day," moved Congress in 1930 to establish a committee under Hamilton Fish to investigate communism. The Fish committee solemnly listened to the dire predictions of CP leaders like William Z. Foster and of patriots like Walter Steele and concluded that legislation was needed to outlaw the Party and to provide for the deportation of alien Communists. A large "Deport the Reds" rally was held in Carnegie Hall in January 1931. In 1931 and 1932 several bills were introduced for the deportation of alien Communists, although none of them passed. The Communist party remained abroad in the land, its numbers swelling yearly.

Eventually, as the 1932 election approached, the Hoover administration did succumb to anticommunist fears. The occasion was the Bonus Army, when perhaps twenty thousand veterans of World War I marched on Washington to demand the immediate payment of bonuses that were not meant to be paid until 1945. When Congress rejected a bonus payment bill some veterans vowed to stay encamped "till 1945," and a shanty town grew up around them. Their persistence was interpreted as an attempt at intimidation, and Hoover finally agreed to use the army to clear them from the Capitol area. His secretary of war, Patrick J. Hurley, and the chief of staff, General Douglas MacArthur, seem to have exceeded presidential instructions in their determination to drive the Bonus Army out of Washington entirely, a purpose accomplished with tanks, fixed bayonets, and tear gas. Hurley believed the veterans represented a communist threat, and MacArthur thought there was "incipient revolution in the air." Other observers doubted these unarmed and ragged men, women, and children constituted much more than a health hazard, but Hoover himself had spoken of "subversive influences" controlling the marchers, and the administration persisted in assigning responsibility to Communists and criminals. In its remaining months in office the Hoover administration suspiciously scanned demonstrations in Washington for signs of Communist conspiracy.

The intensified class conflict and the jumpiness of local and national governments after 1929 were predictable. American capitalism was facing the greatest crisis in its history, and there was sporadic talk of revolution both from resuscitated radicals and from conservatives. Less predictable, perhaps, was the weakness of reaction. No red scare suffused the United States as happened after World War I. The CP was not banned, radicals were not rounded up generally, and socialist publications continued to circulate. The red scare tactics employed by some state and city governments failed to stem the growth of the Communist movement.

The relative weakness of the anticommunist reaction owed a great deal to the deflation of confidence in American institutions. Businessmen were ceasing to be public heroes, and less was heard of the proud boast of One Hundred Percent Americanism. The very size of the catastrophe made nonsense of the traditional assumption that the impoverished had only themselves to blame, and as unemployment mounted toward a quarter of the work force few families remained untouched. In communities where unionism was almost unknown and where there was a close identification between the business leaders and the civil authorities, red scare tactics might be used successfully, but at the cost of reinforcing the image of the owners as heartless enemies of the hungry. The spectacular instances of class conflict often mobilized sympathy for the distressed, as in Harlan County, which became a cause célèbre in the national press when civil libertarians, intellectuals, and journalists poured into the area. The newspaper pictures of armed troops being set on the hapless Bonus Army precipitated enormous criticism. In such a climate the anticommunist cause remained of limited appeal.

Further, if only a few Americans succumbed to the siren song of communism, a goodly number, some of them public officials, believed that social protest should be heard. Several city and state governments were commanded by Progressive Republicans and urban Democrats, and they tended to react to the distress around them with some compassion. Pressure for legislation to protect labor mounted in Congress, where prolabor bills jostled with the antialien bills for attention, and with greater success. In 1932 Congress greatly restricted the power of courts to issue injunctions in labor disputes, and it expressly recognized the legitimacy of collective bargaining. The Supreme Court too tentatively began to provide greater protection for civil liberties, as in the 1931 decision overturning the California conviction that sent a woman to prison for displaying the red flag.

Those patriotic societies that had recently been preaching One Hundred Percent Americanism had lost their momentum. Veterans, after all, were losing their jobs and farms too, and the American Legion was under pressure to support the campaign for the payment of the veterans' bonus. The depression also sapped the membership and disrupted the fund-raising activities of the patriotic societies, and the Legion, the National Civic Federation, and the Daughters of the American Revolution curtailed their antiradical activities. The Veterans of Foreign Wars had to cut back on its Americanism program when the New York bank where it kept its money closed its doors. Because these respectable bodies were abandoning the offensive, organized anticommunism became associated with a number of small fringe groups that sprang up in the depth of the depression.

One was the American Patriots, founded in 1930 by Allen Zoll, who was destined to have a long career in anti-Semitic and anticommunist groups. Also anti-Semitic were the Paul Reveres, organized in 1932 by Col. Edwin M. Hadley. The appearance of Communist organizers in

Atlanta in 1930 precipitated the formation of a local group of fascists or Black Shirts "to combat the Communist Party and to discourage the teachings of Communism and foster white supremacy," but though it appealed to some unemployed white youths, its identification with crime and violence led to its early demise. The Ku Klux Klan too, much shrunken in size and bearing the fears of a now embattled urban lower class, displayed a greater obsession with communism as attempts were made to organize the South's steel, coal, and textile workers and even some black sharecroppers. In the early 1930s the southern Klan was boasting that "Communism Will Not Be Tolerated" and equating it with both unionism and black activism. In Dallas in March 1931 armed Klansmen flogged two Communist organizers for speaking out against racial discrimination, and in Birmingham in 1932 it preyed on Communist supporters of the Scottsboro boys. In the past left-wing groups had on occasion suffered when they had become tinged with violence. In the darkest days of the depression racism and violence were most commonly associated with far-right organizations, and this disreputable image greatly curtailed their appeal.

The New Deal

By the mid-1930s, as the depression gradually eased, anticommunist sentiments were achieving greater force and coherence. A new note had been sounded in the 1932 presidential campaign. An embattled Herbert Hoover charged that the Democratic party had been infected by "the fumes of the witch's cauldon which boiled in Russia." His opponent, he said, was "proposing changes and so-called new deals which would destroy the very foundations of our American system." The charge that Franklin Roosevelt's New Deal was subverting true American principles soon became a familiar one in what one writer dubbed "the Red Decade" because of the alleged pervasiveness of Communist influence. Where the focus of antiradical hostility had once been alien workers, it was now the federal government itself, although communistic ideas were espied everywhere. Anticommunist rhetoric for the first time began to be directed upwards through the polity, and to big business hatred of Roosevelt was added a populistic distrust of Washington.

The reorientation and revitalization of the anticommunist animus had its origins in key events in 1933. One was the inauguration of Franklin Roosevelt in March and his launching of his New Deal program. As Roosevelt redefined American liberalism in terms of an active government and a welfare state, those who had always equated state action with an alien ideology were given pause. "Not long ago," wrote one bemused economist, "economic planning connoted socialism or communism."

Within months of Roosevelt's taking office the United States recognized the Soviet Union (rather belatedly for a major power), a move supported by many conservative businessmen anxious to ease the depression by finding new markets, but opposed by patriotic societies and some leading Catholics and later seen by anticommunists as an act of treason. In retrospect the early course of both Roosevelt's domestic policy and his foreign policy would seem distinctly sinister to those who came to hold him responsible for subverting the cherished American system. In 1933 too, the day after Roosevelt took the oath of office, Adolf Hitler was given absolute power in Germany by the Reichstag. With Mussolini's regime in Italy already attracting some favorable attention in the United States, the advent of Hitler suggested that fascism was the wave of the future and provided those Americans fearful of democracy with a new political model. Ardent American anticommunists, of course, were not necessarily admirers of Nazi Germany, but rather as the Russian Revolution had reinvigorated American radicals, the vigor of European fascism imparted new energy to some right-wing Americans. As in Nazi Germany, also, anti-Semitism became even more closely intertwined with anticommunism.

Early in 1933 the American economic system appeared to be even more discredited than it had been at the end of 1929. Recovery had not come as President Hoover had promised, and economic activity was sagging to a new low. The symbols of America's vaunted capitalist system, the banks, were collapsing across the country, and on the very day that Roosevelt took the oath of office the governor of New York closed the Wall Street banks. The stoicism of the poor was turning to anger, and it was in the years following Roosevelt's election that CP membership swelled most rapidly. This was a period when many intellectuals were captivated anew by the Soviet Union which now displayed an economic and social system that at least worked. Robert Morse Lovett observed that here was "a government acting directly for public ends and not for the protection of private interest," and to Lincoln Steffens the Communists offered "a scientific cure for all our troubles." The New Deal generally gained the allegiance of intellectuals and liberals, although the fascination of some New Dealers with the Soviet experiment deepened the suspicions of their enemies. The rise of European fascism made it possible to see the world in apocalyptic terms, a future holding a mighty showdown between communism and fascism. If this ideological struggle did not touch all Americans, it had a polarizing effect upon their politics. Those who found something to admire in the Soviet system were matched by those who viewed the apparent growth of collectivism both abroad and at home with alarm and who saw in the regimes of Mussolini and Hitler an attempt to resist it.

Within a year or so of the unleashing of the New Deal the makings of a red scare were being deployed against it. The reorientation of anticommunist sentiments was marked by the publication in 1934 of *The Red Network* by Mrs. Elizabeth Dilling, who had been associated with some of the patriotic groups to emerge early in the depression, such as the Paul Reveres. Subtitled *A "Who's Who" and Handbook of Radicalism for Patriots*, the book listed over 460 "Communist, Radical Pacifist, Anarchist, Socialist, I.W.W. controlled organizations and agencies," including the ACLU, the AFL, the National Association for the Advancement of Colored People (NAACP), the Young Men's Christian Association, and the League of Women Voters. It also listed about 1,300 people connected with these subversive groups, among them seventy-four-year-old Jane Addams, the writer Sherwood Anderson, and Albert Einstein, Sidney Hillman, and Eleanor Roosevelt. Its presentation as a kind of factual work of reference was to be much imitated by later anticommunists, and it caused a minor stir when it first appeared, going through four printings in nine months. It was clearly intended to implicate the New Deal in the red network, tracing the supposedly radical connections of Roosevelt's appointees, and it pronounced "shocking" a "comparison" between *The Communist Manifesto*'s "ten measures for socializing a state" and the "Rooseveltian Bills passed by Congress 1933–4." Mrs. Dilling's slapdash compendium was not taken very seriously even by most conservatives, but in implicating the most respected of Americans in the Communist conspiracy it represented a vital change from the days when A. Mitchell Palmer had believed that revolutionaries could be identified from their "lopsided faces, sloping brows, and misshapen features."

"We need a rockbound old American," said Mrs. Dilling, to rescue the government from the "radical tamperers" who were "saddling it with bureaucracy." A part of the revulsion against the New Deal was a populistic distrust of Washington allied to a nostalgia for the small-town past. In the 1920s the Ku Klux Klan among others had protected the integrity of the traditional well-knit community against the invasion of Catholic and Jewish immigrants and modern ideas. By the time of the Roosevelt administration spokesmen of a very different kind were articulating traditional values, some antipathetic to the bureaucratic thrust of the New Deal. The persistence of the depression, despite the furious activity in Washington, aided the emergence of a number of popular "messiahs" peddling panaceas of their own, notably Huey Long of Louisiana, with his "Share Our Wealth" campaign to tax the rich for the benefit of the poor, Dr. Francis Townsend of California, who wanted to boost the economy by giving generous pensions to the elderly, and Father Charles Coughlin of Michigan, the radio priest who preached a version of populism and currency reform.

These figures were turning against the New Deal because it was not doing enough for the distressed, but they also saw their schemes as bulwarks against communism and, as Alan Brinkley has pointed out, drew sustenance from the traditions of Jeffersonian individualism and the autonomy of the local community. Father Coughlin, at first a New Deal supporter, became Roosevelt's fiercest critic. Since his early broadcasting days the priest had condemned atheistic communism, and by the mid-1930s, when he was speaking to the largest radio audience in the world, he was suggesting that the bureaucracy and regulations of the New Deal were communistic. In 1935 Coughlin thought that the power of the Public Works Administration to acquire property implied "a radical leaning toward international socialism or sovietism." Roosevelt, he said, "stands for a poor brand of Russian Communism." Dr. Townsend and Huey Long were also winning mass followings by 1935, and though they were not obsessed with communism in the way Coughlin was, they did detect alien influences in the New Deal. Long identified New Deal tickets with "other tickets in Moscow." "We don't endorse any socialistic program," explained Dr. Townsend. "The Townsend Plan represents an attempt to make the profit system work." His followers, he said, were people "who believe in the Bible, believe in God, cheer when the flag passes by, the Bible Belt solid Americans." The urban Catholic parishes Coughlin spoke for were equally attached to traditional patriotic and community values. In 1936 Coughlin attempted to merge Coughlinites, Townsendites, and Share Our Wealthers into a Union party to "take a Communist out of the chair once occupied by Washington." Anticommunism, it seemed, might be one issue on which populistic instincts could be aroused against the bureaucrats and intellectuals of Washington.

The resentments and restiveness awakened by the depression were also occasionally shaped by the example of Nazi Germany. Some remnants of the Bonus Army were organized into the Khaki Shirts by "General" Art J. Smith, who threatened to march on Washington as Mussolini had marched on Rome, but the movement crumbled after a bloody clash with radicals in New York and a police raid. More enduring was Gerald B. Winrod, a fundamentalist preacher in Kansas since the mid-1920s, who in 1933 identified "Jewish Bolshevism" as the principal menace to American society, not least in its creation of the New Deal. Following a visit to Germany in 1934 he became an increasingly visible apologist for Nazism, his monthly *Defender* advancing from a circulation of 40,000 in that year to 109,000 in 1936.

William Dudley Pelley of Asheville, North Carolina, was another who had been peddling a magazine mixture of religion and politics for some years, and after Hitler's accession to power in 1933 he established the Silver Shirts, his own version of the SS. This organization, which was strongest in the western states and had its greatest concentration in southern California, grew to perhaps fifteen thousand members in 1934 and became known for its quasi-military trappings, its pro-Nazi publications, and its pervasive anti-Semitism, which spilled over into antiunionism and anticommunism. In Salt Lake City in 1933 Silver Shirts savagely assaulted a suspected Communist and left him for dead. Flanking these fascistic groups were organizations of German Americans more directly dependent on Nazi Germany, notably the Friends of New Germany, whose antics attracted much attention if not sympathy, as when they championed the cause in 1935 of the German-born carpenter accused of the kidnap-murder of the Lindbergh baby. They were succeeded in 1936 by the German-American Bund, "a militant group of patriotic Americans," according to its leader Fritz Kuhn, dedicated to rescuing the United States from subversion, which he identified with atheism, miscegenation, international finance, pacifism, and "international so-called Labor Movements." The followings of the various Nazi-inspired organizations were modest, but the publicity accorded them was extensive, and in locating Jewish Bolshevists in both Washington and Moscow they more effectively harnessed the emotions of anti-Semitism to the anticommunist cause. Aiding this process was the undoubted fact that several of Roosevelt's advisers were Jewish.

Also broadcasting a heady mixture of anti-Semitism, anti-Catholicism, and anticommunism was the Ku Klux Klan. Although not the power it had been, the Klan still lived on in many communities in the Midwest and the South, and there were said to be as many as thirty thousand Klansmen in Florida in the 1930s. After an initial flirtation with Franklin Roosevelt, who kept a second home in Warm Springs, Georgia, the Klan quickly turned against an administration that leaned so heavily on the services of Roman Catholics and Jews. In Pennsylvania a Klan chapter attacked the "brain trusters" for plotting revolution, and in Virginia Klansmen accused the New Deal of having "honeycombed Washington with Communists." As it inveighed against Roosevelt, the Klan maintained its vigilance for signs of unions in the textile and steel mills of the South and the citrus groves of Florida. The Imperial Wizard announced in 1936 that the Klan has subordinated "racial and religious matters" to the more important cause of combating "communism" and industrial unionism, and well-publicized violent outrages against labor activists at least did something to tarnish its image in the eyes of outsiders. In the Midwest even the Klan was embarrassed by the actions of an offshoot known as the Black Legion, which had taken root among industrial workers in Detroit in the early 1930s and spread into neighboring states, and which like the Klan punctuated its anti-Catholic, anti-Semitic, and antiblack messages with floggings and bombings, on occasion burning the homes of reputed Communists. Its involvement in a ritual murder of a Works Progress Administration worker in 1936 brought it to national attention and repudiation by the Klan. The violence associated with the Klan and its imitators undoubtedly intimidated many people in the communities where they operated, but it also invoked widespread condemnation and limited their appeal.

While the collectivist trappings of the New Deal were stirring patriotic, anti-Semitic, and populistic suspicions in the wasteland of depression America, more respectable forces were also turning against it. There were a few intellectuals who worried about the advance of statism in an individualistic society, and the Southern Agrarians sought refuge in a tradition-oriented regionalism. Progressive Republicans, too, were often uneasy about the thrust of government power. But the most formidable opponents of the New Deal were in the business community.

Many businessmen were now acknowledging the need for greater government responsibility, but not all. The New Deal had been launched with a rhetorical assault on business irresponsibility and selfishness, and some big businessmen, newspaper tycoons, and conservative politicians were only too eager to discredit it. A surge of strike activity and industrial violence in 1934 redoubled their determination, for many employers attributed the unrest to the encouragement given to collective bargaining by the National Industrial Recovery Act. A general strike briefly paralyzed San Francisco and was called by the *Los Angeles Times* "a Communist inspired and led revolt against organized government," as well as being condemned by a vehement Hearst press. But Roosevelt, who suspected that the strike had been provoked by conservative business interests to discredit labor, resisted pressure to send in troops. Labor hopes and employer determination not to give ground to the principle of collective bargaining also led to bloody scenes among the truckers of Minneapolis and in textile towns in New England and the South. The workers were disillusioned by the administration's failure to uphold their cause, but its fumbling attempts at mediation also confirmed the worst fears of the employers. The sympathy of the national administration was evidently not with business, some elements of which detected communist influences not only in the labor movement but also in Washington.

The citadel of capitalism was also being more directly attacked by the New Deal. Many businessmen disliked the administration's bill to regulate the stock exchanges, introduced into Congress in 1934, which was described by James H. Rand, of Remington Rand, as intended to push the country "along the road from Democracy to Communism." Later in the year the Hearst newspapers launched a sustained campaign against red subversion in Washington, describing the administration as "more

Communistic than the Communists themselves." The Hearst attack on the administration broadened into an attack on its allies in the nation's colleges, abetted by the American Legion, which was submitting teacher loyalty oath bills to state legislatures. The recruitment of a number of academics into Roosevelt's celebrated "brain trust," not least that favorite bogeyman of the right-wingers, Rexford Tugwell, had drawn attention to the connections between the New Deal and the intellectual community, and there were certainly professors and students who felt an attraction to the Marxist blueprint for a new society. One was Sidney Hook, who in 1933 was organizing the new American Workers party, believing that "only communism can save the world from its social evils." Hearst sent reporters posing as students into a number of colleges to gather evidence against left-wing professors, claiming that "Red Radicalism has planted a soapbox on every campus of America." When New York University refused to sack professors Sidney Hook and James Burnham as Hearst demanded, he asked whether the university was to be classified "as an active center for treasonable plotting for the overthrow of the American Government." Other right-wing journals took up the cry against the colleges. The drugstore magnate Charles R. Walgreen made a spectacle of withdrawing his niece from the University of Chicago because of alleged Communist influence there, and the Wisconsin legislature investigated and branded the University of Wisconsin "an ultra liberal institution in which communistic teachings were encouraged and where avowed communists were welcome." The campaign of Hearst, other conservative press barons, and the American Legion fanned the populistic suspicions about pink professors, and enough of a red scare was generated to precipitate teacher loyalty oath legislation in nine states and to cause a number of lost jobs, including that of Granville Hicks at Rensselaer Polytechnic Institute in 1935.

Among those who blamed the "mountebanks and crackpots" of the brain trust for hijacking the Democratic party for the cause of Karl Marx were Al Smith and John J. Raskob, still smarting over losing control of the party to the New Dealers. In 1934 they joined with other conservative Democrats and with executives from Du Pont and General Motors to form the American Liberty League, whose object was "to combat radicalism" and foster the Jeffersonian principles of laissez-faire. If at first uncertain whether to call Roosevelt a socialist or a fascist dictator, most Liberty Leaguers eventually agreed with James A. Reed that the New Deal was flying a flag of "varying shades of Bolshevism, Socialism, and Communism . . . with red predominating." The League rapidly became an anti–New Deal forum, spending twice as much money in 1935 as the Republican party on its frenetic activities, mainly pamphlets and lectures warning that Roosevelt was leading the nation to socialism and ruin. Early in 1936 it staged a massive dinner at the Mayflower Hotel in Washington, at which Al Smith recalled his own rise from newsboy to governor in classic American fashion, asserted that the New Deal spelled the end of such individualism because it was setting class against class and instituting a dangerous "government by bureaucracy," and concluded that the country faced a choice between "the pure air of America [and] the foul breath of communistic Russia." Such hyperbole, and the corporate interests prominently on display, probably alienated rather than attracted support, but the Liberty League represented another attempt to turn the American creed of equality of opportunity to anti-radical purposes.

But despite all the imprecations of the Coughlinites, the superpatriots, the Nazi groups, the Ku Klux Klan, the Hearst press, the American Legion, and the Liberty League, the mid-1930s red scare never gained general credibility. Congress itself officially discounted the idea of a Communist menace. In 1934 the publicity given to the new Nazi groups prompted the House of Representatives to establish the McCormack-Dickstein committee to investigate them, but other forms of subversion also fell within its terms of reference, and it summoned the leaders of the Communist party to appear before it as well. The hearings were unsensational, however, and in 1935 the committee reported that neither fascism nor communism had made much impact in the United States.

Anticommunism was not without its victims in these years, of course, as the broken bodies of labor organizers and the lost jobs of teachers testified, but the attempt to mobilize it against the New Deal proved politically unsuccessful. It was big business that had been discredited by the Great Crash, not labor, and the public mood remained broadly sympathetic to attempts to regulate business and relieve distress. Further, although the emergence of a number of right-wing groups represented the first signs of a new polarization in American political life, for the moment they exhibited several characteristics that limited their appeal. The quasi-military posturings of the Silver Shirts and the Nazi groups, the violence of the Klan, and the anti-Semitism of these and the Coughlinites were forthrightly condemned, while many in the anticommunist chorus, such as William Randolph Hearst and the Liberty League, seemed primarily concerned with protecting their own financial empires. Indeed, the Liberty League looked so much like a front for wealthy paranoids that the Republican presidential candidate in 1936 described its support as the "kiss of death."

Franklin Roosevelt was able to turn the attacks of the Coughlinites and the Liberty League to his own advantage. In labeling him a Communist—Hearst described Roosevelt as "the unofficial candidate of the Comintern"—these elements were in effect caricaturing the real charges against Roosevelt, that the New Deal was more responsive to the needs of labor, the farmer, and the unemployed than to those of the major coporations and the rich and that it was abandoning the traditional American principle of limited government in favor of the positive state. If the Republican presidential candidate himself did not resort to vulgar red-baiting, the vice-presidential candidate accused Roosevelt of "leading us towards Moscow," the Republican platform claimed that American liberties were for the first time "threatened by government itself," and big business contributed liberally to Republican coffers. Roosevelt was apparently delighted to turn the election into a contest between the "economic royalists" and the New Deal reformers, and Hearst-style red-baiting simply confirmed his allegation that the forces of "organized money" were "unanimous in their hate" for him. Roosevelt's landslide victory demonstrated that few Americans took seriously the talk about a communist New Deal. The populist insurgency that Father Coughlin had attempted to raise against the administration failed to materialize in any substantial way, the Union party candidate winning less than 2 percent of the popular vote. Father Coughlin gracelessly conceded that "President Roosevelt can be a dictator if he wants to." Anticommunist rhetoric had for the first time been extensively used against a presidential administration, but it had not proved an electoral asset.

Conservative Reaction

Franklin D. Roosevelt's triumphant reelection exposed the weakness of the line being peddled by Hearst and Coughlin, but it also signaled a regrouping in American politics that was to give a new plausibility to the anticommunist cause. Most important was the growing identification between the New Deal and the labor movement. Measures like the Social Security Act and the National Labor Relations (or Wagner) Act of 1935 had been warmly endorsed by labor, not least by the advocates of industrial unionism inside the AFL. Seeing in the conditions of the 1930s an unparalleled opportunity to organize the mass production industries like cars and steel along industrial lines, militant union leaders urged the AFL to abandon its protection of craft unionism, and when they were rebuffed in 1935, they formed the Committee for Industrial Organization (CIO—later the Congress of Industrial Organizations). In 1936 the AFL suspended the unions connected with the CIO, which forged ahead with its own organizing drive. It also threw its financial and industrial weight behind Franklin Roosevelt. For the first time in its history, the Democratic party received heavy financial contributions from labor groups. The CIO's John L. Lewis also helped to form Labor's Non-Partisan League, which included some AFL unions and was active on Roosevelt's behalf in a number of important industrial states. Over the next few years the spectacular rise in union membership (in both CIO and AFL unions) could be attributed in part to the administration's friendliness toward labor. At the same time the Non-Partisan League (and the new American Labor party in New York) continued to be active in local elections on behalf of New Deal candidates and causes.

The political alliance that was being forged between the New Deal and the labor movement provided Communists with an opportunity to establish a legitimate role for themselves. With the failure of dual unions to make much headway, many Communist workers had been joining AFL unions even before a change of party line in 1934 encouraged them to do so. The Seventh World Congress of the Communist International in 1935 called for a popular front against fascism. After the 1936 presidential election, with its striking demonstration of Roosevelt's strength, American Communists began to ally themselves with the Democratic party. Some of them won influence in the CIO unions as John L. Lewis, eager to build a labor empire to rival the AFL, found that Communists made energetic and skilled union organizers. Others sought participation in farmer-labor groups that voiced the aspirations of radical farmers, some of which by the late 1930s were seeking an accord with the New Deal. Yet others joined relief organizations like the Workers' Alliance, with its close connections with the Works Progress Administration. In 1938 the Communist leader Earl Browder conceded that where socialism was not attainable, "it is a thousand times better to have a liberal and progressive New Deal . . . than to have a new Hoover." Outside the union movement as well as within it, Communists were now attempting to work with the liberal bourgeoisie of the Democratic party. The Democrats did not seek out these radical allies, but some of the more progressive welcomed whatever support they could get in the cause of reform. In such states as Washington and California the Communists established links with the Democratic party. In Minnesota they worked with the Farmer-Labor party, and in New York they won influence in the American Labor party.

The emergence of popular front politics in a number of areas in the late 1930s, however patchy and incomplete, afforded ammunition for the New Deal's enemies. The red scare that had emerged during Roosevelt's first term had lacked credibility because the CP itself was opposed to Roosevelt. When anticommunist sentiments were deployed against Roosevelt during his second administration, they could not be so lightly dismissed. Whether the White House liked it or not, there were Communists in organizations that were supporting the New Deal. They existed in all those reformist drives that so upset the nation's conservatives, whether in industrial unionism, welfare, or civil rights movements. The radicalism of the later New Deal was precipitating a conservative reaction, and the popular front connections at its leftward edge were to prove its Achilles' heel.

The radical reputation and labor connections of the later New Deal gave pause to some of Roosevelt's allies as well as deepening hostility from his old opponents. In an intensified polarization of American politics, the leftist tendencies of the New Deal coalition were paralleled by a resurgence of conservatism on the right. Conservative interests in particular were taking exception to the New Deal's popular front associations, as were the patriotic societies and fascistic groups that were discovering a new vitality. The growing conservative mood gave added leverage to the traditional anticommunist constituencies such as anti-union businessmen, the white South, fundamentalist Protestants, the Roman Catholic hierarchy, and even the AFL. Events abroad also left their mark, emboldening the anti-Semitic critics of Bolshevism and the New Deal, though their influence remained marginal at best. Nonetheless the conservative revival of the late 1930s was accompanied by a renewal of red scare politics, and on this occasion a few wounds were inflicted. They would have been much greater had Soviet actions suggested that international communism was aggressively on the march once more.

Roosevelt's large majority in the 1936 election proved misleading. Although labor and progressive elements contributed to his success in the presidential race, the Democratic majority in Congress was not unequivocally committed to the New Deal. Many of the Democrats elected to Congress, particularly southerners, were of rather conservative stripe, and the course of events in 1937 tended to distance them from the administration. Conservatives had been complaining for years that the New Deal was incompatible with the fundamental political principles of the United States, a view given some legitimacy by the Supreme Court's tendency to strike down New Deal legislation, and Roosevelt's attempt in 1937 to secure a more compliant Court through his Judiciary Reorganization (or "Court-packing") bill seemed like a direct assault on the Constitution. With conservatives able to claim that their warnings had been vindicated, even many liberals were disturbed.

Many congressmen were also perturbed by the spectacular successes of the labor movement in 1937, when large parts of the auto, steel, rubber, electrical, and textile industries fell to the CIO's unionizing drive, in some cases through sit-down strikes when workers occupied factories with apparent impunity. Such labor effrontery would not have been tolerated in the past, and conservatives held the White House responsible.

Further, the renewed collapse of the economy late in 1937 undermined confidence in Roosevelt's managerial skills. The Democratic majorities in Congress proved increasingly unresponsive to Roosevelt's bidding. In the summer of 1937 conservative Democrats began to join Republicans in resisting reform legislation, abetted by Vice President John Nance Garner, who was particularly upset by the sit-down strikes. Central to this emerging conservative coalition were southern Democratic senators who believed that the New Deal was betraying the principles of Jeffersonian democracy and who hoped to regain control of the leadership of the party at the next election. The midterm elections of 1938 produced something of a Republican revival, with the party gaining substantially in the lower house and more modestly in the Senate. The Democrats retained nominal majorities, but with many southern and conservative Democrats voting with the Republicans, the conservative coalition had effectively put an end to the New Deal.

Some of Roosevelt's former allies were themselves losing enthusiasm for the cause of reform. Representatives of the white South were cool toward measures that might raise the price of labor, promote the unionization of black workers, and, through the Court-packing precedent, increase federal pressures for civil rights. Congressman Edward E. Cox of Georgia, in opposing a labor bill, warned "John L. Lewis and his Communistic cohorts, that no second-hand 'carpetbag expedition' in the Southland, under the banner of Soviet Russia . . . will be tolerated." Episcopal bishop Warren Chandler looked to the South, with its strong conservative faith, to rescue the nation from collectivism. Even parts of the labor movement seemed unenthusiastic about New Deal reform. Some AFL leaders were chagrined at the success of the CIO and its closeness to the administration and bitterly eyed the role of the Communists. John P. Frey alleged that "the CIO policy was determined in the headquarters of the Communist Party in Moscow." In 1938 the AFL dissociated itself from Labor's Non-Partisan League and from popular front alignments in New York and Minnesota. Many Roman Catholics too, though traditionally Democratic, were given pause by the New Deal's radical associations. In the 1930s Catholic publications inveighed fiercely against the Republican cause in Spain, which was associated with anticlericalism and communism, and some Catholics harkened to Father Coughlin's diatribes against the "Red New Deal." Other Catholic leaders were sympathetic to labor aspirations, and in 1937 the Association of Catholic Trade Unionists (ACTU) was launched, one of its principal objectives being to resist Communist influence in the CIO. Members of the Roman Catholic hierarchy were deeply distressed by Roosevelt's apparent tolerance of the sit-down strikes and labor radicalism. Constituencies normally friendly to a Democratic administration were beginning to recoil from the growing identification of reform with radical labor and popular front causes.

Interests and groups hostile to the New Deal needed little encouragement to attempt to mobilize public opinion against it. Their apprehension at the course of public affairs was intensified by the realization that the Supreme Court was no longer a pillar of conservative order, for in 1937 it not only upheld the Wagner Act but also struck down two state security laws. Few businessmen came to terms with industrial unionism in the 1930s, and many responded to the rise of the CIO by affixing a red label to it. The National Association of Manufacturers distributed a pamphlet entitled *Join the CIO and Help Build a Soviet America*, and red scare tactics were frequently employed in attempts to halt the surge of unionization. The American Liberty League had only a fitful existence after 1936, but some businessmen turned to the more reputable National Committee to Uphold Constitutional Government, whose leaders were outraged by Roosevelt's support for organized labor and condemned the "insanity and puerility of New Deal economics." Most corporations made their adjustments to the New Deal, but a substantial minority remained belligerently opposed to the new system of industrial relations it was introducing, and rich industrialists like the Du Ponts and E. T. Weir of National Steel were willing to provide funds for organizations committed to representing the administration as communist inspired. The traditional employers' equation of labor unions with communism had been turned against the federal government.

Veterans' groups, too, were emerging from the disarray into which they had been thrown by the crash and according more attention to their Americanism programs. The American Legion summoned its two million members to join in a new crusade against communism. At its 1936 national convention it instructed all posts "to vigilantly combat Communism" and endorsed a study undertaken by its National Americanism Commission entitled *Isms: A Review of Alien Isms, Revolutionary Communism and Their Active Sympathizers in the United States.* If Mrs. Dilling's book could be dismissed as the work of a crank, this production could not be. Its second edition devoted 265 pages to "Communism," three to "Fascism," and fifteen to "Nazi-ism" in the United States and drew attention to the sinister popular front strategy of the Communist International. The assistance of the AFL in compiling the study was acknowledged, as was that of patriotic societies like the American Coalition and right-wing groups like the Associated Farmers of California. The "mission" of the Legion, it was said, was to "acquaint the public with the growth of subversive activities" and to show "that Communism is attempting to undermine our government; that it is reaching into the schools, the churches, agriculture, and, in fact, into every phase of American life." Some Protestant churchmen agreed. Another product of 1936 was the Methodist League against Communism, Fascism, and Unpatriotic Pacificism, which denounced the "Methodist Reds" of the popular frontish Methodist Federation for Social Service. The Southern Baptist Convention also confirmed in 1938 that there was "no room" for "radical Socialism" or "atheistic Communism" in the United States.

Also reacting to the popular front strategy of the Communists was Father Coughlin. "If there must be fronts," he wrote, "let us have the Christian Front." After a period of silence Coughlin returned to the fight in 1938 when he could see the New Deal faltering. Assailing the CIO for its communism and denouncing the administration's "communistic policies," by the end of 1938 Coughlin was identifying Bolshevism with the international Jewish conspiracy, and as the Christian Front took shape it became a vehicle for anti-Semitism. The membership of the new organization remained small, perhaps twelve hundred, although it won some recruits among Irish and German Catholics in the northeastern cities where its members on occasion beat up Jews. Another alumnus of the Union party was Gerald L. K. Smith, a former Huey Long lieutenant and a remarkable orator. In 1937 he founded his patriotic Committee of One Million, railing against the "reds" in the CIO and charging the Roosevelt administration with fostering communism. By the end of the decade his part in the Share Our Wealth campaign was being forgotten and he was establishing links with conservative politicians like Arthur Vandenberg and rich businessmen like Henry Ford.

Both Coughlin and Smith were accused by their enemies of being fascists, although they disliked being identified with those fringe groups that were drawing strength from the dynamic example of Nazi Germany. The growth of fundamentalist churches in the depression also buoyed up the "apostles of discord." Gerald B. Winrod was still attacking the New Deal, supporting isolationism, and placing responsibility for "the scourge of international communism" on "the international Jew." A more sophisticated variant of evangelical Protestantism emerged with Moral Re-Armament, led by Frank Buchman, who in 1936 thanked "heaven for a man like Adolf Hitler who built a front line of defense against the Anti-Christ of Communism." The Silver Shirts, in which Protestant clergymen were prominent, also seemed to be reviving. The German-American Bund too was becoming more vocal, and from 1938 it became very hostile to the adminstration as Franklin Roosevelt's retreat from neutrality became apparent.

The goose-stepping antics, anti-Semitic rhetoric, violent reputation, and alien image of these groups, however, denied them any mass appeal. The relatively peaceful foreign policy of the Soviet Union for most of the

1930s gave their warnings a hysterical cast. They were not even able to work together. George E. Deatherage of West Virginia, sometime leader of the Knights of the White Camelia, in the late 1930s offered his American Nationalist Confederation as a coordinating body, but such meetings of the fascist groups as he was able to call were unproductive. While these organizations were generally anti-Semitic, and strongly so, some were also anti-Catholic and hence not natural allies of the Coughlinites, while the patriotism of others was offended by the subservience of the Nazi groups to Germany. This was a period when members of the American Legion and of the German-American Bund sometimes came to blows. At the end of the decade the Nazi-Soviet Pact threw the right-wing groups further into disarray. Their visceral anti-Semitism and anti-communism made it difficult for them to stomach an accord with the "Jewish Bolshevists" of Moscow.

Perhaps more revealing than the presence of these groups was their continued feebleness. European fascism was as alien a doctrine to most Americans as communism. No American fascist leader was to achieve the authority and eminence that Sir Oswald Mosley did in Britain. But the fascistic groups represented the conservative reaction to the New Deal at its most racist and attenuated, and they did have a role to play in the history of anticommunist politics. They offended many people in public life, not least Samuel Dickstein, a congressman of Russian Jewish descent. In January 1937 he introduced a resolution in the House of Representatives calling for an investigation of all organizations "found operating in the United States for the purpose of diffusing . . . slanderous or libelous un-American propaganda of religious, racial or subversive political prejudices." The undefined "un-American" was criticized for vagueness and the resolution was tabled but three months later Texas Democrat Martin Dies introduced another resolution to investigate "subversive and un-American propaganda." Although Dies's antilabor and antiimmigrant reputation suggested that he had in mind different targets than Dickstein did, the two congressmen joined forces and eventually secured a majority for the resolution in May 1938. Its supporters dwelled less on the Nazis than on the Communist menace and spoke darkly of the Communist penetration of New Deal agencies. It was Dies who became chairman of the House Un-American Activities Committee (HUAC), whose character was further revealed when it excluded Dickstein. The committee was to reflect the dominant force in the House, the new if uneasy conservative coalition of Republicans and rural or southern Democrats. HUAC was to provide the focus for the mounting anticommunist sentiment, which it sought to unite behind it in an attack on the New Deal and its labor and popular front allies.

THE RED MENACE IN GLOBAL AMERICA

.

The hard times of the 1930s tarnished the reputation of American capitalism and crippled the One Hundred Percent Americanism of the previous decade. Businessmen in many communities invoked the communist menace to justify the brutal treatment meted out to strikers and labor activists, but antiradicalism enjoyed neither the government nor the public support it had once counted on. Even the courts displayed some sensitivity to civil liberties. The domestic red menace was not being magnified by Soviet expansionism in Europe. Toward the end of the decade Communists were even making common cause with liberals in government, being tolerated after a fashion as part of an inchoate popular front against fascism abroad and distress at home. Radicals were once more being afforded a measure of protection by middle-class reformers and a revitalized labor movement.

Unregenerate patriots spoke of a communist New Deal, although in a sense the liberal stance of the federal government diminished the prospect of Communist subversion. In Britain the unimaginative reactions of a conservative government to the Great Depression deepened the disenchantment of many intellectuals and young idealists with the capitalist system, and a few of them entered government service secretly dedicated to communist goals and the interests of the Soviet Union. In the United States the reformist aspirations of the New Deal generally won the imagination of young Americans of Alger Hiss's generation, and few if any of them became Soviet spies after the manner of Kim Philby or Guy Burgess. Nonetheless the absence of a popular front in Britain spared its liberal politicians later embarrassment, while the flirtation of the New Deal with popular front politics exacted its price. It intensified the right-wing suspicions of subversion and afforded charges of Communist influence a shred of credibility. Those liberals who resisted the conservative currents of the late 1930s were almost bound to have worked with Communists, something that left them fatally exposed to anticommunist passions a decade later.

Further, many Americans were left uneasy about the growth of both government and union power. The vibrant libertarian traditions of the United States had generally fostered the notions that both positive government and collective bargaining were antipathetic to the sturdy American value of self-help. Although Roosevelt retained the confidence of the greater part of the electorate, the relationship between the state and the citizen was changing in a way that could readily be represented as a betrayal of American ideals. Conservative patriots may have been perverse in suggesting that Washington was falling under the control of Moscow, but the New Deal did lean toward socialism, if socialism is to be equated with government planning, state welfare, and union rights. By the late 1930s the novelties associated with the New Deal were hastening the polarization of American political life. Not only the business community and America's professional patriots, but parts of the labor movement, the Roman Catholic and fundamentalist Protestant churches, and the white South were coalescing in a conservative reaction to the New Deal agenda. The reorientation of the anticommunist animus was being completed by the imperatives of the political system. If there was any unity to this disparate collection of forces, it was a common opposition to that popular front alignment that was linking the Roosevelt administration to the Communist party. For the first time, anticommunism was being fueled by party politics, which in due course was to prove at least as powerful a dynamic as class conflict.

7

FROM
POPULAR FRONT TO
COMMUNIST FRONT
(1938–1948)

•

W<small>HEN</small> the New Deal ground to a halt in the late 1930s, a serious red scare seemed to be in the making. The House Un-American Activities Committee appeared in 1938, and soon anticommunist legislation was being enacted. Labor activists and other radicals, as always, were among the victims of this anticommunist animus, but what gave the cause its coherence was its hostility to the popular front nexus that had taken shape during the later years of the New Deal. In the 1930s anticommunist suspicions had come to rest on the federal government itself, and as the decade drew to a close red scare tactics were being used against the New Deal at its most vulnerable point. World War II, when the Soviet Union became an ally of the United States, averted a full-blown red scare, but as World War gave way to Cold War anticommunist pressures mounted once more. The CIO unions, the Communist party, and those liberal Democrats in favor of sustaining the popular front alignment were cast as the un-American enemies of the United States. These anticommunist passions engaged conservative and even liberal Democrats as well as Republicans and patriotic interest groups. Indeed, the Truman administration itself played a critical role in discrediting popular front politics. By 1948 the labor movement had been curbed, CP leaders were being prosecuted, and popular front groups were being fatally labeled as "Communist fronts." Anticommunism was becoming the new orthodoxy.

The conservative revival that was registered in the midterm elections of 1938 continued erratically over the next decade. Neither Franklin Roosevelt nor Harry Truman could assemble congressional majorities for reform. American politics had become confrontational and disputatious, with no single party or faction in complete possession of the organs of government. The close political rivalry of these years was accompanied by global crises of an unprecedented kind. The waning of enthusiasm for social change in the late 1930s may have been promoted in part by the ominous portents of war in Europe and the Far East. World War II, when it came, brought a measure of mutual accommodation between business, labor, and government in the United States, checking the reaction against the popular front. Sheltered from direct physical attack, the country emerged from the war with its economic system vindicated and conscious of being the greatest power on earth. For a brief moment it savored the fruits of victory, but as it was drawn into ordering the world's affairs it found itself apparently losing the peace as surely as it had won the war. The onset of the Cold War triggered new strains in American political society, particularly as the course of world events seemed to make a mockery of American pretensions. The insecure politicians of this society, no longer able to confine their attentions to the parochial verities of an isolated nation, searched the foreign policy agenda for issues of political gain. The polarization of the world between East and West, with Soviet Russia now unequivocally cast as the enemy, particularly served the interests of those conservative politicians who were beginning to inch back from the wilderness into which the New Deal had cast them.

In the 1940s red scare tactics came to be used almost routinely for partisan and factional advantage, by moderates and liberals as well as by right-wing groups. Anticommunist rhetoric was becoming part of the common coinage of American politics and was related to a complex process whereby the American political order was being repositioned in opposition to the Soviet bloc rather than the Axis powers. The radical elements in the labor movement and on the left wing of the New Deal were being squeezed out of the arena of legitimate politics. This general politicization of anticommunism also owed much to the "nationalization" of American public affairs, as the New Deal, World War and Cold War vastly extended the scope of federal bureaucracy and the responsibilities of the central government. To a significant degree political authority had been shifted from the state capitals to Washington, and the fate of any revived red scare would depend greatly on the attitude of this centralized authority. Anticommunism was immeasurably strengthened when federal bureaucracies were themselves enlisted in the cause.

The Little Red Scare

By 1938 a reaction was setting in against the New Deal. A public opinion poll in June indicated that over 70 percent of those consulted wanted the Roosevelt administration to move in a "more conservative" direction.

Democrats as well as Republicans were recoiling from the pro-labor and relief policies of Franklin Roosevelt, which could be readily caricatured as communistic. One of the manifestations of this suspicious mood was the House Un-American Activities Committee (HUAC), itself sired by a body that was overwhelmingly Democratic. At its birth in 1938 the committee contained five Democrats and two Republicans, and in its early years it was chaired by Martin Dies, a Texas Democrat who had once been a loyal supporter of the administration but who had joined the southern conservative revolt against the New Deal. After the war HUAC would become predominantly a Republican weapon, but its origins can be traced in no small part to dissident Democrats chafing at Roosevelt's dalliance with labor and the popular front.

The Dies committee, as it became known, occasionally gave attention to fascist groups like the German-American Bund, but its principal targets were New Deal agencies such as the National Labor Relations Board and the Federal Theater and Writers Project, New Deal allies like the CIO, and such popular front groups as the American League for Peace and Democracy. During the midterm elections of November 1938 it turned its glare on the popular front auxiliaries of Democratic candidates in California and Minnesota and on the Communist support given to Michigan governor Frank Murphy, a friend of the president and a bête noire of conservatives for the protection he had given to sit-down strikers. Murphy lost the election and elsewhere Republicans made widespread gains, while conservative southern Democrats withstood Roosevelt's attempt to purge them. The Dies committee was not responsible for these New Deal reverses, but they vindicated its continued attacks against that part of the political spectrum inhabited by the CP, popular front groups, and liberal Democrats. "It seems as though the New Deal was hand in glove with the Communist Party," concluded a Republican member after one such session.

In the summer of 1939 the creaking popular front coalition was suddenly devastated by the news of the Nazi-Soviet Pact. When war broke out in Europe in September, the position of American Communists was rendered even more vulnerable, for they now seemed cast as accessories to Nazi aggression, while the subsequent Soviet incursions into Poland, Finland, and the Baltic states further embarrassed them. Shocked American Communists struggled unhappily to defend Soviet actions, while liberals recoiled from their late allies on the left. The Communists denounced the European conflict as an imperialist struggle and gradually turned against the Roosevelt administration, accusing it of trying to drag the United States into war. Liberals, progressives, and New Dealers who had cooperated with Communists in popular front groups resigned from them in large numbers in 1939 and 1940. The CP was being isolated once more, and liberals were prepared to join conservatives in attacks upon it.

The era of the Nazi-Soviet Pact witnessed a strengthening of the anti-communist cause in the United States; indeed, not until the Korean War would so many powerful forces again be mobilized against the CP. Long-standing anticommunist activists were joined by many government officials, CIO leaders, and even civil libertarians. Congress and the state legislatures enacted anticommunist legislation, and organizations that had tolerated Communists sought to exclude them from their leadership. Franklin Roosevelt himself became "very anti-Communist—militantly so" according to his solicitor general—angered at the CP's apparent subservience to Moscow. The red scare of 1939–41 did not reach the proportions of that of 1919, but by implicating the federal government and in its legislative residue it prepared the way for the postwar onslaught on American Communists.

The turning of the tide was discernible in the Hatch Act of August 1939, an anti–New Deal measure that prohibited federal employees from engaging in political activities. Members of organizations advocating the overthrow of the government were also to be denied employment, a thrust at those Communists who had allegedly infiltrated the federal bureaucracy. Early in 1940 Congress reintroduced the 1917 Espionage Act, although the United States was still at peace. Europe was blazing with war, however. That spring Nazi troops occupied Denmark, Norway, and the Low Countries, and by the end of May the British army was scrambling for safety at Dunkirk; in June France fell to German might. If Britain now succumbed the United States would stand exposed before the Nazi aggressor, or so it seemed to a distressed nation, and the president and Congress threw themselves into furious defense preparations. The very speed of German conquests in 1940, it was widely believed, must have owed something to Nazi "fifth column" operations in the fallen countries, and Nazis or their communist allies were perhaps similarly preparing the downfall of the United States.

With Americans weighing the chances of both external attack and internal subversion, those who had long hankered for curbs on dissidents pressed home their advantage. Despite the immigration controls, aliens had continued to attract suspicion, and nativists like Martin Dies had been promoting antialien bills for years. Dozens of bills directed at aliens were introduced into Congress in 1939 and 1940, one of them by conservative Democrat Howard Smith of Virginia. Entitled the Alien Registration Act, and later notorious as the Smith Act, this provided for the registration, fingerprinting, and deportation of aliens, but in the fearful summer of 1940 it also acquired a section that applied to citizens, making it unlawful for any person knowingly to advocate the overthrow of the government by force or even to be a member of any group with that objective. Even A. Mitchell Palmer had been unable to wrest from Congress a sedition measure like this. Although it could be said to guard against Nazi subversion, it was Communist antiwar agitation and the possibility of Communist-inspired strikes in the defense industries that were alarming the bill's conservative sponsors.

A few months later Congress passed the more restrained Voorhis Act, requiring the registration of any organization subject to foreign control or aiming at the violent overthrow of the government, it being assumed that this would ensure the registration of the Communist party, "inasmuch as it is affiliated with the Comintern." But the CP severed its formal ties with Comintern and refused to register. Nonetheless the isolation of American Communists, their linking of the government with capitalist warmongers, and the widespread fear that the United States would soon be at war (with the Nazis and thus with their Soviet allies) had for the first time made possible federal Communist-control legislation. The Smith Act, the first peacetime sedition act since 1798, in particular remained a weapon that would be used to harry Communists for nearly two decades.

The administration deferred to these congressional impulses, though it sometimes sought to moderate them. It also endorsed action against individual radical leaders, resenting their change of line after the Nazi-Soviet Pact. Earl Browder, who had incautiously admitted to once using a fraudulent passport, was arrested late in 1939 and sentenced to four years in prison in 1940. Harry Bridges, a bugbear of the nation's conservatives since his successful conduct of the West Coast maritime strike of 1934—so much so that a provision was inserted into the Smith Act making it a deportable offense for an alien to be a member of a subversive group at any time since being in the country—became the subject of renewed deportation proceedings, though he was eventually saved by the Supreme Court.

With Roosevelt's approval, the FBI was also extending its surveillance of potential subversives, and the old General Intelligence (or antiradical) Division was revived. Mindful of the violent excesses of local officials and vigilantes during the First World War, the president in 1939 directed that investigations into espionage and disloyalty should be the preserve of the FBI, and an understanding to this effect was reached in meetings in 1940 and 1941 with governors, police officials, and state attorneys general, who agreed to avoid using state sedition laws and to discourage vigilante action. Suggestions that the American Protective League should be reconstituted were brushed aside. "Leave it to the FBI" was J. Edgar Hoover's constant refrain, and even when the FBI recruited thousands of legionnaires into its American Legion Contact Program, the objective seems to have been to preempt Legion activity. Much emphasis was placed on the professional expertise of the FBI—in contrast to the "amateur efforts" of "well-meaning citizens." Hoover was not one to minimize the need for his agency's vigilance. "We have a distinct spy menace," he told the American Legion in 1940. "Hundreds upon hundreds of foreign agents are busily engaged upon a program of peering, peeking, eavesdropping, propaganda, subversiveness, and actual sabotage." The FBI did encounter considerable public flak when it was disclosed that it had been using wiretaps and other questionable techniques, although the president, worried about "fifth column" activities, continued to endorse wiretapping in certain cases. Eager to extend his bureaucratic domain and smarting at the criticism, Hoover fulminated against the "rabble-rousing Communist, the goosestepping bundsman, their stooges and seemingly innocent 'fronts,' and last but not least, the pseudo-liberals." Implicated in the Communist cause, he insisted, whether wittingly or not, were ministers of the gospel, schoolteachers, college professors, writers, and "pseudo-liberal" politicians. Making internal security an FBI responsibility may have done something to contain mob action, but it was at the cost of extending the power of a federal agency headed by a passionate anticommunist.

Among the areas of American life that J. Edgar Hoover viewed with suspicion was the labor movement. The sit-down strikes of 1937, the conspicuous role of Communists in the CIO unions, and the connections between labor and the New Deal had already attracted much criticism, and the deepening conservative mood enabled several states to enact curbs on labor, such as those on secondary boycotts. As the nation was flung into its massive mobilization effort, and as the CP turned on the administration for its favors to the Allies, government and employers began to fear that the Communist unionists would disrupt the defense industries. Unreconstructed corporate leaders, eager to return to the days of the open shop, struck patriotic poses and cast strikers as subversives. Although conventional labor grievances largely accounted for a strike at Allis-Chalmers in Wisconsin in 1941, the United Auto Workers local was led by Communists who were accused of sabotaging the defense effort. Roosevelt himself complained that the strike was "a form of alien sabotage, inspired and directed by Communist forces." When a strike broke out at the North American Aviation Company in Inglewood, California, led by local union officials following the "Communist Party Line" according to the attorney general, the administration sent in troops to reopen the factory. Henceforth, said one cabinet officer, the "subversive and communistic elements" would be treated "as enemies of the country." In the early summer of 1941, according to opinion polls, over three-quarters of the public believed that Communists were responsible for strikes in the defense industries.

Conflict within the labor movement increased its vulnerability. The AFL and the CIO were locked in a tremendous struggle for the allegiance of the nation's workers, and tactics like union raiding and scabbing increased their mutual bitterness, their resort to strike action, and public disenchantment. Red-baiting flourished in this unhappy atmosphere. AFL leaders in the Gompers tradition had been hostile to socialists of any hue since the First World War and before. The Communists in the CIO presented irresistible targets, and the conservative AFL leader John P. Frey told the Dies committee in 1938 that the Communists controlled ten CIO unions and had infiltrated the Democratic party. After the Nazi-Soviet Pact such accusations became difficult for the CIO to ignore. Most CIO leaders supported Roosevelt's reelection in 1940 and the course of his foreign and defense policies, and a gulf opened up between them and their Communist allies. In 1940 John L. Lewis was succeeded as CIO president by Philip Murray, a Catholic who had long distrusted the Communist element, and Murray made it a condition of his acceptance that the CIO annual convention pass a resolution condemning "the dictatorships and totalitarianism of Nazism, Communism and Fascism as inimical to the welfare of labor, and destructive of our form of government." Liberal CIO leaders like Murray and Sidney Hillman suspected there were Communist machinations behind the defense industry strikes of 1941 and began exploring ways of easing Communists out of CIO positions. By summer there were signs that the CIO and the administration might cooperate in securing the dismissal of Communist employees in defense plants.

Communists, indeed, were being placed beyond the pale of legitimacy in many areas of American public life. The patriotic assault on "subversive" school textbooks, in abeyance since the 1920s, was revived in 1939. Some progressive educators, associated particularly with Teachers College of Columbia University, had been influenced by Marxism and had seen in education an instrument to reconstruct society along collectivist lines. By the late 1930s this group had turned against Marxism, but some of their texts remained to inflame right-wing sentiments. Thousands of schools had adopted Harold Rugg's social studies texts, which the Advertising Federation of America attacked in 1939 for their unfavorable references to advertising. The American Legion took up the cause in 1940, denouncing "Treason in the Textbooks," and the National Association of Manufacturers financed a study that assailed the Rugg books and other texts. Prompted by the Legion and the Hearst press, school districts throughout the country banned the books. At a hearing in

Georgia, a police captain pointed at Rugg and shouted, "There sits the ringmaster of the fifth columnists in America, financed by the Russian government." School boards were not alone in succumbing to red scare pressures. Even the American Civil Liberties Union, charged by the Dies committee with being a Communist front, passed a resolution in 1940 barring from its governing committees any member of an organization supporting "totalitarian dictatorship," and to make the message clearer, it expelled from its board of directors CP member Elizabeth Gurley Flynn.

Some state governments also reacted against the popular front tendencies of the New Deal era. In Massachusetts, California, and Oklahoma a rash of "little Dies committees" imitated HUAC in Washington. California governor Culbert Olson, who had been elected with popular front support, rapidly distanced himself from his old allies on the left and in 1940 invited the legislature to bar the CP from the ballot, to which it enthusiastically agreed. In Washington State, where popular front politics had also been strong, the legislature refused to admit a member who had once been in the CP. In 1939 New York passed an act prohibiting the state employment of anyone advocating the forcible overthrow of the government. In 1940 the legislature launched an investigation of the New York City school system, which was said to harbor hundreds of Communist teachers. The Rapp-Coudert committee went about the process of exposure carefully, and its hearings became a model for later congressional probes. The city's board of higher education in 1941 obligingly banned members of "Communist, fascist, or Nazi" groups from employment in the city's colleges and dismissed twenty CP members uncovered by Rapp-Coudert. During the era of the Nazi-Soviet Pact Communists were being defined in the United States as totalitarians who could have no respect for democracy and civil liberties and who conspiratorially followed the orders of Moscow—in short, as Stalinists. The implication that communism was un-American won wide public support; a Gallup poll in May 1941 found that 71 percent favored outlawing the CP. The Party itself was savagely wounded by the Nazi-Soviet Pact and the "little red scare"; before the Pact, membership had been reaching toward one hundred thousand, but in early 1942 it stood at only fifty thousand.

The Revived Popular Front

What checked the gathering forces of anticommunism was the Nazi invasion of the Soviet Union in late June 1941. American Communists were able to align themselves once more with the majority sentiments of the American people. They rallied to the support of Franklin Roosevelt, and they called for a pro-Allies foreign policy. In December the Japanese attack on Pearl Harbor precipitated the United States' entry into the Second World War, and no one supported the war effort more enthusiastically than the Communists. Most American unions adopted a "no-strike pledge," to which Communist officials strenuously adhered, and Earl Browder swung his party's influence to increasing productivity, averting wildcat strikes, and even moderating wage demands. Popular front alliances were revived, as best they could be, and Communists, liberal CIO and AFL leaders, employers, and government officials found ways of cooperating with one another in the interests of the war effort.

This domestic popular front paralleled the international popular front represented by the Allied powers. Comintern was dissolved in 1943, so that Moscow no longer seemed to be directing fifth column activities in other countries, and in the same year Roosevelt, Churchill, and Stalin pledged themselves at Tehran to postwar collaboration. A new cooperative world seemed to be in the making. In 1944 American Communist leaders wound up the Communist party and replaced it with the Communist Political Association, which was to be not a party but a pressure group that would support progressive candidates in the two major parties. For hard political and military reasons, leavened perhaps by dreams of a postwar era of world peace abroad and class harmony at home, liberals and Communists were once more forging connections and pledging themselves to the improvement of American democratic society.

The anticommunist tide ebbed. The government itself no longer had an interest in harrying Communists and indeed was eager for the cooperation of Communist workers in the defense industries. The alliance with the Soviet Union and the newfound cooperativeness of American Communists together restored the latter to the legitimate political arena. Earl Browder was pardoned by Roosevelt and released from prison in 1942. The government and the media engaged in a campaign to improve the Soviet image in the United States. Roosevelt spoke warmly of Joseph Stalin and told Americans in 1943 that "I believe that we are going to get along very well with him and the Russian people—very well indeed." The administration apparently encouraged the production of such Hollywood movies as *Mission to Moscow* and *Song of Russia*, which cast the Soviet Union in a fairly benign light. A genuine idealism strengthened the cooperative mood. In 1943 the former Republican presidential candidate Wendell Willkie published *One World*, a report of his recent tour around the globe, in which he spoke admiringly of the gains ordinary Russian people had made under the Soviet system, found much in the Soviet Union that reminded him of the United States, and insisted that "we do not need to fear Russia. We need to learn to work with her." The book quickly became a best-seller. American Communists basked in the new warmth of the Soviet-American accord.

Bodies like the American Civil Liberties Union commented on the lack of repression in the United States in the war years. In 1944 the ACLU reported on "the extraordinary and unexpected record . . . in freedom of debate and dissent on all public issues." There was much less hostility to the war than there had been in the First World War, and the administration felt less need either to resort to patriotic propaganda or to suppress resistance. The federal government was largely successful in preempting the area of internal security and in persuading state and local officials not to pursue subversives themselves, and there was little vigilante activity. J. Edgar Hoover willingly extended his bureau's political surveillance, but his agents managed to conduct themselves with reasonable propriety. The loyalties of federal employees and of defense plant workers were checked, and though there were a few cases that disturbed civil libertarians, for the most part these procedures won broad acceptance, particularly after the Civil Service Commission reminded its investigators in 1943 that their concerns were strictly with loyalty, not with "unorthodox" views.

There were some groups that were not safe from official and unofficial harassment during the war, generally those not aligned with the popular front or those identified, however questionably, with the Axis powers. Virtually the only left-wingers to oppose the administration's foreign policy after the Nazi invasion of Russia were the Trotskyite members of the Socialist Workers party (SWP), who, as it happened, were strong among the Teamsters of Minneapolis, where war broke out between rival unions in 1941. The Teamster's conservative national leaders drew the attention of the administration to the advocates of "foreign, radical governments" in Minneapolis, and the government obliged by raiding the SWP headquarters and bringing indictments under the new Smith Act against twenty-nine members, securing prison sentences for eighteen of them. The CP's *Daily Worker* patriotically applauded the Minneapolis indictments. But it was right-wing groups that were most vulnerable, having been stranded by the course of world events outside the spectrum of acceptable politics. Father Coughlin's *Social Justice* was banned from the mails, and a mass sedition case was launched against "native fascists," netting leaders of fascistic organizations like Gerald Winrod and William Dudley Pelley, right-wing critics like Elizabeth Dilling and Lawrence Dennis, German agents in the United States, and leaders of the German-American Bund. This bizarre case dragged on interminably, until with the ending of the war the indictments were dismissed. More serious was the evacuation of eleven thousand Japanese Americans from the West Coast, lest they engage in sabotage, and their internment in "relocation centers." Those who could somehow be identified with the enemy cause were not socialists or communists, but their treatment demonstrated that "un-American" minorities could still be refused their constitutional rights. Any group denied political legitimacy in the future would remain vulnerable to harassment and persecution.

Cold War

The truce in the campaign against American Communists and other radicals survived the ending of the Second World War. Civil libertarians feared a reprise of the Big Red Scare, but it did not come. In 1946 the ACLU noted with some surprise the absence of illiberal behavior across the country. Communists were less likely to be heckled, mobbed, or arrested, it seemed, than the patriotic anti-Semite Gerald L. K. Smith, who was occasionally denied a forum. For the moment the United States and the Soviet Union were still clumsily fumbling for ways of cooperating with one another in the postwar world, and the launching of the United Nations was some sort of symbol of the vaunted new era of global peace. Domestically the wartime popular front nexus lived on, and those liberals, progressives, and Communists who were part of it looked forward to renewing the New Deal at home and even to creating a "New Deal for the world," with the major powers working for a better life for oppressed people everywhere. The radical left was still assured of a constructive role in American political life. When Franklin Roosevelt died in April 1945 Earl Browder expressed the hope that his successor would carry out "Roosevelt's legacy."

But although a red scare did not envelop the United States as quickly after the Second World War as after the First, America's radicals were hardly safe. For one thing, they were tied to liberal allies whose own fortunes had been ebbing for some years, despite the aspirations being kindled by the ending of the war. After Franklin Roosevelt's smashing victory in 1936, the Democratic proportion of the presidential vote slowly shrank with each succeeding election, part of a long-term trend that would continue into the 1950s. The congressional midterm elections showed steady Republican gains in 1938 and 1942, a process that would culminate in the stunning Republican victory of 1946. Roosevelt hoped to defy the swing of the pendulum and fought the 1944 election on a reform program—a "second bill of rights." Predictably, there was considerable red-baiting of administration candidates, not least because the CIO and its formidable Political Action Committee (CIO-PAC) under Sidney Hillman were working hard to deliver the labor vote to Roosevelt. The Republican vice presidential contender charged that the Democratic party had become the "Hillman-Browder Communistic Party with Franklin Roosevelt at its front."

Roosevelt was reelected, more because he was seen as an experienced world leader than for his reform proposals, but the voters also put more Republicans into the Senate than they had done since the days of Herbert Hoover. Further, over a third of Roosevelt's electoral vote came from southern states, most of whose representatives in Congress were hostile to reform. The conservative coalition would continue to block New Deal legislation. Liberals hoped that the return of peace would revitalize their cause, but they were even less in command of the nations' councils than they had been before the war, and conservatives eager to take apart the New Deal heritage were already training their sights on its Communist acolytes.

As right-wing politicians maneuvred for advantage, the various anti-communist interest groups awaited their opportunity. Patriotic societies like the DAR remained resolutely opposed to popular front politics. The ranks of the American Legion and the Veterans of Foreign Wars were being replenished by the thousands of veterans returning from the war. The zeal with which business had apparently cooperated with the war effort, and the return of full employment, had restored public confidence in the country's industrial leadership, and some businessmen emerged from the war eager to reverse the labor gains and the "socialist" legislation associated with the New Deal. The United States Chamber of Commerce in particular was readying itself for a sustained campaign against the influence of Communists in American public life. Such interests as the AFL, the Roman Catholic Church, Protestant fundamentalists, the right-wing press, and the white South were as obdurately hostile as ever to communism, whether domestic or foreign. In some respects the anticommunist congregation had been augmented, for groups like Polish Americans and Hungarian Americans were distressed at the way their old homelands, and their relatives there, were becoming subject to Soviet control. The passion and self-confidence of the disparate interests opposed to communism were greater than they had been for years.

What contained these forces was an international configuration that still reflected something of the wartime alliance between the United States and the Soviet Union, and a domestic configuration in which the Democratic–popular front alignment, although on the defensive, could still hope to outface its opponents. Neither the international nor the domestic formation was very stable, however. Even before Roosevelt's death in April 1945 tensions were growing between the United States and the Soviet Union, and by March 1946 they were sufficiently marked for Winston Churchill to speak of "an iron curtain" descending across the European continent.

Domestically, too, the idealism projected by the popular front disguised a host of rivalries and mutual suspicions. Long-serving trade union officials, for example, who in years past had bitterly fought off Communist forays into their territory, could not easily put their trust in their newly acquired allies. There was dissension within the CP itself over the propriety of collaborating with the bourgeoisie after the war, and Browder's rival William Z. Foster anticipated a new and determined capitalist assault on labor at home and the Soviet Union abroad. Outside the popular front, but within the Democratic party and the labor movement, were liberals and moderates who had no desire to perpetuate the political entanglement with the Left. Many radical intellectuals had become disenchanted with the course of the Soviet experiment in the 1930s and despised the "Stalinism" of American Communists. There were influential liberals who regarded with cynicism the frequent changes in the Communist party line, which seemed to prove that American Communists were not their own masters. That the CP should seek succor in Moscow in its fledgling and persecuted early days was perhaps understandable, but by the late 1930s it had achieved a measure of acceptability, and the sudden shifts in line in 1939 and 1941 in response to well-publicized world events suggested that Communists were at best unreliable allies and at worst the agents of a foreign power. Further, there were many liberals who believed there was little to choose between the totalitarianism of Nazi Germany and that of the Soviet Union, and in the postwar world it seemed to be the Soviets who were extinguishing democratic freedoms across a large part of Europe.

In the three years following 1945 the fragile liberal–popular front coalition gradually came apart, cracking under the pressure of world events and domestic discord. When Roosevelt died it lost the one man who possessed the stature, charm, and evasiveness necessary to keep it together. A few weeks later the accommodationist strategy of American Communists was wrecked by the publication of the celebrated article by the French Communist leader Jacques Duclos, apparently reflecting the views of Moscow, attacking Earl Browder for dissolving the CP and thereby abandoning the class struggle for a reformist policy that could never deliver a communist United States. The subsequent convulsions among American Communists resulted in Browder's replacement as leader by William Z. Foster, and the conversion of the Communist Political Association back into the Communist party, accompanied by militant class rhetoric. The revived CP did not reject the popular front, but its distrust of "class collaborationism" and its more radical stance made such alliances difficult to effect. Further, the Duclos episode put a weapon into the hands of those liberals who wanted to repudiate the popular front, for it seemed final proof that whenever Stalin grunted American Communists would snap to attention.

Such liberals were becoming increasingly convinced that any association with a totalitarian element could only compromise the cause of democratic reform. They had earlier founded the Union for Democratic Action (UDA), which excluded Communists from membership, and as Cold War tensions surfaced the UDA began a campaign for the allegiance of the bulk of the old New Dealers. In May 1946 its leader James Loeb called on liberal organizations generally to ban Communist members, warning that popular front groups were likely to become Communist fronts. Within the labor movement too there were those who wanted to end the wartime alliance with the Communists. In the mighty United Auto Workers between 1945 and 1947 Walter Reuther won a protracted battle for control of the union against a popular front coalition in which Communists were strong. In the CIO itself president Phil Murray for the moment tried to steer a middle course between pro- and anticommunist factions, though in September 1946 he declared that organized labor wanted "no damn Communists meddling in our affairs." In November Reuther and the anticommunists persuaded the national convention to "resent and reject efforts of the Communist Party or other political parties and their adherents to interfere in the affairs of the CIO." The onset of the Cold War was making it difficult for liberals to remain linked to Communists.

Eager to deepen the divisions in the liberal–popular front coalition and to wrest what advantage they could from the course of domestic and foreign affairs, the nation's conservatives harped on the dangers of labor and the Left. The government's "reconversion" program did not proceed smoothly, being plagued by leaping prices and restive workers, and the ending of the war released unions from their "no-strike" pledge. Some five million workers went on strike in the year following the Japanese surrender, and 1946 saw more strikes than any other year in American history, enabling newspapers to cultivate images of widespread industrial chaos. The Hearst press represented the strikes as part of a "clear and distinct revolutionary pattern . . . timed to serve Russia's political interests." The United States Chamber of Commerce determined to mount a propaganda campaign against American Communists, and in 1946 it distributed two hundred thousand copies of a pamphlet entitled *Communist Infiltration in the United States*, focusing on Communist subversion in the labor movement and in government. "The Reds have a lot to do with our current, very serious labor situation," insisted a Chamber of Commerce official. No doubt many Americans shrugged off these allegations by anticommunist zealots, but the strikes were generally unpopular, and public opinion moved against labor. Employers were worried about their loss of control over the workplace, consequent upon the Wagner Act and the exigencies of war, and were determined to resist the strikers' demands in an attempt to reclaim their "right to manage."

The swing away from the Democrats became marked in the midterm elections of 1946, when the Republicans won control of both houses of Congress for the first time since 1928 and, except in the South, swept the state governorships too. The Republican national chairman thought that Democratic policy bore "a made-in-Moscow label," deplored "the infiltration of alien-minded radicals" into the government, and assailed the administration's "brazen public alliance" with the "radical-dominated" CIO-PAC. Public opinion polls during the election campaign showed a two-thirds majority in favor of new curbs on unions, a cause the Republicans were identified with. The antilabor sentiment engendered by the strike wave probably increased Republican majorities. Liberal candidates and those endorsed by the CIO fared notably badly in the elections, including a number who had been associated with the popular front strategy.

The notion of a broad alliance of liberals and radicals had suffered a severe rebuff in the 1946 elections, and pressure on the administration to dissociate itself from the left was becoming all but irresistible. The Republicans interpreted the election results as a repudiation of the New Deal, and dozens of antilabor bills were presented to the new Congress. The United States Chamber of Commerce maintained its propaganda campaign, early in 1947 publishing reports alleging extensive Communist penetration of government and of the labor unions. The idea that there was Communist subversion in the United States was beginning to gain some credibility. In 1945 classified documents had been found in the office of the magazine *Amerasia*, and though their innocuous nature meant that the resulting legal charges were fairly nominal, the Hearst press generated a red scare and for years right-wingers complained of a cover-up. The episode at least seemed to demonstrate that the New Dealers in the government were capable of leaking official information to their left-wing friends.

Another scare was precipitated in 1946 when the Canadian government uncovered a Soviet spy ring. This was authentic enough and fed suspicions of Soviet espionage in the United States as well, enabling J. Edgar Hoover to step up FBI investigations of possible Communist subversion. Public opinion polls in the wake of these scares showed large majorities believing that there were Russian agents in the United States and that Communists should be barred from government jobs.

The new Republican majorities in the Eightieth Congress, propelled by a mixture of conviction and political opportunism, had every incentive to use the labor and communist issues as ways of discrediting the heritage of the New Deal and embarrassing the administration. The White House, while determined to maintain New Deal reforms, quickly concluded that it would be wise to preempt Congress wherever possible.

This strategy was to lead the Truman administration on a fateful and controversial course, which in the view of some scholars meant that it bore much responsibility for the later McCarthyite red scare. Even before the new Congress assembled, Truman appointed a Temporary Commission on Employee Loyalty to consider the need for permanent procedures to screen government employees on loyalty grounds. As he was thus protecting himself from the Republican charge of tolerating Communists in government, he was also increasingly perceiving the Soviet Union as an enemy abroad. American-Soviet relations had continued to deteriorate, with the Soviet Union seemingly replacing Nazi Germany as the epitome of totalitarian expansionism, and when the financially crippled British government found that it could not maintain its presence in Greece and Turkey, Truman had to decide whether the United States should assume the responsibility for resisting communist influence in those areas. This was a momentous decision, for never before had the United States been militarily implicated in Europe in time of peace, and when Truman asked Congress for military and economic assistance in March 1947 he sought to mobilize public support for this radical departure by conjuring a new battle for freedom. "I believe that it must be the policy of the United States to support free peoples who are resisting attempted subjugation by armed minorities or by outside pressures," he said, and he accepted Senator Arthur Vandenberg's advice to "scare hell out of the American people" by dwelling on the totalitarian alternative that somehow threatened even the United States. Like Wilson during World War I, Truman was faced with potentially crippling domestic opposition, and he was resorting to ideological pressures to create a new foreign policy consensus. Even many anticommunist liberals were dismayed by the belligerent tone of the Truman Doctrine, which allowed no role for the United Nations, and as the Soviet Union was transformed from an ally into an enemy, popular front liberals and Communists found themselves increasingly at odds with the administration.

The same month witnessed the domestic counterpart of the Truman Doctrine, the adoption of a loyalty program after the report of the temporary commission. With Congress itself beginning to consider legislation to outlaw the CP, the administration's strategy, like that of Roosevelt during the war, was an attempt to make loyalty and security issues the preserve of the executive. Since HUAC was being allowed more license than ever before by the conservative Eightieth Congress, the Truman loyalty program perhaps did avert a new round of anticommunist legislation, but it was at the cost of extending the functions of those bureaucratic agencies engaged in political surveillance, chief among them the FBI. Federal employees were to be screened for "disloyalty," a concept that was not clearly defined but could include membership in or even "sympathetic association" with any organization "designated" by the attorney general as "totalitarian, Fascist, Communist or subversive." Individuals could thus be proscribed simply for their beliefs or thoughts. The hastily devised procedures were open to abuse, and individuals subject to a full-scale investigation might not be told the precise charges against them or even the identities of those providing evidence, so that cross-examination was impossible. Considerable arbitrary power was accorded to the attorney general, whose responsibility it was to compile the list of subversive organizations, which he could do without holding hearings or allowing for an appeal. With the list's publication, what had been compiled by hearsay was widely treated as an authoritative judgment.

It is doubtful that Truman realized the precedents his program was setting or the power being accorded to federal bureaucracy. The CIO-PAC likened the loyalty program to "the infamous sedition laws of 1798," and Philip Murray asked the president why it was necessary when the country had just survived a world war without one. The reason for its introduction, as Truman effectively conceded when he spoke of the need to forestall HUAC's red-baiters, was political; the security program was largely the creation of the highly partisan and closely fought politics of the 1940s.

But the Republican Eightieth Congress was not going to abandon its attacks on the New Deal. Its resurgent conservatism was enshrined in the Taft-Hartley Act of 1947, passed over Truman's veto. Employers had long been complaining that the Wagner Act had tilted the balance in industrial relations in favor of the unions, and the antilabor sentiment and Republican revival following the postwar strike wave gave them the opportunity to secure a new labor law strengthening their managerial prerogatives. The Taft-Hartley Act also reflected the temper of the Eightieth Congress by requiring union officials employing National Labor Relations Board services to execute anticommunist affadavits. The anticommunist oath was directed at the CIO unions, which were said to contain Communists, and greatly increased the pressure on the CIO to dissociate itself from the CP.

The more fervent anticommunists in Congress amplified the communist issue via HUAC, now composed exclusively of Republicans and southern Democrats and revitalized with a greatly increased appropriation. It was in this congressional session that HUAC became a household name, not least through its celebrated hearings on the Communist infiltration of Hollywood in the fall of 1947. In November, fearful that untoward publicity would affect the box office, the studio executives announced the dismissal of those Hollywood witnesses who had boisterously defied HUAC, the small beginnings of a blacklist that would later deprive hundreds of their jobs. In 1947 HUAC in fact attracted as much criticism as applause for its Hollywood hearings, which were abruptly terminated, but its power was demonstrated when the unfriendly Hollywood Ten were given prison sentences for contempt of Congress. HUAC was also paying attention to the major labor unions, student radicals, popular front groups like the Southern Conference of Human Welfare, and the CP itself—in short those constituencies that had been associated with the leftward edge of the New Deal coalition.

Outside Congress too the pressure from a range of energetic anticommunist interests was unremitting. The United States Chamber of Commerce represented the views of many small businessmen and some big ones in its periodic imprecations against the New Deal, labor unions, and anything resembling socialism, and in 1948 it sought to stimulate the grass roots with a pamphlet entitled *A Program for Community Anti-Communist Action*. Countless newspapers and private publishers provided outlets for anticommunist propaganda. From 1947 a New York group with close contacts with the FBI published a weekly newsletter entitled *Counterattack*, the most prominent of a number of such newssheets devoted to exposing "Communist fronts" and the nefarious activities of American radicals and liberals. The principal veterans' organizations maintained their vigilant watch for communist influence in the government, the schools, the cinema, and elsewhere, as in a 1948 publication of the American Legion entitled *The "Red" Exposure: "A Study of Subversive Influences."*

The Roman Catholic hierarchy, through such spokesmen as Francis Cardinal Spellman and Bishop Fulton J. Sheen, repeatedly warned of "the yellow travelers in the United States and those whose hearts bleed for Red Fascism," and such groups as the Catholic War Veterans, the Knights of Columbus, and the Association of Catholic Trade Unionists energetically deployed their resources in the fight against communism. The fundamentalist churches were also experiencing something of a revival, and new organizations like the National Association of Evangelicals assailed the "revolutionary" activities of the New Deal and the infiltration of government, the unions, and churches by "reds." White southerners darkly attributed the civil rights initiatives of the Truman administration to the influence of international communism, and when the civil rights plank in the Democratic platform of 1948 provoked the creation of a States' Rights party, its candidate, Strom Thurmond, represented white supremacy as a bulwark against communist subversion. Some of the anticommunist groups and individuals were on occasion given information and cooperation by the FBI, under the brooding influence of J. Edgar Hoover, who was able to use the Cold War to extend the political surveillance of his formidable bureaucracy.

Encouraged by such constituencies, HUAC reached its apotheosis in the Eightieth Congress, which expanded its appropriation from a reluctant $50,000 in 1945 to a record $200,000 in 1948. In some ways its unruly behavior under J. Parnell Thomas hurt rather than helped its reputation, as did the public sympathy accorded to the Hollywood Ten when they went to prison. But at the prompting of Republican members Karl E. Mundt and Richard Nixon it was finally giving sustained attention to the formulation of anticommunist legislation. J. Edgar Hoover advised HUAC that it would be unwise to outlaw the CP, which would simply reemerge in a new guise, and the Mundt-Nixon bill sought to put it under public surveillance by requiring it and its fronts and its individual members to register with the Justice Department. The bill passed the House in 1948 with the backing of Republicans and southern Democrats although the Senate failed to act on it. The operations of HUAC were hardly an unqualified success in these years, and on occasion it experienced embarrassing rebuffs from the White House and other critics, but it did something to foster the suspicion of communist subversion by flailing away at the New Deal, the labor movement, the popular front, and the Communist party and the dubious connections between them.

Harried by the antilabor and anticommunist offensive of the Republican Congress and increasingly subject to the Cold War perception of the CP as a Soviet agency, the faltering popular front–Democratic alliance was prised apart. Early in 1947 the popular front elements formed the Progressive Citizens of America (PCA), which condemned the administration's "imperialism" and its abandonment of New Deal reform and hinted at the formation of a new left-liberal party. The anticommunist liberals in the Union for Democratic Action retaliated by forming Americans for Democratic Action (ADA), which attracted several prominent New Dealers and which explicitly rejected any association with either Communists or fascists. One of its organizers described it as "a declaration of liberal independence from the stifling and paralysing influence of the Communists and their apologists in America." These liberals had little affection at this stage for the Truman administration, but they were clearly repudiating the popular front strategy, and in the course of 1947 the government's policies widened the gulf between it and the PCA but brought it closer to the ADA.

The Marshall Plan in particular, with its commitment of American resources to rebuilding the European economy, accelerated this political realignment. It was close to the earlier liberal dream of a New Deal for the world—Taft disparagingly called it a "European TVA"—and though it implied an effort to build markets for American goods and to contain international communism by economic means, its apparent subordination of military to humanitarian principles appealed to liberal sensibilities. The PCA denounced the imperialist and globally divisive nature of the plan, but it was the ADA that was proving successful in recruiting the bulk of the old New Dealers, and the ADA aligned itself with the administration. The old popular front persuasion, which had offered American Communists some protection, was being isolated.

Nonetheless, recalling the exhilarating days of the New Deal and the potency that labor, farm, and liberal movements had so recently shown, PCA liberals believed there was potential widespread support in the country for a left-liberal alternative to the Truman program. New Dealers had once ruled the land and just might do so again, and at the end of 1947 Henry Wallace acceded to PCA pressures to lead a new third party. American Communists lent their support to this Progressive party, which thus became an attempt to rebuild the popular front, albeit in rebellion against the powerful Democratic party instead of in alliance with it. The presidential election of 1948 was to be the testing ground of this new political force.

Even without the foreign policy crises of 1948, when the Soviet Union seemed to emerge yet more starkly as the enemy of freedom, the Progressive party was perfectly positioned to draw the fire of the various anticommunist interests. Not only had the CP rallied to its cause, but it had failed to win the allegiance of powerful noncommunist allies who might have given it some legitimacy. Democratic party loyalists reviled it, most of the old prominent New Dealers refused to join it, civil rights and liberal farm groups shrank from it, and the CIO itself, earlier caught between its PCA and ADA wings, at first refused officially to endorse either and subsequently gave strong support to the president. It was easy for superpatriots like Gerald L. K. Smith to warn that Stalin was on the loose on the American continent "under the guise of the Progressive Party." The press almost unanimously represented the party as a Communist front, and respectable newspapers like the *New York Times* deployed such headlines as "Communists in Control." Perhaps even more damaging were the red-baiting assaults emanating from within the liberal community. While Truman lashed at the "do-nothing" Eightieth Congress, he also rebuked "Henry Wallace and his Communists." The ADA in particular turned its anticommunist animus against the Wallace candidacy, publicizing the connections between prominent

Progressive party supporters and the suspect organizations on the attorney general's list and depicting Wallace as a Communist dupe. With the Progressive party so widely reviled, local anticommunists harassed it at every turn. In North Carolina Wallace himself was pelted with eggs and tomatoes, and his running mate, Senator Glen Taylor, was arrested in Birmingham, Alabama, for attempting to speak to an integrated audience. The Birmingham police chief, Eugene ("Bull") Connor, explained, "There's not enough room in town for Bull and the Commies."

The evolution of foreign affairs in 1948 sealed the Progressives' fate, identifying them even more firmly with a Soviet enemy. A kind of popular front government, containing both Communists and noncommunists, had existed in Czechoslovakia, and when it collapsed under Soviet pressure and Czechoslovakia apparently became a Soviet satellite, as it had once been a Nazi satellite, Stalin's blandishments seemed no more trustworthy than Hitler's. The "fall" of Czechoslovakia greatly increased support for the Marshall Plan in the United States and intensified distrust of the real Communist motives in Wallace's popular front. In June the Russians again appeared as the aggressors when they imposed a blockade of Berlin, and American public opinion moved more firmly behind Truman's Cold War policies. By making the "fight for peace" and a conciliatory attitude toward Russia the basis of his campaign, Henry Wallace seemed to be serving Soviet interests. Whatever the involvement of the CP in the Progressive party, its critics could plausibly represent it as being directed from Moscow.

While the Truman administration was squaring off to the Soviet Union abroad and the Wallace insurgency at home, it was also acting more and more on the assumption that American Communists were Soviet agents. In December 1947 it made public the attorney general's notorious List of Subversive Organizations, thereby encouraging the harassment of the listed bodies, which found themselves losing financial support, members, and access to public platforms and exposed to the unkindly attentions of superpatriots. In 1948 radical aliens, particularly union leaders, again began to be arrested with a view to deportation, and the Smith Act was once more employed when twelve Communist leaders were charged with conspiring to organize the CP as a body advocating the violent overthrow of the government. Such moves threatened the very existence of the CP, which could hardly operate without leaders; not since the era of the Nazi-Soviet Pact had an American administration sought to banish Communists from public life. The exigencies of foreign and domestic politics had brought the Truman government to share the right-wing view that the CP was the organ of an international communist conspiracy.

As Democrats and Republicans maneuvered to put themselves on the

8

THE
REPUBLICAN
OFFENSIVE
(1948–1952)

•

THE OUTCOME of the 1948 presidential election left the United States poised on the brink of an intensive red scare. Since the late 1930s the communist issue had been a regular presence in national politics, but its potency had been limited. The ill-judged performances of HUAC had probably done it as much harm as good; no federal communist-control legislation had been enacted since 1940 (other than the anticommunist affidavit in Taft-Hartley), and only a handful of dissidents had lost their jobs and none had yet gone to prison, although the Hollywood Ten were on their way there. The anticommunists had helped to place popular front politics beyond the pale, but they had not yet won ascendancy over American public life. Truman's unexpected victory in 1948 ironically gave them their opportunity.

American Communists were left more exposed than they had been since 1941. New Deal liberalism had been supplanted by ADA liberalism, with its determined repudiation of the radical Left. The Truman administration itself was seeking to remove Communists and other loyalty risks from its own agencies and had begun to prosecute top Communists under the Smith Act. The weakness demonstrated by the CP (via the Progressive party) in the 1948 election rendered it exceedingly vulnerable, for even labor leaders were drawing the conclusion that association with it was a distinct political liability. And Republican party leaders, seething at their defeat, were concluding that if the Democrats could win advantage by adopting an anticommunist stance, so could they. Some Republicans, of couse, had regularly used the communist issue against the administration, but after 1948 their party embraced it with a vehemence hitherto exhibited by no major party in American politics. For the next four years the most powerful and sustained impulse behind the anticommunist cause was the Republican party's determination to ends its prolonged exile.

By 1950 the United States was succumbing to its second Big Red Scare. In that year Senator Joseph McCarthy began brandishing his lists of communists in the State Department, the Internal Security Act was passed over Truman's veto, and Republican candidates appeared to profit considerably in the November elections from red-baiting tactics. Communists and their liberal sympathizers were once more being hounded out of American public life. The Republican party owed part of its success to the support of the traditional anticommunist constituencies, some of which, like the veterans' organizations, had gained in influence since the Second World War. But it was the evolution of the Cold War itself, with the "fall" of China, the Soviet development of atomic weapons, and the Korean War, that really gave the Republicans the opportunity to assail the administration with being "soft on communism." Truman had used anticommunist sentiments against Henry Wallace, but never before had one major party attempted to deploy the full force of the anticommunist persuasion against the other.

To a considerable degree, politicians were following imperatives of their own. As Theda Skocpol and others have argued, politicans may form a distinctive class, relatively independent of economic interests and the social formation. Bureaucrats too may have their own interests to pursue. For significant numbers of party politicians and senior bureaucrats in the Cold War era, anticommunism became an important means of serving not only their ideals but their fortunes.

The Spy Cases and Foreign Reverses

It was the Hiss case that first let Republicans seriously implicate the reigning Democrats in the communist conspiracy. In the summer of 1948, when the electioneering president was accusing Congress of being the "worst" in history, a Republican-dominated HUAC listened to former Communists Whittaker Chambers and Elizabeth Bentley testify that there had been Communists in the Roosevelt administration, among them Alger Hiss, who had been a senior official in the State Department and still had prominent Democratic friends. When Hiss denied the charges, Chambers, with Richard Nixon's encouragement, escalated them, dramatically producing documents suggesting that Hiss had been a spy. Hiss had once been in the Department of Agriculture with the suspect Henry Wallace, and he had later been at the Yalta Conference, where right-wingers believed that Roosevelt had sold out to Stalin, and so he was ideally cast to personify the old Republican charge that Communists had penetrated to the very heart of the New Deal. Protected from an espionage indictment by the statute of limitations, Alger Hiss was formally charged with perjury in December.

Even before the trial of Alger Hiss, politicians and public figures were moving to dissociate themselves from the radicalism that had been doomed by the election of 1948. The CIO was preparing to expel Communists from its ranks, and the administration was trying to put Communists behind bars. The Republicans for their part were eager to use the Hiss case to affix the tag of treason to the Democrats. Other loyalty cases hit the headlines with a frequency that suggested that the administration was trying to fortify itself on the issue and its opponents to exploit it. In March 1949 Judith Coplon, a Justice Department official, was arrested for espionage, promising another sensation that would embarrass the incumbent Democrats. In May the government resumed its campaign against Harry Bridges, this time accusing him of perjuring himself in an earlier denial that he was a Communist. As the Smith Act and the Hiss, Coplon, and Bridges cases wound their way through the courts in 1949, extensive press coverage conjured up images of widespread disloyalty and espionage. HUAC, too, was probing espionage, but with greater decorum, airing suspicions that Communists had penetrated American atomic establishments during the war. Public opinion continued to move against the Communist party, and by the end of 1949 Gallup was reporting that some 68 percent of Americans—a higher figure than any obtained since 1941—believed it should be banned.

The powerful forces within the American polity that were already poised against domestic radicalism in 1949 were strengthened yet further by tensions arising from international politics. The course of events abroad seemed to corroborate fears that subversion had indeed taken place in the United States. In China the nationalists were succumbing to the Red Army, and right-wing Republicans attributed the "loss" to inadequate American support—the result, they said, of the influence of communist sympathizers in the State Department. The Republican charge had a certain resonance for Americans, who believed that they had "won" the Second World War and that the United States was a benevolent colossus capable of ordering the affairs of the world—one, indeed, that had long exerted considerable influence in China.

In September it was announced that the Soviet Union had exploded an atomic bomb, years before the date predicted by American scientists, and one plausible explanation was that the Soviets had had access to American secrets. HUAC had already published a report entitled *Soviet Espionage Activities in Connection with the Atom Bomb*. Its suspicions were not altogether ill founded; in February 1950 it was revealed that Dr. Klaus Fuchs, a British scientist who had worked at Los Alamos during the war, had indeed spied for the Soviet Union. As evidence mounted

from abroad of communist influence in the United States, the trials of
Alger Hiss spectacularly confirmed conservative suspicions that the
New Deal bureaucracy had been riddled with Communists. A well-
educated, upper-middle-class lawyer, Hiss was the very personification
of the young reformers who had been attracted to Washington by Franklin Roosevelt and who had acquired influential positions in the State
Department during the wartime alliance with Russia. When Hiss was
eventually convicted in January 1950, in effect of being a Soviet spy, the
long-standing conspiracy theory seemed vindicated. Not only were the
New Deal's unconventional experiments in "socialism" explained, so
were the reverses in postwar foreign policy. The Republicans now had
an issue with which to end the overlong rule of the Democrats. (In Britain, by contrast, the Conservative opposition could not easily use the
Fuchs case against the Labour government, since Fuchs's spying had
begun during the war when the government was a coalition under Winston Churchill.)

The purge of Communists from American public life had already
begun. After the floundering Wallace campaign of 1948, the CIO drew
the lesson that it would not wreck itself by ousting its enfeebled Communist element. With hopes dashed that Taft-Hartley would be
repealed, it seemed wise to accommodate to the law. At its national convention in the fall of 1949 Philip Murray insisted there was but "one
issue, and one issue alone, and that is . . . Communism," and he submitted Walter Reuther's resolutions barring members of "the Communist Party, any fascist organization, or other totalitarian movement"
from the CIO executive board and giving the board power to expel affil-
iates that served the purposes of such organizations. The resolutions
were passed, the convention promptly expelled two Communist-
oriented unions, and in the following year nine others were sent after
them. A few unions purged themselves, and several dozen unions—CIO
and AFL—adopted rules barring Communists from holding office.

Other liberal bodies were also ridding themselves of the Communist
liability. The Congress of Racial Equality had always been wary of asso-
ciating itself with other distracting causes, but its 1948 convention
determined not to allow "Communist-controlled" groups to affiliate
with it. The National Association for the Advancement of Colored People (NAACP) also resolved in 1950 to expel any Communist-led
branches. In 1949 the ACLU adopted a resolution opposing "any form
of the police state or the single party state, or any movement in support
of them," and in 1951 its 1940 resolution banning Communists from
holding office was embedded in the ACLU constitution. In 1949 too the
National Education Association barred Communists from membership
and proposed that CP members should not be employed as teachers, and

in the same year the board of regents of the University of California precipitated a celebrated furor by requiring a loyalty oath of professors. The American Bar Association formally registered its hostility to Communists in 1948 and by 1950 was recommending that lawyers take a loyalty oath.

State and local governments also began to shed Communists and other recalcitrant employees. In 1948 Los Angeles County employees began to lose their jobs for failing to take a loyalty oath, and in 1949 fifteen states introduced various communist-control laws, one of the most widely admired and imitated being Maryland's Ober Law, which attempted to outlaw subversive organizations and required loyalty oaths from all public employees, including teachers and librarians. Communists—and others who could not bring themselves to execute loyalty oaths—were becoming the victims of the widespread conviction that the CP was part of an international conspiracy directed from Moscow, and of the competition as politicians and others in American public life sought to demonstrate their patriotism. Even before Senator Joseph McCarthy belatedly spotted Communists in the State Department in February 1950, the Cold War, in interacting with a political system in which precarious politicians were buffeted endlessly by a host of revitalized patriotic and conservative interests, had transformed American Communists and their sympathizers into public lepers.

Senator Joseph McCarthy

During the election of 1948 Republican spokesmen had routinely but vainly attempted to use the communist issue against the administration, but by the start of 1950 their charges were beginning to bite. When Alger Hiss was convicted in January, Karl Mundt demanded the removal of other federal employees "whose Soviet leanings have contributed so greatly to the deplorable mess of our foreign policy," and other Republicans eagerly seized on this proof (and soon that offered by Judith Coplon's conviction in March) that the bureaucracy had been penetrated by spies. The bombshell of Klaus Fuchs's arrest seemed further evidence for the charge. Early in February the Republican National Committee adopted a "Statement of Republican Principles and Objectives" that decried "the dangerous degree to which Communists and their fellow travelers have been employed in important Government posts." J. Edgar Hoover, never overfriendly to the Truman administration, confirmed the presence of an enormous fifth column in asserting that there were over a half-million Communists and fellow travelers in the United States. On Lincoln Day—9 February—Republican speakers across the country laid into the administration for harboring Communists. The Hiss case, according to Congressman Richard Nixon, was but "a small part of the whole shocking story of Communist espionage in the United States."

One such speech was given by a hitherto rather obscure Republican senator from Wisconsin, Joseph R. McCarthy. It was in Wheeling, West Virginia, that he flourished his imaginative "list of names" of 205 Communists in the State Department, which next day in Denver became "207 bad risks" and in Salt Lake City "57 card-carrying members of the Communist Party." For nearly two decades Republicans had been espying communist influence in the government, but here was a United States senator claiming to possess a specific list of Communist employees and documentary evidence to substantiate it. The press was electrified, and a mystified Washington wondered what McCarthy could have stumbled on. The list never in fact existed—McCarthy's speeches wove together garbled and inaccurate extracts from dated documents—but his claim to hard information gave him the spotlight, and in subsequent months he mastered the techniques of keeping it trained on him. Within about three months of his Wheeling speech McCarthy was enjoying vital support in the opinion polls, some 39 percent of respondents believing that his hunt for Communists was "a good thing for the country." For the next four years he would rarely be out of the headlines.

In many respects McCarthy's significance has been ludicrously exaggerated, and it is questionable whether he merits much attention here. He did not inspire the anticommunist cause, to which he came very late. He contributed no new ideas, fashioned no legislation, commanded no coherent organization; he only briefly chaired a Senate committee, and that a minor one, and his tactics did lasting harm to his own mission. Further, he probably inflicted less damage on the CP as such than his Democratic colleague Pat McCarran, who pushed through the Internal Security Act and headed the Senate's own—and more effective—version of HUAC. Yet before the eyes of the country and indeed of the world it was McCarthy who became the personification of American anticommunism, and for a time press and politicians, bureaucrats and businessmen, Congress and White House treated him as a power in the land. This phenomenon in itself was remarkable.

There is little evidence that McCarthy foresaw such celebrity for himself. His cause took off in February 1950 in part because he unexpectedly hit upon a style that would command attention and in part because the political climate was favorable to his Communists-in-the-government charge. This favorite Republican thesis had been gaining credibility in the previous six months, which had witnessed Mao Tse-tung's proclamation of the People's Republic of China, the announcement of the Soviet atomic bomb, and the conviction of Alger Hiss, symbol of the espionage in the State Department that was responsible for these communist successes. McCarthy's essential charge was that Hiss had not been alone, and the scale of American reverses lent him some plausibility. Since 1947 the Truman administration had been vigorously preaching the need to contain the creeping Soviet menace, yet both Czechoslovakia and China had "fallen," and the Russians had developed nuclear weapons with suspicious speed. McCarthy, it seemed, could answer the question why the United States, with all its power and enviable example, was losing the Cold War. The same month that brought McCarthy's speech also brought news of the arrest of Klaus Fuchs for espionage. A few months later war broke out in Korea, and that summer Julius and Ethel Rosenberg were arrested as spies, further evidence that Communists had successfully breached American security. Better than anyone, partly through sheer audacity, McCarthy was able to tap the vein of suspicion that traitors in the government were selling out the United States to the Soviet Union.

As McCarthy caught the headlines with charges of spies in the State Department, he found aid being eagerly proferred to him from many quarters. His fellow Republicans, several of whom shared his suspicions of Democratic foreign policy, were willing enough to lend support and protection to the senator's brutish harassment of the administration. The press itself obligingly amplified McCarthy's charges, and right-wing publishers established close connections with him. J. Edgar Hoover and the FBI provided McCarthy with data, and scattered through other government bureaucracies was a host of informants willing to play a surreptitious role in the anticommunist campaign. McCarthy's celebrity also brought him money and the assistance of a number of wealthy right-wing business interests. Without this coterie of well-placed supporters, McCarthy would never have been able to sustain his cause.

Perhaps McCarthy's most important asset was his status as a Republican senator. McCarthy had been elected to the Senate in 1946. Since that time the Washington news corps had developed a low opinion of this ill-informed and headstrong politician, but by virtue of his office a United States senator commanded some attention from other officeholders, press, and public. Further, McCarthy was casting in savage and telling form a charge that right-wing Republicans had been making for years. For many on the Republican right, American foreign policy from the late 1930s onward had been characterized by the subordination of legitimate American interests and responsibilities in the Far East to the questionable interests of Europe, and the abandonment of China to the communists was the consummation of Democratic perfidy. Republican senators of this stripe, like Styles Bridges and Bourke Hickenlooper, instinctively rallied to McCarthy's side. Even many moderate Republicans frequently guarded McCarthy from Democratic attempts to expose him as a fraud, loyally if not always enthusiastically voting to sustain their party colleague in roll calls in the Senate. The respected Republican leader in the Senate, Robert A. Taft, though perfectly aware of McCarthy's cavalier way with facts, was delighted at the discomfiture of the Truman administration and advised McCarthy, "If one case doesn't work, try another." Once it became clear that McCarthy could not be shrugged off as a buffoon after the manner of Martin Dies or J. Parnell Thomas, his Republican colleagues, for a mixture of partisan and ideological reasons, gave him encouragement and protection.

McCarthy, as it happens, did have the makings of a buffoon, and he was so treated after 1954, but the intensity and pervasiveness of anti-communist feeling in the early 1950s ensured him a receptive audience. The press played a key role in transmitting McCarthy's alarms to the public. Quality newspapers like the *New York Times* and the *Washington Post* berated the senator, but the greater part of the press was right wing and generally supported him, although some conservative papers shrank from his methods. Even those reporters and editors who prided themselves on political independence from their business-oriented proprietors could be manipulated by McCarthy. The newspaper ethic of the day was "straight reporting," relaying the news without adornment, which in this case meant confining a story to what McCarthy actually said, without injecting suspicions about his credibility or motivation. McCarthy's far-fetched accusations were thus soberly reported as the pronouncements of a United States senator. Further, his tangled charges about Communists in government inevitably became simplified into such headlines as "McCarthy Insists Truman Oust Reds," leaving the casual reader with the impression that there were reds to be ousted. A columnist in the *New York Post* might patiently take apart McCarthy's fabrications, but small newspapers across the country simply plucked his statements from the wire services. Better than most politicians, McCarthy knew reporters' deadlines and how to create last-minute stories that could not be checked.

The reportorial conventions and news technology of the period, then, suited McCarthy's purposes admirably, and most newspaper proprietors, themselves hostile to the Truman administration, were content to allow him a good press and support him in their editorial columns. Some press barons went further. The Hearst newspaper chain, which had been deploying red scare tactics against Democratic administrations since the mid-1930s, swiftly moved to the senator's side. "Joe never had any names," remembered William Randolph Hearst, Jr. "He came to us. 'What am I gonna do? You gotta help me.' So we gave him a few good reporters." The Scripps-Howard newspapers performed similar favors and provided strong editorial support, and McCarthy established a particularly close connection with Colonel Robert R. McCormick's chain of newspapers, among them the *Chicago Tribune* and the *Washington Times-Herald*, whose newsmen sometimes wrote his speeches. Close to McCarthy, too, were staunchly anticommunist columnists and radio commentators like Westbrook Pegler, George Sokolsky, Frederick Woltman, and Fulton Lewis, Jr. These newsmen provided McCarthy with material and contacts and helped him to identify witnesses, whom on occasion they probably coached. When McCarthy delivered his first slapdash anticommunist speeches he had been more or less on his own, but as he triggered a response, this supportive coterie of well-informed, well-connected, and well-financed press interests, seeing an opportunity to promote their right-wing and anticommunist doctrines, willingly provided him with the services he needed to keep going.

Money also sometimes flowed from press coffers into McCarthy's pockets. In his years as a senator McCarthy had shown himself willing on occasion to perform political favors for grateful business lobbies, and wealthy lobbyists driven by ideological convictions were soon offering their checkbooks and other resources to the cause. One well-organized interest group was the China Lobby, which vigorously supported the Chinese Nationalists, led particularly by the rich importer Alfred Kohlberg, who had helped finance a number of publications suggesting treason in high places and who placed his services at McCarthy's disposal. A cluster of midwestern businessmen, hostile to the moderate Republicanism of Wall Street, helped McCarthy with funds, as did several wealthy Texans. "We all made money fast. We were interested in nothing else," said one Texas oil man. "Then this Communist business burst upon us. Were we going to lose what we had gained?" To oil barons like Clint W. Murchison, H. R. Cullen, and H. L. Hunt, communism meant big government and the New Deal heritage, and they adopted McCarthy with enthusiasm, feeding him stock market tips and generous campaign donations. "His idea of getting the Reds out of the government," said Hunt, "well, I think that's wonderful." Such ideological and economic interest groups seized on McCarthy for their own purposes, providing him with invaluable technical and financial assistance. As he achieved celebrity status, McCarthy also found cash gifts from worried citizens arriving daily in the mail. They helped him to expand his staff, pay for investigations, and buy information.

Some information was supplied free. J. Edgar Hoover, ever a cautious man, was sometimes alarmed by McCarthy's tendency to shoot from the hip, but perhaps because of this he tried to ensure that at least some of the senator's ammunition was reliable, discreetly culled from FBI files. At Hoover's suggestion McCarthy hired a former FBI agent as an investigator and put other former FBI men on his payroll, and the staffs of the nations' two foremost Communist hunters kept in frequent contact, at least until 1953. Tips also flowed into McCarthy's crowded offices from a variety of sources, some anonymous, within other government agencies, whether zealous anticommunists eager to help the cause or disgruntled employees settling old scores. McCarthy's network of informants within the executive branch itself added considerably to his potency.

Finally, what completed McCarthy's power was his own personality. He was shrewd enough to pick out both helpful allies and vulnerable victims, at least during his heyday, and he was unscrupulous enough not to be inhibited by the truth. He was not a spellbinding orator, but at his public appearances he often staged theatrical entrances and delighted his audiences with pugnacious and sarcastic speeches, gripping them with documents pulled from his bulging briefcase. Insisting that "McCarthyism is Americanism with its sleeves rolled up," he presented himself as a folksy prizefighter waging a lonely and courageous battle against Washington's "bright young men who are born with silver spoons in their mouths." Traditional Republicans supplied the core of his public support, but such a style also stirred some populist sentiments among poorly educated manual workers, ethnic Catholics, and small businessmen.

At Senate hearings McCarthy eschewed procedural niceties and often confounded witnesses, counsel, and fellow senators with the enormity and sheer irrationality of his assertions. Like a drunk—and he sometimes had been drinking—McCarthy simply could not be reasoned with. His wild punches, nonetheless, on occasion hit their mark, and for some years he was too valuable a political weapon for his Republican colleagues and his ardent anticommunist backers to abandon. When some of his congressional critics lost at the polls, his vaunted electoral clout reached mythic proportions.

It was in February 1950 that McCarthy first captured widespread attention with his charge of a specific—if variable—number of Communists in the State Department and whetted the public appetite with a few names. The Senate quickly established a subcommittee chaired by Democrat Millard Tydings to investigate these confusing allegations, and though Tydings expected to expose McCarthy as a fraud, the latter was able to use the occasion to add to his list of suspects, several of whom proved not even to be government employees, let alone Communists. Demonstrations of his inaccuracies, however, did not faze the senator, who brazenly named a Johns Hopkins professor, Owen Lattimore, as "the top Russian espionage agent" in the United States. Lattimore was a distinguished authority on China and had at times advised government officials, but he was also a bête noire of the China Lobby for allegedly serving the interests of the Chinese Communists, and it was Kohlberg who prompted McCarthy's sensational charge. McCarthy summoned Louis Budenz, a former CP official making a new career as an authority on communism, who testified that Lattimore had been a part of a Communist group at the Institute of Pacific Relations. Even this was far removed from being the "top" Russian spy, and several witnesses effectively refuted the charges against Lattimore and other individuals. Eventually the Tydings committee cleared everyone who had been named and harshly condemned McCarthy, but because its report was the work of its Democratic majority and was accepted by the Senate on a party vote, McCarthy's strength was hardly dented. The Republicans were standing by their man, enabling McCarthy to dismiss the Tydings Report as a Democratic "whitewash" of the administration. And by the time it was published, the country was at war.

Congressional Anticommunism

The Korean War, after bringing a momentary surge of popular support for the president, added credibility to the Republicans' charges of the subversion of American Far Eastern policy. It cemented the anticommunist consensus and provided the backdrop for the prolonged red scare known as McCarthyism. Ever since the advent of the Cold War there had been talk about the likelihood of a third world war, which in the wake of Hiroshima and the Soviet A-bomb promised an end to civilization itself. Although American troops had been committed to Korea in the hope of stopping Communist aggression—the administration could not risk another "China"—the war was easily seen as the harbinger of the apocalypse. As respected and moderate a figure as the governor of California, Earl Warren, declared that "our country is at war, ostensibly with North Korea, but actually with the Soviet Union," and spoke "not just of a possible but a probable third world war." In August 1950 the Gallup Poll reported that 57 percent of those surveyed believed the country already was "actually in World War III." As Americans confronted the possibility of nuclear holocaust, Republicans attributed the North Korean invasion to Democratic weakness and treachery. American boys were dying, said McCarthy, because "a group of untouchables in the State Department sabotaged" the aid program for South Korea. The arrest of the Rosenbergs supplied further evidence of the presence of spies. "If our far eastern policy was not betrayed," asked the right-wing columnist George Sokolsky, "why are we fighting in Korea?" The reverses subsequently encountered by the supposedly invincible Ameri-

can forces and the later sacking of General Douglas MacArthur intensified and prolonged the Republican party's use of the communist issue
against the administration.

In September 1950 the conservative bloc in Congress demonstrated its
contempt for Truman's loyalty program by passing the Internal Security
Act by large majorities over a presidential veto. Deriving the terms from
the earlier Mundt-Nixon Communist-registration proposals, which the
Republican Policy Committee added to its "must list" after the outbreak
of the Korean War, Senator Pat McCarran presented an omnibus measure requiring Communist and Communist-front organizations to register with the government. A new body, the Subversive Activities Control
Board, would ensure that they did. Liberal senators and the White
House tried to head off the proposals with an alternative measure providing only for the detention of subversives during an "internal security
emergency," which they presumably believed would rarely be invoked,
but the tactic misfired and the detention provision was added to McCarran's bill. Truman vetoed the bill because it would "interfere with our
liberties," but the Korean War and the approach of the midterm elections guaranteed its passage. "The feeling on Capitol Hill," reported the
New York Times, "is that it is too risky politically to vote against anti-
Communist legislation." Pat McCarran explained that Congress had to
"fortify the home front even as we are today fortifying our boys on the
battlefield of Korea." At its final appearance, every Republican senator
present voted for the bill; a mere ten Democratic senators held out
against it.

Truman's loyalty program had been largely confined to federal
employees; the Internal Security Act subjected private associations and
individuals to political surveillance and exposure. Bodies registered
under the act had to label their publications as those of a "communist
organization." The loyalty and trustworthiness of Communists at any
point in American society, not only in government, were being officially
questioned, serving to legitimize the emerging purge of "subversives" in
Hollywood, education, and private industry, a process that congressional committees enthusiastically set about assisting. This escalation of
the federal government's Communist-control program generally won
the endorsement of the public. An opinon poll reported that 90 percent
favored the immediate removal of Communists from industries that
would be important in wartime, suggesting that the Republicans and
conservative Democrats who had pushed through the Internal Security
Act could wrest yet further political advantage from the anticommunist
cause.

The Republicans' noisy assaults on the communistic tendencies of
their rivals reached a crescendo with the midterm elections of 1950. Dur-

ing the Korean crisis Truman nominated General George Marshall to be secretary of defense, moving Senator William E. Jenner to denounce the appointment as a respectable front for "the vicious sell-out" of American soldiers who were "dying even now" because of "treachery." Senator Taft more moderately thought the nomination in line with the State Department's "sympathetic attitude toward Communism in the Far East." Republican candidates took up the theme. A Republican victory, according to Everett Dirksen in Illinois, would let Stalin know "that there will be a housecleaning of his sympathizers and party-liners such as this country has never seen before." Richard Nixon characterized his senatorial opponent in California, Helen Gahagan Douglas, as "the Pink Lady" and reported her as "committed to the State Department policy of appeasement toward Communism in the Far East."

As the most audacious proponent of the thesis that the Democrats were the party of treason, Joe McCarthy was in great demand by Republican audiences, and GOP leaders were content to let him have his head. "The public may agree with the intellectuals that McCarthy has never proved a single one of his charges," observed a Republican politico, "but I'm sure the public is still saying, 'There must be something to this.' " McCarthy campaigned for Republican candidates in over a dozen states, calling the Democrats the "party of the puppets of the politburo" and accusing them of using the Tydings committee to "whitewash" the State Department. There was a personal element in this, for McCarthy had been angered by Millard Tydings's disdainful attitude during the hearings. With Tydings running for reelection in Maryland, McCarthy entered the state for the pleasure of speaking against him. He also procured considerable funding, staff, and press assistance for Tydings's Republican opponent, John M. Butler, investing his campaign with a full complement of dirty tricks.

The outcome of the November elections seemed to substantiate both McCarthy's personal power and the effectiveness of red-baiting tactics by Republican candidates. In Maryland the stately Tydings, who had held his seat for twenty-four years, was defeated decisively—thanks, it was said, to the conspicuous role of McCarthy in the campaign. Another McCarthy target, the Senate leader Scott Lucas, lost to the right-wing Republican Everett Dirksen in Illinois. Elsewhere, too, Republicans who had used the communist issue against their opponents, such as Richard Nixon in California and Wallace Bennett in Utah, won well-publicized successes. But in contrast to 1946, the Republican gains were not enough to win control of either the House of Representatives or the Senate, and later analyses showed that they could be attributed to a number of causes. In Maryland, for example, the surprise outcome was probably at least as much the result of the long-term growth in the

Republican vote as of anything McCarthy did. Further, by November the Korean War was going badly, and this was probably the most important single reason for the modest Republican gains. But the war itself was inseparable from the right-wing charge of foreign policy mismanagement, and at the time both press and politicians generally shared Marquis Childs's verdict on the 1950 elections: "In every contest where it was a major factor, McCarthyism won." As the new Congress assembled, another reporter noted "a general expression of fear" among the Democrats "that what had happened to Mr. Tydings, with all his standing in the Senate, could happen to any other man in the Senate." Politicians generally were drawing the conclusion that anticommunism could be an effective political force, while Democrats were reflecting that McCarthy was not a man to be crossed and Republicans noted that he was a weapon to be used.

Although Republicans had not won control of Congress, Democratic majorities had been reduced and the conservative bloc had completed its ascendancy. The Internal Security Act had all but declared open season for the hunting of subversives, loosely defined, both inside and outside government, and congressional conservatives were determined to use their traditional powers of investigation vigorously. HUAC remained the instrument of anticommunists in the lower house, but was joined in 1951 by the Senate Internal Security Subcommittee (SISS), so that senators too could win some Communist scalps. Senator McCarthy for the moment continued to hunt alone, allowed a roving license by his complacent Republican colleagues. Although the congressional investigating committees were nominally under Democratic control in the early 1950s, they were chaired by members of the conservative bloc and served Republican interests in loudly amplifying the communist issue. The committees' power to summon witnesses and to command television cameras made them formidable proponents of the anticommunist cause.

Under the restrained management of the gentlemanly John S. Wood of Georgia, HUAC in the early 1950s was even achieving a measure of respectability. Its Democratic leaders showed little inclination to take on the administration, but they did find ways of attracting media attention to the communist menace. In these years the committee perfected the techniques of exposure. Irritated by the number of witnesses who were shielding themselves behind the Fifth Amendment and refusing, it seemed, to answer even the most innocuous questions lest their answers prove incriminating, HUAC in 1950 persuaded the House to approve fifty-six contempt citations. The courts generally upheld the right of witnesses to take the Fifth Amendment, however, and when the Supreme Court confirmed the Smith Act convictions in 1951, pressure on witnesses and defendants to resort to the Fifth increased even further, for being an active Communist might in itself be a crime. The result was that HUAC and other congressional committees found themselves with even longer parades of witnesses resolutely taking the Fifth, but they were able to turn the situation to their advantage. Use of the Fifth Amendment protected witnesses from prison but not from their employers, and HUAC was soon smugly subpoenaing hostile witnesses, knowing that their appearance would lose them their jobs. Often such charades would be played out before television cameras, showing patriotic congressmen doing their duty unencumbered by the need to substantiate charges of disloyalty. As one HUAC member remarked to a witness, "Your refusal to testify so consistently leaves a strong impression that you are still an ardent follower of the Communist Party and its purpose."

No area of American life was more calculated to command media attention than Hollywood, with its stables of celebrities, and HUAC returned to its old stomping ground in the spring of 1951. The committee had retreated from its 1947 encounter with the film world in some disarray, but by 1951 it was immeasurably stronger. The last of the Hollywood Ten had finally gone to prison in September 1950, a somber reminder of the fate that could await hostile witnesses, and the foreign policy reverses and spy cases had vindicated HUAC's raison d'être. When the Hollywood producers made it clear that they would dutifully extend the blacklist to all employees who took the Fifth, the pressure on witnesses became intense. Many of those who were subpoenaed were not Communists themselves, although some were former Communists or popular front liberals, and they faced the agonizing choice of either informing on their friends or losing their jobs. Edward Dmytryk, who had gone to prison as one of the Hollywood Ten, made his peace with HUAC by naming a few Communists already known to it, and he was able to return to work. The committee was beginning to take on itself the function of "clearing" those whose careers had been threatened when their names had surfaced in anticommunist propaganda, and the price was usually naming others. Hundreds were not cleared, and the Hollywood blacklist grew apace. The intimidation of Hollywood, a process begun in 1947, was successfuly completed in the early 1950s.

Hollywood was not HUAC's only target. During the Korean War it probed the defense industries and also gave much attention to suspect unions, such as the United Electrical Workers, the largest of those expelled by the CIO, in which campaign it was sedulously assisted by the rival union, the International Union of Electrical Workers. The techniques of exposure afforded a standing temptation to political candidates, employers, and anticommunist union factions to invite HUAC to undertake a probe, supply it with the names of those they wanted harmed, and watch these unfortunates impale themselves on the Fifth. HUAC and its subcommittees swooped on Baltimore, Los Angeles, Chicago, Albany, San Diego, Philadelphia, and several other communities too, often becoming embroiled in such local political maneuverings. HUAC was not doing much to frame anticommunist legislation in these years, but the ritual naming of names by friendly witnesses and the long strings of dour Fifth Amendment witnesses left the impression that the United States was liberally sprinkled with Communists.

SISS served the Republican cause even more effectively, though it also demonstrated that anticommunist passions transcended party lines. Its first chairman was Pat McCarran, the highly conservative Democrat who bore major responsibility for the Internal Security Act and, in 1952, the Immigration and Nationality Act, both of which resumed the thrust of an earlier generation in making aliens more readily deportable. One of SISS's first and most influential acts was to investigate the Institute of Pacific Relations (IPR), an academic research center that in effect was accused of manipulating the State Department to deliver China to the Communists. The IPR did serve as a meeting ground for diplomats and academics with an interest in China, and if it could be shown to be a Communist front the old Republican complaint against Truman's Far Eastern policy would in large measure be vindicated. Some of those with links to the IPR were Communists, and when the SISS forced a number of IPR witnesses to take the Fifth, the case against it seemed to be made. The former Communist witnesses also played their part. Louis Budenz testified that the CP had looked on the IPR as "the little red schoolhouse for teaching certain people in Washington how to think with the Soviet Union in the Far East." A less friendly witness was McCarthy's old target, Owen Lattimore, who was subsequently indicted for perjury for denying that he was a Communist sympathizer. In 1952 the SISS reported that "but for the machinations" of a group in the IPR, "China would be free." The right-wing charges against the administration had been proved, at least to the satisfaction of a Senate committee.

Senator McCarthy himself, exhilarated by the demonstration of his power in the 1950 elections, continued his pugnacious assaults on the White House, press critics, and personal enemies. In June 1951 he capped Senator Jenner by describing the secretary of defense, George Marshall, as part of "a conspiracy so immense and an infamy so black as to dwarf any previous venture in the history of man." This mind-boggling charge embarrassed Republican leaders, but they did not disavow their impetuous colleague, who resumed his attacks on the State Department and played a role in denying Senate confirmation as a United Nations delegate to Philip Jessup, one of the much maligned "China hands." The improprieties of the notorious Maryland election were investigated by a Senate committee, and the "back-street" tactics of McCarthy's agents were exposed and condemned. Citing this and other instances of misconduct, Senator William B. Benton, a Connecticut Democrat, called for McCarthy's expulsion from the Senate, and a subcommittee unhappily began to investigate McCarthy himself. The Wisconsin senator denounced the "completely dishonest" investigation as serving Communist goals, and hampered by his obstructive tactics, it dragged on into the campaign of 1952.

The Republicans again sought to extract maximum advantage from the communist issue in the election. Early in the year Republican county chairmen identified as one of their most effective arguments the proposition that "the Democratic party has let too many Communists get into important Government positions in Washington," and 54 percent of Independent voters surveyed agreed that it was a "strong" one. Karl Mundt defined the Republican platform as "K_1C_2—Korea, Communism, Corruption," and the three issues became increasingly difficult to disentangle. The nomination of the moderate Dwight Eisenhower for president was balanced by that of HUAC graduate Richard Nixon for vice president. As the nemesis of Alger Hiss and Helen Gahagan Douglas, Nixon personified Republican anticommunism. Joe McCarthy, himself still the subject of a Senate probe, was cheered at the Republican National Convention, and GOP leaders like Robert Taft commended his assaults on the "pro-Communist" State Department. Senator Jenner warned that another Democratic victory would ensure that "the Red network will continue to work secretly and safely for the destruction of the United States." The Republican party swung into the campaign yoked to the thesis of its right-wingers that the Democrats had been responsible for "twenty years of treason."

The Truman Administration

Although it was the Republicans, aided by a few fiercely right-wing Democrats like Pat McCarran, who constituted the driving force behind the political anticommunism of Truman's second term, they were not alone responsible for the anticommunist consensus that was enveloping American public life. The Democratic administration, after all, had legitimized the use of political tests with its loyalty program, and its red-baiting of the Wallace campaign had invited those to its right to resort to similar tactics. Truman could protest the methods of the Internal Security Act and of Senator McCarthy, but he could not disavow their declared objective of flushing Communists from positions of influence. The Democrats and the Republicans—or administration and critics—were divided by means, not by ends. Communists and their sympathizers had no significant protectors anywhere in American life, and the pace of their removal from federal and local government, trade unions, company plants, schools, and voluntary associations gained momentum with each passing year.

The Truman administration was itself deeply implicated in this process, even if many of its actions were in response to Republican criticisms. Having conceded that Communists endangered American security, the administration was obliged to develop its own Communist-control measures, and the loyalty program had patently failed to defuse the issue. Further, the unnerving escalation of the Cold War did nothing to improve the public image of American Communists or the administration's regard for them, and there were federal officers and agencies who were themselves vehemently anticommunist. Whatever the balance of defensive and offensive instincts in propelling the government's anticommunist measures, the very commitment of the government to the cause, the immense legitimating authority that it brought to it, added immeasurably to its potency.

In May 1950 the nation's foremost authority on communism, the director of the FBI, told a radio audience that "Communists have been and are today at work within the very gates of America. There are few walks in American life which they do not traverse. . . . Wherever they may be, they have in common one diabolic ambition: to weaken and to eventually destroy American democracy by stealth and cunning." For the most part the White House, the Justice Department, the State Department, and other executive agencies accepted this diagnosis. Harry Truman might have flinched at J. Edgar Hoover's tendency to see Communists at every turn, but he did not contradict him, and he accepted that the powers of the federal government had to be directed to extirpating communist subversion.

The Truman administration, of course, had been seeking to remove Communists from public life since the early days of the Cold War. The Smith Act defendants had been convicted in 1949, and when the Supreme Court upheld the convictions in 1951 the commitment of the judiciary to the anticommunist campaign was made plain. The Justice Department was thus given license to harass the Communist party. The FBI soon arrested second-string and local CP leaders in New York, Baltimore, Cleveland, and elsewhere, subjecting them to trials that rested on the premise that the CP represented a conspiracy to overthrow the government. For the most part the defendants were found guilty and given prison sentences. The government and the courts had accepted the right-wing—and Trotskyite—view that the CP was a Soviet-directed conspiracy dedicated to the overthrow of American democracy, and they had found a way of removing its leaders from public life. Playing a part in this drama were several former Communists like Louis Budenz, some-time managing director of the *Daily Worker*, and FBI agents like Herbert Philbrick, celebrated for his infiltration of the CP, who testified to the highly disciplined, conspiratorial, and revolutionary nature of the international communist movement. Not only did such witnesses persuade the courts that the CP was a tightly organized criminal conspiracy, as they testified before congressional committees and television cameras an indelible impression was created in the public mind of an amoral and ruthless force single-mindedly bent on destroying American institutions. By the end of 1956 over one hundred CP leaders had been convicted under the Smith Act, although, since their appeals afforded them bail and eventually reached into a less repressive era, only about a quarter of them served prison terms after conviction. Nonetheless the Smith Act, passed during the little red scare of 1940, was being used in the 1950s effectively to outlaw the Communist party, which protected itself as best it could by going underground.

The anticommunist drive of the Justice Department was most sensationally illustrated by the Rosenberg case. After the British scientist Klaus Fuchs confessed in London in 1950 that he had supplied atomic secrets to the Soviets, some while working at Los Alamos during the war, the trail led back somewhat circuitously to Julius and Ethel Rosenberg, who were supposed to have played a part in relaying this and other information. The charge against the Rosenbergs, who were of lower-class Jewish immigrant origins, was in effect that they were running an atomic spy ring, although the questionable nature of some of the evidence left many unconvinced of their guilt. The government, however, was determined to win a conviction, and the case was pressed in the spring of 1951 when anticommunist sentiments were at their height. The jury found Julius and Ethel Rosenberg guilty of conspiracy to commit espionage, and the judge, who vouchsafed the opinion that the Rosenbergs were part of a "diabolical conspiracy to destroy a God-fearing nation" and that they had given the Soviet Union the atomic bomb and so brought on the war in Korea, sentenced them to death. The trial and the subsequent appeals attracted enormous publicity and pleas for clemency from throughout the world but in June 1953 sentence was carried out. Meanwhile Klaus Fuchs, who had undoubtedly delivered important atomic secrets to the Soviet Union, both during and after the war, spent nine years in a British prison.

No federal agency was more committed to the assault on Communists than the FBI, with its director's obsessive fear of subversion. Hoover lost no opportunity to communicate his fears to the White House, congressional committees, the American Legion and other patriotic audiences, and the public at large. The outbreak of the Korean War gave him another chance to secure a presidential statement confirming that the FBI "should take charge of investigative work in matters relating to espionage, sabotage, and subversive activities," and its surveillance extended into virtually every walk of life. The FBI's extensive bureaucratic apparatus was itself staffed by men who often enough were veterans or of Irish and Catholic background, middle-class white males who shared the anticommunist perspective. As these agents discreetly compiled dossiers on Communists, radicals, and political activists, Hoover himself emerged as a principal propagandist of the anticommunist cause. He spoke and wrote extensively on the issue, pointing out that the American CP compared favorably in size with the Russian CP at the time of the Bolshevik revolution and arguing that for every CP member there were ten others willing to accept Communist leadership. "A disciplined Party of hard-core fanatical members is now at work," he was to explain in *Masters of Deceit*, "with their fellow travelers, sympathizers, opportunists, and dupes." The FBI swapped favors with HUAC, McCarthy, the American Legion, right-wing columnists, and others prepared to cooperate in its war against communism. Whether or not there was a Communist conspiracy, there was something approaching an anticommunist conspiracy directed by the FBI.

The power of the FBI expanded with every extension of the loyalty program. The federal program that Truman introduced in 1947 for screening government employees progressively tightened its grip. In April 1951, after attacks by Senator McCarthy, Truman issued a new directive enjoining the dismissal of federal employees whose loyalty remained in doubt. In December the Loyalty Review Board assumed the right to review *any* decision of a lower review board, even where the individual had been cleared. In his nearly six years of responsibility, Truman presided over some twelve hundred dismissals (against Franklin Roosevelt's score of a little over a hundred in World War II), and thousands of other civil servants resigned as their activities and associations came under scrutiny. Brief membership years earlier in an organization listed by the attorney general might be enough to secure dismissal, and some employees found themselves investigated because they had incautiously made favorable remarks about Russia, possessed books on communism, or associated with others who belonged to suspect groups. Very few who left the government's employment under these pressures were actually CP members. Many held rather modest posts, such as clerks or supervisors, but the civil service did lose a few of its most distinguished members, particularly in the State Department, on which Senator McCarthy fastened his glare. One was John Vincent Service, who had been director of Far Eastern affairs and one of the

"China hands" said to be responsible for Chiang Kai-shek's downfall, fired after a loyalty review in 1951.

The executive branch of the government was not content with prosecuting CP leaders and placating Republican critics by forcing suspect members out of the civil service. Its vigilance against the international communist conspiracy could be displayed in any corner of American life to which federal responsibility was extended. Immigration was one such area, and if small by earlier standards, it was increasing sufficiently to touch occasional nativist nerves. In 1950 immigration reached nearly a quarter-million, and the old identification of the alien with the radical was once more being made. Truman's attorney general himself noted that over three-quarters of CP leaders were of "foreign stock." The extension of Soviet power over central and Eastern Europe meant that many Americans had relatives behind the Iron Curtain, arguably exposing those Americans to communist solicitation and blackmail. Legislation of 1950 and 1952, carrying the imprint of the nativist and anticommunist Pat McCarran, broadened the grounds on which aliens could be deported, reduced their legal protection, and eased the way to stripping naturalized Americans of citizenship. The outbreak of the Korean war was followed by an increase in the number of political deportations. Native radicals also found themselves subject to bureaucratic harassment. From 1947 American Communists were denied passports, and in the early 1950s the denial was extended to anyone, in Dean Acheson's words, whose "conduct abroad is likely to be contrary to the best interest of the United States." The Passport Office was manned by zealous anticommunists, who contrived to withhold passports from Linus Pauling, Owen Lattimore, Paul Robeson, W. E. B. Du Bois, and hundreds of others, and even from a justice of the Supreme Court, William O. Douglas, when he wanted to visit China. Visas could also be denied to prospective foreign visitors, a policy that disrupted several scientific conferences and led to such bizarre outcomes as the exiling of Charles Chaplin, a British subject who had lived in the United States for decades but went abroad in 1952 and found he was not permitted to reenter. Once the Truman administration had endorsed the proposition that Communists were subversives, zealous bureaucrats happily busied themselves with the task of regulating the lives and activities of any alleged subversives who strayed into their sights.

·

What helped to make the second Big Red Scare so irresistible was the mutual reinforcement provided by the different branches of government. The well-publicized rows between executive and legislature obscured the fact that they were tending to validate one another's activities. In any case, liaison between the two was often greater than was apparent. Truman appointed Republicans to the loyalty review boards in the hope of disarming his congressional critics. J. Edgar Hoover quietly supplied information to red-baiting congressmen. Private lobbies, like the American Legion, the Chamber of Commerce, and anticommunist unions, cultivated relationships with both executive officials and legislators, exchanging data on the red menace. For American radicals there was little respite from the stranglehold they were being subjected to by the combined actions of the executive and the legislature. The Supreme Court offered no relief, because it too shared the perspective of the Truman administration and put little check on the Communist-control programs being elaborated by Congress and the White House. Indeed, the Court stamped its imprimatur on them, most notable in its *Dennis* decision of 1951 upholding the Smith Act.

The Communist-control measures of the Truman administration, extensive though they were, failed to quell Republican charges of Democratic complacency, incompetence, and treason on security and loyalty matters. During the campaign of 1952 Republican orators made much of the scandals associated with the Truman White House and its unhappy handling of the Korean War, but the communist issue was one of their most frequent ploys. Senate Republicans published a booklet entitled *Communism in Government,* which detailed "the Red Record of Democratic Administrations." Dwight Eisenhower, who detested McCarthy and disavowed "witch hunts," told a campaign meeting that a Republican administration "will find the pinks, we will find the Communists, we will find the disloyal." Even the Americans for Democratic Action, which had done so much to detach the Democratic party from its former popular front associations, was widely condemned by Republican speakers, the GOP national chairman describing it as "an organization dedicated to the promotion of Socialist schemes in America." The outcome of the election, in which the Republicans won control not only of the presidency but also of both houses of Congress, seemed to confirm the potency of the issue. In Connecticut McCarthy's Senate critic William Benton lost his seat—yet another sign, it seemed, of McCarthy's invincibility. Again later analyses were to show that both anticommunist rhetoric in general and McCarthy's activities in particular of themselves did little to account for the Republican successes, but as in 1950 the political community credited red-baiting with considerable electoral clout. The influential commentator Arthur Krock reflected that "the voting majority indicated approval of the objectives of . . . McCarthyism." The Republican harnessing of the anticommunist cause had apparently accomplished its purpose.

9

THE
ANTICOMMUNIST
CONSENSUS
(the 1950s)

•

B<small>Y</small> 1950 an anticommunist consensus had settled on American public life. The principal organs of government, the major political parties, the trades union movement, leading church spokesmen, and many public and private institutions across the land were agreed that Communists had no legitimate role in American society. Party competition had done much to create this climate of opinion, but the Republican victory at the polls in 1952, which largely nullified the partisan advantage to be gained from the communist issue, did nothing to abate anticommunist sentiments. The Korean War had also played an important part in confirming to Americans that Communists were the mortal enemies of the United States, but when it ended in 1953 the anticommunist consensus remained intact, at least for the moment. A Communist Control Act passed Congress in 1954 with the overwhelming support of both major parties and was accepted by the administration. It was this consensus among America's political leaders and most powerful institutions that made possible the second Big Red Scare. This scare threatened not so much lives as livelihoods, and through the first half of the 1950s many thousands of citizens lost their jobs because their beliefs were deemed insufficiently American.

The vigor of anticommunist passions in these years cannot be explained solely by reference to party competition and Cold War tensions. The sociological formations and political infrastructure of the period also favored the anticommunist cause. Economic growth, a great religious awakening, a revived white racism, and archaic electoral arrangements contributed in different ways to a red scare culture, as did the veterans' groups and other patriotic organizations, reinvigorated by World War II and the Korean War. A public mood broadly if not actively hostile to the Soviet Union and its ideology was being exploited by energetic pressure groups and insecure political elites. What gave the anticommunist cause its force was the incessant and complex interplay between popular opinion, private interest groups, and public officials.

When the Republicans ceased to use red scare tactics against the federal government, the anticommunist crusade lost some of its sense of direction but not its potency. A government and bureaucracy staffed by committed anticommunists had no difficulty in finding vulnerable targets. Since party leaders and government officials had united in an anticommunist accord, victims increasingly tended to be outsiders or low in the power structure, if not necessarily in social standing. Further, since elaborate communist-control measures had been put into place by 1950, the "clear and immediate" danger to the republic had largely been averted. Many saw the menace as more insidious. Communists who had been flushed from government, perhaps, could no longer engage in treason or sabotage, but they were left with the sinister alternative of reaching into American minds. Increasingly, popular fears of communism focused on the possible subversion of the institutions that molded opinion. Such a definition of the communist menace also gave the citizenry a role to play in the great crusade. The FBI might screen government employees, but local patriots could mount a surveillance of schools, libraries, and movie theaters. They could also on occasion reaffirm their democratic faith by assailing persons of prestige. America's populist traditions were being aligned with the anticommunist thrust of political leaders and government bureaucracy.

Anticommunist Constituencies

The political and bureaucratic classes bore a major responsibility for the magnification of the communist issue in postwar America. But their preoccupation with an internal Communist threat would not have reached the obsessional degree it did without the encouragement and aid of a variety of interest groups and constituencies, which in turn were emboldened by the government endorsement of their cause. The course of American economic and social history in the decade or so after 1945, and the evolution of the Cold War itself, tended to strengthen further those constituencies and lobbies that were prone to worry about red subversion. The anticommunist consensus in Washington was rooted in and sustained by a broad popular approval and by the active assistance of influential elements in the polity.

The conservative coloring of American political culture in the 1950s owed much to a heightened confidence in the socioeconomic system of the United States. The Great Depression was receding into memory; American capitalism had been vindicated by its performance in the

Second World War, and the sustained period of economic growth after the war muffled critics of the system. Between 1945 and 1960 the gross national product increased by some 250 percent, and phenomenal statistics were constantly on hand to testify to the vigor of the world's foremost economy. The nearly 25 percent unemployed rate of 1933 had plummeted to 2.5 percent in 1953, not because of socialism but because of capitalism. As the triumphant course of the American economy and other Western economies discredited Marxist predictions of their imminent demise, the limitations of the Soviet system became ever more apparent. The beacon lit by the October Revolution of 1917, and fanned by the collapse of the Western economies after 1929, had dimmed. The human cost of Stalin's industrialization program was being weighed, and even radical intellectuals were recoiling from the totalitarian nature of the Soviet regime. Postwar Eastern Europe seemed to offer neither spiritual freedom nor material comfort. The example of American capitalism did not entrance all intellectuals, but few were able to offer a convincing alternative.

The rehabilitation of the American economic system was helped along by image-conscious businessmen themselves. Advertizing had become a major industry in its own right, and Madison Avenue played an important role in promoting the ethic of free enterprise and in displaying the benign nature of American products. Businessmen were more active in proselytizing for their cause than they had dared to be in the 1930s. "I am convinced that businessmen must write as well as speak," wrote one of them, "in order that we may bring to people everywhere the exciting and confident message of our faith in the free enterprise way of life." Corporations established and enlarged public relations programs, and business values were promoted at every opportunity. Business groups carefully forged closer links with educators. A Chamber of Commerce spokesman told a mass meeting of teachers in 1950: "Working together, we can help keep the United States the free and happy country we want it to be for the youngsters in your classrooms." In many communities "B-E day" (Business-Education) became an annual event for teachers. The Advertising Council in the mid-1950s promoted the concept of "People's Capitalism," seeking through speeches, articles, and conferences to show that capitalism benefited the workers and that class lines were disappearing. Television, dependent on commercial sponsors, for the most part relayed wholesome images of American business, and radio stations, magazines, and newspapers, themselves owned by successful businessmen, generally endorsed the free enterprise system. The pervasive dissemination of business values need not have been marred by the crudities of McCarthyism, but it did contribute to an atmosphere in which free enterprise was identified with "the American way" and socialism or communism with un-Americanism.

The sanctification of the free enterprise system freed many businessmen to indulge their anticommunist convictions. "The spies, traitors, and the misguided fools who promote Communism constitute our number one industrial security problem today," pronounced the National Industrial Conference Board in 1952. The major corporations regularly dismissed workers who had appeared before congressional and state investigating committees, and many established security departments to screen employees. The bureaucratic procedures government used to remove disloyal elements were being employed by business. Some firms introduced their own loyalty oaths, and in 1955 the American Security Council was established to compile dossiers on suspect Americans for sale to employers. Although—or because of—employing such discreet communist-control measures, big businessmen tended to distance themselves from the rude tactics of Joe McCarthy. But small businessmen showed some sympathy for the crusading senator, as did oilmen, newspaper proprietors, and others able to run their businesses like the entrepreneurs of old, their acquisitive individualism unhampered by the bureaucratic embrace of boards of managers. Such business elements formed a major constituent of Cold War anticommunism and helped to fund those groups and individuals at the cutting edge of the cause.

The heyday of free enterprise also witnessed a revitalization of American religion. As in the 1920s this resurgence of piety could embolden critics of American society, such as the Reverend Martin Luther King, Jr., but for the most part the religious currents harmonized with the conservative ideology of the age. Between 1950 and 1960 the percentage of the American population with a church affiliation jumped from 55 to 69, an increase unprecedented in the twentieth century. The reasons for this religious revival were complex, but it was at least partly shaped by Cold War tensions. Religion might quiet the anxieties of an uncertain world; more to the point, the confrontation with the "atheistic communism" of the Soviet Union invited comparison with the spiritual strength of the United States. President Eisenhower set an example by attending church and opening cabinet meetings with prayer; in 1954 the phrase "under God" was added to the Pledge of Allegiance. What both distinguished Americans from Russians and confirmed their superiority, it seemed, was a belief in God. Senator McCarthy himself defined the modern crisis as "a final, all-out battle between communistic atheism and Christianity."

Evangelical Protestantism in the United States had been a powerful force poised against political and economic radicalism since before the

Civil War, and it was a major beneficiary of the postwar religious awakening. The National Association of Evangelicals (NAE), representing only a million members in 1945, spoke for over ten million by 1952 and continued to expand. The NAE attempted to distance itself from the crude fundamentalism of the past, but its publications denounced "reds" in the churches and in the government and insisted that "Christianity . . . alone can safeguard free enterprise from perversion." One revivalist who rose to prominence during the anxieties of the Korean War years was Billy Graham, whose evangelicalism was married to a political conservatism that led him to denounce the foreign policy "betrayals" and to congratulate the congressional investigating committees for "their work of exposing the pinks, the lavenders, and the reds who have sought refuge beneath the wings of the American eagle." Previous evangelists had tried to convert their audiences by invoking images of hellfire; Graham deployed the horrors of nuclear war and a communized United States. "Only as millions of Americans turn to Jesus Christ at this hour and accept him as Savior," he explained, "can this nation possibly be spared the onslaught of demon-possessed communism." Billy Graham was only the most successful of the evangelists urging born-again Christianity as the antidote to the communist virus. Important also in spreading the word was the proliferation of evangelical and fundamentalist schools, radio stations, publishing companies, and magazines.

The NAE and the evangelists associated with it represented the "moderate" or "modern" wing of American fundamentalism, but an unreconstructed fundamentalism remained potent, and its churches were also booming in the 1950s. Some of these groups made the anticommunist cause their central objective. The Reverend Carl McIntyre attempted to rally the fundamentalist sects in his American Council of Christian Churches, founded in 1941 and ultimately speaking for some 1,500,000 members. He campaigned for the open shop and against the United Nations, the communist conspiracy and the welfare and civil rights programs that had been develping since the New Deal. The Australian-born Dr. Frederick C. Schwarz launched his Christian Anti-Communist Crusade from Iowa in 1953, moving to California in 1956. It sought to combat communism by sponsoring lectures and broadcasts, providing courses for missionaries, holding church services, and publishing books and pamphlets. The South and Southwest, the heart of the "Bible Belt," proved particularly susceptible to such groups. Dr. George S. Benson, president of the Church of Christ's Harding College in Arkansas, inaugurated his National Education Program in 1948, using broadcasts, free newspaper columns, textbooks, and school study outlines to "immunize our people to Communist infiltration and propaganda."

Similar techniques were used by the flamboyant Reverend Billy James Hargis, who in 1950 launched from Oklahoma what became known as the Christian Crusade, in an attempt to save the American Eden from the satanic invasion of communism. The influence of these ultra conservative groups cannot be measured, but the funds that poured into their coffers suggest that their followings were not insignificant.

It was not only evangelical and fundamentalist Protestantism that was receptive to the arguments of the anticommunist persuasion. The Roman Catholic church was expanding too, another denomination with a historic hostility to the Soviet regime. Some 20.3 percent of the United States population in 1955 was Roman Catholic, up from 16.1 percent in 1940. The extension of Soviet control over a large part of Catholic Europe intensified the American Catholic distaste for international communism. The imprisoned József Cardinal Mindszenty in Hungary and Archibishop Aloysius Stepinac in Yugoslavia became popular martyr figures in the United States. Francis Cardinal Spellman of New York was the foremost anticommunist spokesman of the American Catholic hierarchy, warning that the United States was in imminent danger from the "Communist floodings of our own land." His admonitions were echoed by Archibishop Richard J. Cushing of Boston and by the anticommunist ideologue Bishop Fulton J. Sheen, whose frequent publications and broadcasts spelled out the un-American nature of communism. The patriotism of many Catholic laymen was demonstrated by their fraternal organization, the Knights of Columbus, and by the Catholic War Veterans (CWV). In 1949, for example, the CWV undertook a national drive employing films, educational courses, and press advertisements to expose communist infiltration. The Association of Catholic Trade Unionists, liberal on welfare issues, helped to strengthen the anticommunist stance in the labor movement.

Not all Catholics, of course, succumbed to the anticommunist persuasion, but there were signs that the communist issue could affect Catholic voting behavior. Some Polish Catholics, agitated by the abandonment of their homeland, seem to have defected to the Republicans in 1946. In the celebrated Maryland senatorial election of 1950, when Millard Tydings was defeated by a McCarthy-backed Republican, Catholics appear disproportionately to have deserted the Democrats. In 1952 more Catholics voted for a Republican presidential candidate than ever before, perhaps because of the Communists-in-government charge. Senator Joseph McCarthy, a Roman Catholic himself, established friendly relations with Catholic leaders and, although a Republican, was popular in many Catholic if Democratic communities, as in Boston. A Gallup poll of May 1954 showed McCarthy winning the support of 56 percent of Catholics and 45 percent of Protestants. There were many Roman Catholics who were distinctly hostile to McCarthy, but few had good words to say about communism.

The patriotic impulses animating the religious resurgence of postwar America eased the conquest of the anticommunist consensus. If most Americans preferred the temperate anticommunism of Dwight Eisenhower to the indiscriminate zeal of McCarthy, there were organized groups within each major faith zealously beating the patriotic drum. Even Judaism, the religious form most resistant to the anticommunist animus, housed a few admirers of McCarthy. Like some recent Catholic immigrants, a few—very few—Jews found in anticommunism a means of proving their American identity. The Rabbi Benjamin Schultz, Roy Cohn, and others promoted their views through the American Jewish League against Communism. To a greater or lesser degree, all denominations were being aligned against the un-American communist menace. Religious commitment, of course, was also capable of inspiring radical and pacifist movements, though these were weak in the 1950s. Clerics who did aim to change society sometimes had to make their own accommodation to the anticommunist consensus. When the Reverend Martin Luther King and other black ministers organized the Southern Christian Leadership Conference, the word Christian was inserted in the title to ward off allegations of communism.

If chambers of commerce and many religious leaders could be counted on to promote conservative and patriotic values, so could the veterans' groups that laced the land. The American Legion had been replenished by the Second World War, and the Korean War supplied it with yet more recruits. In 1950 the Legion had about 2.5 million members; the Veterans of Foreign Wars (VFW) had grown from 250,000 before the Second World War to over a million after it. Both the Legion and the VFW maintained their Americanism programs and cultivated close contacts with schools, churches, civic groups, and politicians. The Legion's national convention in 1950 voted that CP members should be tried for treason. Veterans pressed their old interest in combating the subversion of young minds, the VFW holding in 1953 that children should be compelled to study officially approved history. The Legion and the VFW enthusiastically encouraged the congressional investigation committees and kept their own files of individuals and organizations suspected of subversive tendencies, which they obligingly opened to state and federal investigators. The veterans' groups sponsored local antisubversion seminars, presented public and college libraries with anticommunist literature, and supported such enterprises as the All-American Conference to Combat Communism, an annual event of the 1950s. Vigilante excesses involving veterans were not unknown but were much less frequent than in 1919–20. The FBI and the police authorities did not welcome incursions into their territory.

But the very legality and respectability of the veterans' activities enhanced their influence, and veterans were a conspicuous presence in state legislatures, school boards, and community groups. In an age of pressure group politics, the major veterans' organizations had become formidable lobbies for patriotic causes. Many veterans, of course, had benefited from the GI Bill of 1944 (and later from the more modest Korean War GI Bill) and the consequent federal services that helped to supply them with college educations, jobs, and mortgages. In the 1950s one in five new housing units was bought with the assistance of the Veterans Administration. Veterans who had joined middle-class and suburban America no doubt had good reason to believe in the virtues of the American way of life.

Other patriotic societies also made their contributions to the anticommunist persuasion. Such traditional groups as the Sons and the Daughters of the American Revolution energetically sustained their promotion of patriotic values, taking particular interest in school textbooks. Influential in some communities were the newly formed Minute Women of the USA, which by 1952 had chapters in twenty-seven states. Dedicated to the "traditional American way of life," this organization tended to attract upper-middle-class and often Republican women prepared to devote their time to supporting right-wing candidates for office, harassing speakers held to be communistic, bombarding elected officials with letters and telephone calls, and maintaining a surveillance of local communities for signs of "un-American activities." Loosely scattered across the land were a host of other local bodies of varying degrees of effectiveness. The Ohio Coalition of Patriotic Societies sponsored anti-subversion seminars; the Hawaii Residents Association published bimonthly exposures of local communists; in Idaho the Shoshone County Anti-Communist Association mounted radio programs and parades to warn citizens of the red menace. Those interested in enlisting in the war on communism could usually find outlets for their energies.

Patriotism had also become a marked characteristic of the labor movement, in which the anticommunist unionists continued on their triumphant course. The left-wing unions expelled by the CIO rapidly lost members to the rival unions that preyed on them. The largest of the ousted unions, United Electrical (UE), found itself confronted by a newly organized International Union of Electrical Workers (IUE), led by the vehement anticommunist James Carey. By 1956 the UE, which had once boasted half a million members, had dwindled to 75,000, while the IUE had reached 400,000 and the corresponding AFL electrical union was even larger. Other expelled unions either collapsed, contracted, or replaced their Communist leaders. The deradicalization of the labor movement helped make possible its unification—in 1955 the CIO and AFL merged once more. It was formally declared that "the merged federation shall constitutionally affirm its determination to protect the American trade union movement . . . from the undermining efforts of Communist agencies and all others who are opposed to the basic principles of our democracy." The labor movement had joined the anticommunist consensus, and prominent trade unionists were conspicuous at almost every point of the great crusade. Senior union figures usually graced the annual All-American Conference to Combat Communism. At its 1955 meeting George Meany, who that year became the first president of the merged AFL-CIO, warned against the "spirit of Geneva," which was concealing Moscow's goal "to dominate the entire world with their godless ideology of communism."

Business, labor, veteran, and patriotic lobbies accorded considerable attention to influencing city councils and state legislatures. The environment of state politics tended to favor conservative interests. Even in the 1930s state governments had tended to react to New Deal initiatives with suspicion and reluctance, and the great economic expansion of the postwar era had helped to rehabilitate the conventional wisdom of local political elites. Rapidly growing urban populations were imperfectly represented in the state legislatures, in which malapportionment favored middle-class property owners and rural elements. Liberal-minded governors returned by statewide electorates, like Earl Warren in California and G. Mennen Williams in Michigan, not infrequently found themselves at odds with illiberal legislators, often old-fashioned Republicans for whom the New Deal remained a dangerous experiment in socialism. Several such legislatures, as in Michigan and Ohio, set up their own "little HUACs" to root out communistic elements in their states. These bodies on occasion liaised with HUAC itself or with SISS or the FBI, providing one another with information and mutual corroboration and thus lacing a kind of anticommunist network across the United States.

The most resolutely conservative part of the country remained the Deep South; its white politicians were often more responsive to the demands of wealthy planters, town bankers, and low-wage industrialists than of their limited electorates. A number of liberal politicians were elected in the South in the immediate postwar years, but by the early 1950s southern liberalism was in retreat. The revival of the race issue largely accounted for this, and a favorite weapon deployed by racist politicians was the red scare. Communists and other radicals had been outspoken champions of black rights. In 1950 the staunch New Dealer

Claude Pepper lost in the Florida Democratic senatorial primary after his opponent had denounced "the Red Record of Senator Claude Pepper." Individual states sometimes advertised their patriotism by such measures as the 1953 Alabama law requiring school textbooks to carry a statement of the author's attitude toward communism.

Nonetheless the South, Texan oilmen apart, did not evince much enthusiasm for Senator McCarthy, whose Catholicism and Republicanism made him an alien figure to most southern voters. What really aroused racist and anticommunist passions there was the Supreme Court's *Brown v. Topeka* decision of 1954, demanding an end to segregated schools, and southern leaders like Senator James Eastland of Mississippi charged that the Court had been "influenced and infiltrated by Reds." State sovereignty commissions and un-American activities committees appeared in several southern states to defend the region's peculiar traditions. In Louisiana a legislative committee in 1957 attributed the growing racial unrest to the international communist conspiracy, implicating the NAACP, the ACLU, and Martin Luther King's Southern Christian Leadership Conference. The white South, with its influential representation on congressional committees, had its own reasons for joining the anticommunist crusade.

The interests and constituencies that ardently supported the various campaigns to expose communists and combat red subversion may not have embraced the most prestigious of American institutions like the top corporations or top universities, but neither did they represent the dispossessed. For the most part, organized anticommunism did not mobilize blacks, migrant agricultural laborers, new immigrants, or low-paid workers. Small businessmen, the Knights of Columbus, the Christian Crusaders, well-paid unionists, veterans, Minute Women, and the local political elites in the Midwest and the South did not represent the whole of "Middle America," but they did typify a part of the propertied and middling orders of American society. In the depression unemployed white youths had sometimes used red scare tactics against working blacks in their own desperate search for security, but the anticommunist forces of the 1950s were themselves the beneficiaries of the affluent society. This perhaps reinforced their conviction about the superiority of American civilization and their distaste for its critics. Affluence at least meant that their associations were well funded. Further, their respectability enhanced their influence. No longer was anticommunism encumbered by the alien and violent reputations associated with some of its exponents in the 1930s. The Silver Shirts had disappeared from view, and the Klan had withdrawn to the most discredited redoubts of southern racism.

Quite apart from the legitimacy accorded the cause by government institutions like the FBI, anticommunism in society at large in the 1950s was primarily associated with authentically American bodies such as the National Association of Manufacturers, the American Legion, the National Association of Evangelicals, the AFL, and the Daughters of the American Revolution, which generally diffused the wholesome values of the middle class. As in previous eras in American history, without significant support or protection from the middle class and propertied working class, radicals were exceedingly vulnerable, and in the 1950s suburban and middle-class America seemed to enjoy a not inconsiderable influence with government and media.

The Politics of Anticommunism

Presiding over the anticommunist consensus for most of the 1950s was the Eisenhower administration. The Republicans may have had little partisan use for the communist issue after 1952, but they had promised to be even more vigilant than the Democrats, and the change of administration increased the number of committed anticommunists in high government office. J. Edgar Hoover now had an administration more to his liking, and the FBI, Justice, State, Defense, and other departments energetically discharged their patriotic duty in dismissing, prosecuting, and deporting the Communists they thought they discovered. The bureaucratic purge acquired its own momentum and the anticommunist animus was directed less against political opponents than against Communists and other suspect elements outside conventional politics or in modest civil service positions.

In 1953, anxious to deliver on campaign promises of flushing reds from government, President Eisenhower established a new federal program that expanded the criteria under which employees could be dismissed as security risks and making more use of the power of "summary dismissal." When Truman's program was launched the focus had been on *loyalty* risks; by the Eisenhower era employees could be dismissed as *security* risks, even where they could not be shown to be disloyal. Determined to show itself more vigilant than the Democrats, the administration was soon playing the "numbers game," boasting of the multitude severed from federal employment under the new regime, which increased as the 1954 elections approached. Vice President Nixon claimed that the administration was "kicking the communists and fellow travelers and security risks out of government . . . by the thousands." In Eisenhower's first three years perhaps fifteen hundred were sacked for security reasons, more than Truman had managed in twice the time. Thousands of others left the civil service "voluntarily."

Many of those dismissed had held jobs in the lower or middle ranks of the federal bureaucracy—as secretaries, clerks, supervisors, special assistants, engineers, economists, and administrators. However tenuous their association with communism and however lowly their position, it seemed, national security demanded their removal from office. A few major figures fell foul of the program. One of the most celebrated was J. Robert Oppenheimer, whose popular front associations before the Second World War had not precluded his directing the atomic bomb program during the war. The security community had never been entirely happy about Oppenheimer, and his criticism of Cold War defense strategy and his doubts about the hydrogen bomb earned him further enemies in the armed services, particularly the air force. By the 1950s he had returned to academic life, but he remained a consultant of the Atomic Energy Commission until 1954, when a review board concluded that he was a security risk because "his past associations with persons known to him to be Communists extended far beyond the tolerable limits of prudence and self-restraint."

While the bureaucratic search for security risks intensified, the federal government continued its assault on the CP itself. Some forty-two CP leaders were indicted under the Smith Act between 1953 and 1956, sometimes for "knowing" of the party's revolutionary intentions rather than conspiring in them. The scope of other communist-control programs also tended to broaden, as zealous bureaucrats sought to please their masters by finding new reasons to withhold passports or visas or to invoke denaturalization or deportation proceedings. The Eisenhower administration, perhaps more sensitive to nativist pressures than its predecessor, increased the number of aliens expelled for political reasons; such deportations peaked at sixty-one in 1954. The powerful federal bureaucracies, by ranging ever more widely and indiscriminately in their quest for Communists and their sympathizers, were inviting Americans to consider the preservation of civil liberties a lower priority than the containment of domestic communism.

This was also the message of the congressional investigating committees, their energies recharged by Republican chairmen who had furthered their careers with the communist issue. For two years HUAC was headed by a former FBI agent, Harold H. Velde, who had campaigned for Congress with the slogan "Get the Reds out of Washington and Washington out of the Red." In 1953–54 HUAC held more days of public hearings than ever before, some 147 in all, and listened to over 650 witnesses, even if many did no more than plead the Fifth. Those fruitful hunting grounds of anticommunist committees, the left-wing unions and Hollywood, were visited yet again, although HUAC also fastened its suspicious sights on education and even the churches. Also setting an example to the nation and its host of anticommunist constituencies was the Senate Internal Security Subcommittee (SISS), which staged well-publicized investigations of communist influence in education, the unions, and leading newspapers. Government was now less suspect than the molders of opinion. In 1955 the SISS chairmanship fell to the passionate white supremacist Democrat James Eastland of Mississippi, who energetically used the communist issue and his powers of subpoena to defend the segregationist South from the subversive designs of the civil rights movement. Protected and legitimized by the anticommunist consensus in public life, and themselves bipartisan bodies, HUAC and SISS were less intent on embarrassing the administration or political rivals then on vindicating their existence by sniffing out vulnerable targets wherever they might be in American society. They were given information and assistance not only by the FBI, but also by the state "little HUACs" and by patriotic lobbies like the American Legion and anticommunist unions. At its birth in 1938, HUAC had been an instrument of political dissidents in revolt against the administration; by the 1950s it was part of a political establishment that was preying on powerless dissidents.

The Republican electoral victories of 1952 also brought a new committee into the great hunt for subversives. Joseph McCarthy himself as a leading Republican senator had to be given a committee to chair. In fact the Republican leadership, concluding perhaps that McCarthy had served his political purpose, attempted to sideline him by allowing him only the chairmanship of the insignificant Committee on Government Operations. But this committee carried in its wake an investigative subcommittee with authority to scrutinize "government activities at all levels," and McCarthy determined to use it to pursue his crusade against communism. As the subcommittee chairman, McCarthy commanded a federally funded staff and budget and a kind of quasi-legitimacy in employing his extensive network of bureaucratic informants. Indeed, the Republican victory meant that some of McCarthy's friends were able to secure jobs in the administration, such as the former FBI agent R. W. Scott McLeod, who became chief security officer of the State Department and enthusiastically set about ridding it of "drunks, perverts, or Communists." This did not save the department from McCarthy's own inquisition, and his subcommittee's first major hearings concerned the Voice of America program, which Republicans had long suspected of soft-peddling anti-Soviet propaganda because of the influence of "Communists, left-wingers, New Dealers, radicals and pinkos." Such influences apparently extended into the American information libraries overseas, and McCarthy's aides Roy Cohn and David Schine were let loose on a tour of Europe searching for subversive books. McCarthy himself summoned a number of bewildered authors to appear before his subcommittee in what sometimes proved to be rowdy sessions. The State Department fired or accepted the resignations of several of those connected with the programs that had so offended McCarthy.

It was the various subcommittee hearings of 1953 that established McCarthy's reputation as an investigator and greatly augmented his public recognition. In April Gallup polls reported that 19 percent of Americans were favorable to the senator and 22 percent unfavorable, but by August the figures were 34 and 42 percent. If his methods were generating more critics than sympathizers, he was at least at the center of much public attention, and by the end of the year his popularity was increasing. His 1953 junketings climaxed with a probe of Fort Monmouth, New Jersey, the site of important army radar laboratories—in which, he alleged, there was a Communist spy ring. At first the army cooperated with McCarthy, but it resisted when he sought to interrogate the members of the loyalty board responsible for clearing personnel at Fort Monmouth. McCarthy found a stick to beat the army with when he learned of the case of Irving Peress, an army dentist of "disloyal tendencies," according to an army probe, who nonetheless had been promoted to major before being hastily bundled out of the service with an honorable discharge. By this time the army was developing its own grievances against McCarthy, not least because Roy Cohn was applying intense pressure on it to obtain favorable treatment for his friend David Schine, who had recently been drafted. As 1954 opened, Senator McCarthy and the army were moving irresistibly toward confrontation. In January McCarthy reached a 50 percent favorable rating in the Gallup poll, his highest ever.

Previously when McCarthy had gone out on a limb, as in his demonstrably preposterous accusations in 1950 about Communists in the State Department, his fellow Republicans had generally rescued him. In 1954, however, the Republicans were themselves in command of the federal government, and the Eisenhower administration had been fretting at McCarthy's demands ever since it took office. J. Edgar Hoover too, distressed at McCarthy's indiscretions, had already withdrawn FBI assistance. Eisenhower had never liked McCarthy, and he took particular exception to the contemptuous treatment of his old service, though the senator's apparent popularity meant he had to be treated cautiously. In February McCarthy summoned Irving Peress's commanding officer, General Ralph Zwicker, vainly demanding to know who had been responsible for the dentist's discharge and informing the general that he was "not fit to wear that uniform." Secretary of the Army Robert T. Stevens attempted to defend his officers but buckled under the intense pressure McCarthy applied. Eisenhower himself called for "fair play" at congressional hearings, a mild slap at the senator, who incautiously responded by suggesting that the president's stand was responsible for "the gleeful shouting of every un-American element." Some of McCarthy's allies began to desert him as he turned on the White House, and Vice President Nixon went on the radio to condemn McCarthy's methods. In the Senate fellow Republican Ralph Flanders delivered a devastating attack on McCarthy for "doing his best to shatter" the Republican party through his clownish one-man crusade against "a pink Army dentist." On network television Edward R. Murrow showed clips of McCarthy at his most loutish. McCarthy had been attacked often enough in newspapers, but the more timid medium of television had never previously been used against him. Emboldened, perhaps, by these signs of White House and public support, the army counterattacked by releasing a report on Roy Cohn's harassment of the army to secure privileges for David Schine. Battle was now joined between the army and McCarthy. The investigative subcommittee determined to hear both sides, and for this purpose McCarthy yielded the chair to Karl Mundt.

The celebrated hearings, in front of the now almost customary television cameras, began in April 1954. The sales of television sets rose, and people stayed home to view the excitement. Millions watched McCarthy's endless points of order, the revelation of the favors Cohn had wrung from the army for Schine, the exposure of the doctoring of a photograph by McCarthy's staff, the refusal of the executive branch to permit its employees to disclose confidential conversations within it, and the pillorying of secretary of the army Stevens. The dramatic highlight came when McCarthy gratuitously smeared a young man in the firm of the army's counsel, Joseph Welch, who transfixed his audience with his rejoinder: "Until this moment, Senator, I think I never really gauged your cruelty or your recklessness." Television and film newsreels repeated the exchange, and newspaper headlines echoed Welch's words. Before the hearings Gallup had reported a 46 percent "favorable" rating for McCarthy, against 36 percent "unfavorable"; when they ended in June the balance had shifted to 34 percent "favorable" and 45 percent "unfavorable." McCarthy had been mortally wounded by the hearings, which exposed as never before his unprincipled and bullying methods. In July Senator Ralph Flanders introduced a resolution of censure into the Senate, and a committee was again set the task of reviewing McCarthy's conduct. On this occasion it allowed him little room for histrionics, and the Republicans on the committee finally joined the Democrats in firmly recommending censure. The Senate discreetly postponed the censure debate itself until after the midterm elections, in which McCarthyites fared badly, but in December 1954 it voted by sixty-seven votes to twenty-two to "condemn" McCarthy.

All the Democrats present voted against McCarthy, as did half of the

Republicans, a final demonstration that the senator was no longer protected by party solidarity. Nonetheless, twenty-two Republican senators, mainly midwestern conservatives, stood by him, validating Adlai Stevenson's earlier gibe that the Republican party was "half McCarthy and half Eisenhower." But it was the Eisenhower half that was in the ascendancy, and as McCarthy's relations with the administration grew ever more bitter even his sympathizers found it difficult to defend him. Further, the Democratic successes in the 1954 elections ended Republican control of the Senate and deprived McCarthy of his prized chairmanships. Increasingly a loner and repeatedly rebuffed by establishment figures, McCarthy also came to be ignored by the press. Deprived of the oxygen of publicity, his spirit broken and his health destroyed by heavy drinking, McCarthy stumbled blindly around the political stage until his death in 1957.

McCarthy in the end had destroyed himself, more by failing to observe the demands of party loyalty and senatorial propriety than by his anticommunist zeal as such. No one in public life questioned the need for vigilance against Communist subversion, and even his nemesis Joseph Welch told McCarthy on one occasion, "I admire the work you do, when it succeeds." McCarthy's subcommittee apart, the congressional investigating committees sustained the red hunt through the 1950s, and liberals in Congress did little to obstruct them. In 1954 only one congressman voted against HUAC's appropriation, and only one senator voted against the appropriation for McCarthy's subcommittee. The commitment of the political community to the anticommunist consensus even after the mockery of the army-McCarthy hearings was demonstrated by the Communist Control bill, introduced in the Senate in August 1954 by Hubert H. Humphrey with the support of other liberal senators. This declared the Communist party to be "the agency of a hostile foreign power" and imposed penalties for membership. The legal status of the CP had been in some doubt since the Smith Act was upheld in 1951; now membership in it was clearly a crime.

The Senate liberals sponsoring the bill perhaps intended it to weaken the Internal Security Act, for attaching criminal penalties made CP membership a matter to be determined by the courts, with their respect for due process and constitutional rights, rather than by congressional committees and executive agencies. But conservatives removed the penalty provisions, and most Senate liberals accepted the amended bill in order to display their own anticommunist convictions. In its final form the Communist Control bill passed the Senate without opposition and the House with only two negative votes. Yet little use was made of the act, which symbolized the capitulation of self-proclaimed liberals to red scare politics. It was concocted shortly before the midterm elections of 1954, when several Senate liberals were seeking reelection, and its purpose was to protect liberals by sacrificing Communists: it made membership, not associations, the test of political untouchability.

Saving American Minds

During the heyday of the anticommunist consensus, McCarthy's aberrations apart, government and congressional investigators as well as the patriotic lobbies were dwelling not so much on the possible communist penetration of the bureaucracy as on communist influence in other walks of life. The political system itself attracted less attention by the early to mid-1950s than institutions like trade unions, education, and the media. The political drives that had sustained the use of red scare tactics against party rivals between 1938 and 1952 were largely spent. The Eisenhower administration, in part the product of the successful conservative exploitation of anticommunist politics, could not plausibly be represented as soft on communism. But the dynamics of party and Cold War tensions had brought convinced anticommunists to high office even as they had removed popular front liberals from political life. The communist issue could no longer be used with much effect against political opponents, and new targets had to be found to legitimize the anticommunist consensus.

If there were few communist sympathizers in public life, there was some reason to believe that the anticommunist faith was not shared by all Americans. In opinion polls conducted in 1954, over three-quarters of respondents believed Communists should be stripped of citizenship and over half thought they should be jailed; yet some 13 percent and 34 percent, respectively, opposed those positions. When asked whether it was more important "to find out all the Communists even if some innocent people should be hurt" or "to protect the rights of innocent people even if some Communists are not found out," 58 percent plumped for red-hunting and 32 percent for civil liberties. In Michigan in 1950 over a third of voters in a referendum were against a state antisubversion bill; in California in 1952 about a third of voters were opposed to adding an anticommunist amendment to the state constitution. Such figures call into question the pervasiveness of the anticommunist consensus. Perhaps as many as a third of Americans were not subscribers to the cause. But two-thirds or more were, and politicians not unnaturally responded with greater alacrity to majority opinion than to the minority. The anticommunist stance of the majority was translated into near unanimity in the elected councils of the nation. The members of those government bodies could no longer find communist apologists among their own number, but outside the political establishment were those whose doubts about the anticommunist consensus rendered them suspect.

By the early 1950s the country was well protected by antisubversion measures of various kinds—restrictive immigration laws, the federal loyalty security programs, and the Internal Security Act, not to mention the various state sedition laws. Further, CP leaders were being put behind bars. As had occurred after the Big Red Scare, once the immediate danger of espionage and sabotage had been contained, suspicions focused on more subtle forms of subversion. Only a few Americans seriously believed that Communists were actively engaged in espionage in the United States (8 percent according to one poll), but substantial numbers (in polls varying between 24 and 31 percent) were worried about Communist "Conversion and Spreading Ideas." Not a few agreed with a Nebraska housewife that "they are getting into schools and teaching the children things and it's the young minds that are easy to influence." The institutions that molded and manipulated opinion were especially open to suspicion—schools, the cinema, libraries, newspapers, the churches. The intellectual prestige that members of such institutions often enjoyed also incited in some Americans a leveling zeal. The evolution of the Cold War encouraged such fears of a creeping ideological subversion. As the prospect of an immediate nuclear holocaust receded, Americans readied themselves for a prolonged glacial confrontation with the Soviet Union. In such a struggle, Communist conspirators might be expected to reach into American minds before destroying American bodies.

Ever since the Big Red Scare, patriotic Americans had fretted over the possible communist infiltration of education, religion, and the media. In the 1950s their warnings were accorded a measure of credibility. The widespread image of Communists as unscrupulous, duplicitous, and single-minded conspirators under the absolute control of an enemy power made it difficult to believe that Communist teachers and others were engaged in innocent activities. The very nature of the Cold War itself, as East and West awaited each other's internal collapse, fostered expectations that subversion could be of the most insidious kind.

Further, this was an era when many Americans believed that the human personality could be readily manipulated. A serious academic literature had grown up on the subject of "brainwashing," whose effectiveness seemed to be confirmed by reports that American prisoners of war in Korea had had their fundamental values changed by such techniques. Intellectuals, intrigued by the earlier impact of Nazi propaganda, had developed the field of communcations research. Many liberals worried about the growing public relations industry and the powers of advertising, one focus of concern being subliminal messages. Some psychologists, legal experts, and parents attributed juvenile delinquency to the influence of the media; crime and horror comics were said to be seducing the young. The "inner-directed" American, with his own internalized values, according to sociologist David Riesman, was being replaced by the "other-directed" person who took cues from peers. For a generation that imputed so much potency to the techniques of indoctrination, conditioning, and manipulation, there was nothing inherently implausible in the proposition that Communists were using education and the media to influence malleable American minds. As it happened, those institutions credited with molding opinion did contain their share of radicals and liberals critical of the anticommunist consensus, and the elitism they sometimes betrayed attracted populist resentment. The well-publicized "exposures" of alleged communists in Hollywood or Harvard served to fulfil the paranoid prophecy.

No less an authority than J. Edgar Hoover had long pointed to the subversive potential of teachers. "Every Communist uprooted from our educational system is one more assurance that it will not degenerate into a medium of propaganda for Marxism," he told Congress. This was an endeavor to which congressional committees, state legislatures, local school boards, and patriotic societies could each make a contribution. The public school systems were particularly vulnerable to the whims of local politicians because they were the one large bureaucratic enterprise that was subject to state rather than federal control. Many eagerly enlisted themselves in the Cold War by introducing antisubversive devices in the schools. In 1950 teachers had to sign loyalty oaths in twenty-six states, and the number increased to thirty-two before the end of the decade.

Sometimes teachers were required to inculcate patriotism, and several states expanded the teaching of American history and civics. Business groups, as noted earlier, developed links with the schools to promote the free enterprise system. Patriotic societies added their own scrutiny, and occasionally textbook controversies broke out. Among the groups specializing in the exposure of "subversive" texts were the Sons of the American Revolution and the Conference of American Small Business Organizations. Although the book banners rarely won outright victories, teachers learned to be circumspect in the materials they used.

Some states went beyond requiring loyalty oaths of teachers. In New York the 1949 Feinberg Law required an annual report on all teachers, who could be disqualified for membership in a subversive organization, and in 1950 a court ruling permitted the board of education to dismiss teachers who refused to answer the questions of congressional committees. The hunt for subversive New York teachers, begun in 1940, was resumed, and members of the left-wing Teachers' Union were soon being suspended or fired. Through the 1950s about four hundred New York City schoolteachers lost their jobs as a result of loyalty investigations. In Philadelphia, which HUAC visited regularly between 1952 and 1954, several teachers were fired for "incompetence" after taking the Fifth Amendment. California law provided for the dismissal of schoolteachers who attempted to indoctrinate their pupils with communism or who refused to answer questions put to them by official investigating bodies. In 1955 a California legislative committee reported itself "deeply gratified" at the progress made by school districts in firing teachers who had taken the Fifth. In general public opinion strongly endorsed this purge. A poll of 1954 showed that 91 percent favored firing high-school teachers who were admitted Communists. The United States Supreme Court upheld the doctrine that the schoolroom was a "sensitive area" in that it shaped "young minds" and that the school authorities could legitimately "screen" teachers "as to their fitness to maintain the integrity of the schools as a part of ordered society."

As in the Smith Act trials, it was usually assumed that subversion or potential subversion had been adequately demonstrated if the person charged could be shown to be a Communist (which in itself might be inferred from the taking of the Fifth). Since the CP was defined as a conspiracy to overthrow the republic, further evidence of criminal intent was redundant. SISS confidently concluded in 1953 that "Communist teachers use their positions in the classroom and in extracurricular activities to subvert students and other teachers and the public to promote the objectives of communism," though few instances of teachers actually deviating from their prescribed duties were ever found. Populistic suspicions about the professional claims of teachers strengthened legislative attempts to make educational institutions more accountable, particularly in respect to higher education. In this sector the housecleaning began at the University of Washington in 1948 when three professors were dismissed after a probe by a state "little HUAC." Controversy followed at the University of California, which first introduced its own loyalty oath and in 1950 became subject to a state loyalty oath. Through the early 1950s uncooperative California professors at state-funded colleges were losing their jobs. The pressures on the academic community increased in 1952–53 when SISS and HUAC conducted major investigations, and prestigious institutions like Harvard and Massachusetts Institute of Technology were implicated in the communist conspiracy, at least in the eyes of their critics. Over a hundred college teachers were interrogated in 1953 by congressional committees. During the years of the anticommunist consensus, hundreds of academics lost or were denied jobs or were refused promotion. The pressures on them did not

THE ANTICOMMUNIST CONSENSUS

all come from outside the universities. Most college presidents and many professors themselves agreed that CP membership, with its conspiratorial associations, was incompatible with a university position. Yet many of the academic victims had never been CP members; they had declined on principle to cooperate with loyalty investigations and thereby rendered their patriotism suspect.

The need to protect American minds from indoctrination was similarly the rationale for the purge of the entertainment industry, although exception was also taken to the role of entertainers in raising funds for the Communist party. The president of the Screen Actors Guild, Ronald Reagan, spoke in 1951 of the CP's old hope "eventually to control contents of films and thus influence the minds of 80,000,000 movie goers." Producers were even more submissive to public pressures than were college presidents. Although the off-Broadway theater could afford to be daring, Hollywood and broadcasting were traditionally averse to offending audiences or sponsors. Film studio heads, from the famous sex scandals of the 1920s onward, had been leery of stars who transgressed the mores of Middle America, and radio and television producers had learned that advertisers did not want their wholesome products linked with anyone controversial. Sponsors and theater managers shrank from being harassed or picketed by patriotic lobbies, with the attendant unwelcome publicity and threat to revenues.

The cinema, hardly surprisingly, had been the first major industry to capitulate to blacklisting pressures in 1947, although the immediate victims were restricted to the Hollywood Ten. By the early 1950s its resilience had been further weakened by an antitrust decision that forced the studios to relinquish their theater chains and by a dramatic drop in movie attendance following the spread of television. HUAC found Hollywood personalities much more cooperative when it resumed its scrutiny in 1951 than they had been in 1947, although perhaps 250 or more actors, writers, and directors were recalcitrant enough to be added eventually to the blacklist. Patriotic citizens again enlisted in the Cold War. Local posts of such groups as the American Legion and the Catholic War Veterans were more alert to the menace of red subversion and on occasion picketed films, to the distress of studio executives, who feared that banks would not fund features starring stigmatized actors. Such action, for example, forced the cancellation in several cities of Charles Chaplin's *Limelight* (1952). The film industry established its own clearance procedures and made an arrangement with the American Legion in 1952 permitting the Legion a role in the process. Neither the Legion nor HUAC paid much attention to the content of films. Naming names was held to be sufficient to flush out those giving comfort to the communist conspiracy, whether in the form of financial aid or as purveyors of propaganda. Television and the mainstream theater also succumbed to black-listing pressures.

Education and the media were not the only institutions suspected of promoting subversive ideas. The press was protected to a degree by its general conservatism and by the conspicuous anticommunism of some major proprietors, but the patriotism of liberal newspapers was sometimes questioned. McCarthy made frequent attacks on the "left-wing press," attributing the survival of the Communist movement to the "Communist utilization of the so-called respectable newspapers and radio stations," and SISS conducted an investigation into the influence of Communists in the press. After several *New York Times* journalists had been interrogated by SISS, the newspaper said that it would not wittingly employ Communists in its news or editorial departments. The American Newspaper Guild, which represented over twenty-seven thousand North American newsmen, voted in 1954 to bar Communists from membership, although in the following year it thought better of the move. Libraries too were vulnerable to charges that they housed politically seductive material, and from time to time, often after lobbying by local patriotic groups, suspect books or magazines were removed or librarians lost their jobs.

Even the churches were not immune. In the 1930s a few church groups, such as the Methodist Federation for Social Service, had supported popular front positions, and conservatives had long suspected them of advancing the cause of communism under the guise of religion. The most tireless chronicler of "subversive" church activities was Dr. J. B. Matthews, who in July 1953 published an article in *American Mercury* entitled "Reds and Our Churches," which opened with the arresting sentence, "The largest single group supporting the Communist apparatus in the United States today is composed of Protestant clergymen." In the same month HUAC interrogated Methodist bishop G. Bromley Oxnam, who had been accused by one of its members of a long "record of aid and comfort to the Communist front." But the anticommunists overreached themselves in their attack on organized religion, which was more widely seen as an antidote to "atheistic" communism. Matthews's article precipitated such a furor that he was obliged to resign his new position with Senator McCarthy's subcommittee. The anticommunist consensus was not invulnerable.

The anticommunist obsession with education, the media, and even the churches reflected fears about the subversive potential of these institutions, outrage that distinguished persons associated with them might be lending their prestige to malevolent causes, and popular resentment at the arrogance occasionally displayed by the intelligentsia. But the assault on these bodies, as on such radical unions as survived, also reflected the fact that not all Americans shared the values of the anti-communist consensus. A significant minority doubted the need for communist-control measures, and radicals and libertarians did tend to be clustered disproportionately in colleges and schools, labor and civil rights groups, and parts of the entertainment industry and the press. In the eyes of local patriots, such dissidents seemed to be giving comfort to America's enemies.

These spheres also contained their share of influential believers in the presence of a malign communist conspiracy. In some cases these contrasting perspectives represented ancient political rivalries, and right-wing elements were able to use the anticommunist consensus to settle old scores. The targets of the anticommunist activists may not always have been Communists, and there were conservatives among them who suffered because they refused to submit to the new tests of loyalty, but they were not figments of fevered imaginations. For the most part, they were men and women whose ideals stood as a reproof to McCarthy's America.

.

The anticommunist consensus was held firmly in place by the mutual reinforcement of the executive, legislative, and judicial branches of government, and this unanimity in the high councils of the nation was sustained by and in turn sustained popular and interest group convictions that American communism was a Soviet weapon in the Cold War. Economic expansion in an unusually dangerous international setting tended to strengthen the more conservative constituencies of the American polity, and in complex ways the promptings of class, religion, and race reinforced anticommunist values. The ideological showdown between the United States and the Soviet Union quickened patriotic pulses, and the Manichaean image of a bipolar world divided between God and Satan evoked popular fears of satanic emissaries at work within a vulnerable American society. In contrast to the first Big Red Scare, the anxious patriotism of the 1950s rarely spilled over into vigilante violence, despite the populistic instincts that had been awakened. Popular sentiments and government policies interacted smoothly enough. With the government purging itself of security risks, middle-level politicians and local patriots exercised a logical vigilance over people's susceptible minds. The tradition of an active replublican citizenry came to life once more.

The anticommunist ascendancy represented the completion of a political cycle that had begun in the 1930s. There had then been a conservative revolt against the dominant New Deal and its popular front allies, but not until the Eisenhower years were conservatives safely placed in government. In fact, Republicans of the stripe of Robert Taft and Joseph McCarthy felt the conservative restoration had not gone far enough, but it had been aided by the anticommunist crusade, which could not be lightly abandoned even where its partisan purposes had been effected. Where once the communist issue had been used to attack those high in government, the anticommunist accord secured in Washington in the 1950s meant that probes now tended to be directed downward and outward in the polity, interacting with patriotic lobbies and vigilant local citizens in pursuit of the elusive enemy. Yet the political dynamic that had destroyed the popular front and raised anticommunist conservatives to power had played itself out. Public opinion was soon to take on a more liberal coloring, and one branch of government was to defect from the anticommunist consensus.

10

THE
EBBING OF
ANTICOMMUNISM?

•

T HE anticommunist persuasion, in its pervasiveness and intensity, was never again to achieve the success of the early and middle 1950s. By the second half of that decade the anticommunist consensus was coming apart, and by the 1960s those Americans who insisted that the United States was being subverted by a red enemy within were being widely ridiculed as extremists. The ultimate revitalization of American conservatism by the New Right of the 1970s owed more to the discrediting of liberalism than to fear of revolutionary socialism. The "evil empire" might still be abroad, but it was an external threat. Some influential Americans who had feared an internal communist conspiracy relocated the menace outside American borders, in Cuba or Nicaragua. This replacement of domestic undermining by hemispheric subversion represented the adjustment of Cold War patterns of thought to new geopolitical conditions; but though it legitimized assaults on radical regimes in Latin America, it afforded no grounds for a new witch-hunt inside the United States.

The judiciary was largely responsible for first prising open the chinks in the anticommunist armor of the 1950s. At about the time the Supreme Court was knocking down the walls of segregation, it was also moving to deprive the government of its instruments for controlling domestic communism. For those given to right-wing attitudes on race, internal security, and the Constitution, the Court under Chief Justice Earl Warren took on a sinister and even malevolent aspect, arrogating to itself legislative and dictatorial powers to transform the nature of the American polity. But the Supreme Court was part of a larger political culture that was itself changing. The conservative revival that had begun in the late 1930s had run its course by the mid-1950s. The Democrats won control of both houses of Congress in 1954 and increased their majorities in 1958, and liberals in both major parties, now impeccably anticommunist, seemed to be gaining ascendancy. By the early 1960s a "liberal consensus" was replacing the anticommunist consensus. This liberal moment was itself in part made possible by the weakening of those configurations that had in the past contributed to red scare politics. Class conflict of the traditional kind was receding as a postindustrial society replaced the industrial order; nativism had declined with immigration, and even southern white racism was on the defensive; and a firmer line was being drawn between religion and politics. Most important, the anticommunist cause had long ceased to be driven by the imperatives of party politics. Anticommunist crusaders still sounded the alarms, but they had been nudged to the political sidelines.

The erosion of the anticommunist consensus was also made possible by changing perceptions of the Cold War. The end of the Korean War and the death of Stalin in 1953 rendered the Soviet Union somewhat less menacing, and two years later the superpowers were conferring at Geneva. Since the Cold War seemed to be turning into a long-term contest for the good opinion of mankind, American political leaders became more sensitive to the need to display the merits of "the American way." In a longer perspective, the growth in importance of Third World countries, the advent of the European Community, and the schisms within the "Communist bloc" made the image of a bipolar world increasingly anachronistic. That image was still powerful enough in the 1960s to pull the United States into the Vietnam War, but the unhappy course of that war for Americans did not trigger the kind of passions that had fed Joseph McCarthy during the Korean War. The glimpses of a fragmented world abroad and a pluralistic society at home undermined the Manichean and apocalyptic appeal of the anticommunist cause.

The Anticommunist Consensus Undone

The army-McCarthy hearings and the Communist Control Act of the summer of 1954 might be said to mark the high tide of Cold War anticommunism. Thereafter the anticommunist persuasion began to lose some of its potency, though it never entirely disappeared. Those exigencies of both international and national politics that had helped to establish the anticommunist consensus were themselves beginning to fade. The series of devastating foreign policy reverses of 1948–51 was disappearing into the past, and the Korean War ended in 1953, reducing international tension and removing one of the reasons for public anger with the State Department. The United States now possessed a formidable defense arsenal, the NATO alliance had been cemented, and it seemed that Soviet expansionism had been more or less contained. Joseph Stalin was dead, and in 1955 President Eisenhower met the new Soviet leader at a summit conference in Geneva. The "spirit of Geneva" marked some thawing in American-Soviet relations, and talk of "peaceful coexistence" between East and West signaled the postponement of Armageddon. The Far Right seethed as the Eisenhower administration thus succumbed to Soviet wiles—McCarthy attacked the president's participation in the Geneva Conference—but these events were tending to undermine its appeal. The survival of the United States no longer seemed under immediate threat, and if anything the stridency of the McCarthyites began to seem a greater menace to world peace than the pacifist impulses of left-wingers.

The slackening of global tension was accompanied by changes in American politics that also tended to blunt the edge of domestic anticommunism. Between 1948 and 1952 the Communists-in-government charge had been predominantly a Republican weapon, and Republicans had little further use for it when they took control of White House and Congress in 1953. For another eighteen months or so Joe McCarthy remained a loose cannon on the Republican deck, but for that very reason he eventually had to be maneuvered overboard. Politicians of all persuasions, of course, remained obediently anticommunist, as was demonstrated by the Communist Control Act, but by 1954 both major parties had effectively immunized themselves against the suspicion of succoring reds. In the midterm elections of that year Vice President Nixon did claim that the CP "had determined to conduct its program within the Democratic party," but the charge lacked credibility, and the Democrats indeed regained control of both houses of Congress. Liberal Democrats too fared well in the elections, which was seen as further proof that red-baiting was losing its bite. Their electoral successes meant that the congressional investigating committees were restored to the Democrats, and if a few of them, such as Senator James Eastland as chairman of SISS, were ferociously anticommunist themselves, they were less interested in using the communist issue for partisan causes. Anyone who accused Eisenhower of being a communist dupe was likely to be regarded as a crank.

Slowly, politicians began to show more respect for civil liberties. In part this was a reaction to the excesses of Senator McCarthy, whose extraordinary behavior was discrediting the anticommunist movement by the summer of 1954. "McCarthyism" was becoming almost as damaging an epithet as "soft on communism," and the senator's disastrous confrontation with the army probably did something to cut short the larger anticommunist crusade. Congress debated codes of fair procedure for its investigating committees, and though none was adopted, committee chairmen knew they had come under critical scrutiny from bar associations, civil liberties groups, and a significant portion of the press. The greater sensitivity to individual rights owed something to the evolu-

194

tion of the Cold War. As a nuclear holocaust seemed less imminent and as the Cold War was increasingly perceived as a long and laborious struggle for people's minds and hearts, the need to flourish the virtues of American civilization before the rest of the world became more compelling. McCarthyism, like southern white racism, was marring America's international image, and the more prestigious newspapers, leading politicians, and other public figures began to speak out more boldly against injustice and abuse. The American political tradition itself, with its cultivation of individual liberties, could be—and was—turned against indiscriminate anticommunism.

In the winter of 1954–55 the tide was turning. Liberal Democrats were cheered by their electoral successes in November. When at the end of the year two distinguished government officials fell foul of the security program, despite the flimsiness of the charges against them, there was widespread condemnation. In December McCarthy himself was censured. Senator Hubert Humphrey, who had recently been using the Communist Control Act to wave his anticommunist credentials, called for the creation of a bipartisan Commission on Government Security to review the whole security program. Another critical Senate liberal was Thomas C. Hennings, whose Subcommittee on Civil Rights changed the latter part of its title to Constitutional Rights in January to free it to embark on a broad-ranging examination of modern rights and liberties. In the same month shock waves were felt in the administration itself when Harry P. Cain, sometime right-wing Republican and McCarthyite and a member of the Subversive Activities Control Board, fiercely and publicly assailed the security program and called for its replacement. This attack from an impeccably conservative source attracted extensive publicity. The "Cain Mutiny" erupted again in March when Cain demanded that the security program be divorced from politics and that its most questionable features, such as the attorney general's List, be abolished. Another painful blow to the program came in early 1955, when Harvey Matusow, one of the government's regular former Communist witnesses who had helped put a number of CP leaders behind bars, revealed that his testimony was fictitious. He soon elaborated, claiming to have lied frequently in his five years as an informer and witness and accusing other former Communist witnesses of lying too. Civil liberties lobbies and activists and a growing number of newspapers pressed home the attack. The Ford Foundation's Fund for the Republic, for example, gave the New York Bar Association a grant to examine in depth the legal implications of the security program. Far from protecting the national interest, it was increasingly being suggested, the security program was damaging it.

Most destructive to the anticommunist bureaucratic apparatus was the attitude being taken by the Supreme Court, now headed by Earl Warren. If defectors in the administration and critics in Congress were undermining the various security measures erected since 1947, it was the judicial branch of government that delivered the fatal blows. In February 1955 Earl Warren observed during a speech that the contemporary American public might reject the Bill of Rights itself were it submitted for ratification, a common enough gibe of liberals but disconcerting when coming from the chief justice of the United States. Later that year the Court began to query both the government's security program and the free-ranging probes of Congress. In *Peters v. Hobby* a security dismissal was invalidated because the right procedures had not been followed and the job in question was not sensitive. On another occasion the Supreme Court warned Congress that the power to investigate "must not be used to inquire into private affairs unrelated to a valid legislative purpose." For years the various executive and legislative Communist-control (or security) operations had insistently pushed their boundaries outward and grown ever more indiscriminate; finally the Supreme Court was signaling that they must be reined in.

The Court's purpose was made clearer in 1956. A major blow to the nation's dedicated anticommunists came in April with *Pennsylvania v. Nelson*, which held that Congress had legislated so extensively on internal security as to make it a federal responsibility. State sedition laws in general had no validity, a decision that let the Pennsylvania Communist Steve Nelson go free. Soon after, the Court ordered the reinstatement of a Brooklyn professor who had been sacked for taking the Fifth, recognizing that his constitutional rights had been abridged. In June the Court struck again at the federal security program, reducing the president's powers of summary dismissal and restricting the scope of the program more explicitly to "sensitive agencies."

It was a year later, however, that the Court delivered its knockdown blows to the internal security lobbies. Early in June 1957 the Supreme Court ruled (in *Jencks v. U.S.*) that the defense should have access to the confidential information supplied to the government by FBI informers. This decision not only made it more difficult for the Justice Department to secure convictions under the Smith Act and other statutes, it also threatened to expose the operations of the hallowed FBI. Justice Tom Clark, who as attorney general had helped put Truman's loyalty program in place, raged that the government's intelligence agencies "may as well close up shop, for the Court had opened their files to the criminal and thus afforded him a Roman holiday for rummaging through confidential information as well as vital national secrets."

Two weeks later, on 17 June 1957, the Supreme Court handed down three devastating decisions that marked the day as "Red Monday." In

Watkins v. U.S. the Court rebuffed HUAC by dismissing a contempt citation on the grounds that the questions the witness had refused to answer were not relevant to a legitimate legislative inquiry; *Sweezy v. New Hampshire* struck down a similar contempt citation in a state probe. Finally, in *Yates v. U.S.*, the Court reversed fourteen Smith Act convictions and greatly reduced the scope of the act, arguing that the "abstract doctrine" of advocating the overthrow of the government was not in itself illegal and that the prohibition on organizing subversive groups applied to their initial formation rather than to their continued survival. The Smith Act, in the words of a lower court judge, was left "a virtual shambles," incapable of enforcement, and prosecutions under it were henceforth generally abandoned. Taken together, the various decisions of June 1957 hampered the prosecution of political dissidents, circumscribed the powers of congressional investigating committees, further restricted the antisubversive activities of state agencies, and crippled what had been the most effective of the anticommunist laws. The iron lock in which the executive and legislative branches of government had together held American Communists was being broken.

This judicial dismantling of a large part of the anticommunist machinery provoked a mighty storm of vituperation, and measures were introduced into Congress to curb the powers of the Supreme Court. In 1958 the most formidable of the anti-Court bills, supported by a coalition of Republicans and southern Democrats reminiscent of the one that had sustained HUAC in the 1940s, was beaten back, albeit by a narrow Senate vote. Emboldened perhaps by the stand of the Supreme Court and responding to the more libertarian spirit that was invading American political culture, northern Democrats and some liberal Republicans were insisting that constitutional rights not be subordinated to the needs of internal security. The anticommunist consensus was crumbling.

Anticommunism Marginalized

Soon after the anti-Court bill was defeated in 1958, the Democrats substantially increased their majorities in both houses of Congress. The Democratic ascendancy was confirmed in 1960 with the—albeit narrow—election of John F. Kennedy to the presidency, wedded to a political image that was widely labeled liberal. In the Republican party, too, liberals of the stripe of Nelson Rockefeller and Henry Cabot Lodge were close to the centers of power, though bitterly resisted by conservatives like Barry Goldwater, who felt the party had conceded too much to the New Deal heritage. By the early 1960s the "liberal consensus"—which linked its faith in capitalism to respect for civil rights, civil liberties, and a modest welfare state—had become the new orthodoxy. But the liberals of the 1960s were more the heirs of Americans for Democratic Action (ADA) than of the New Deal with its left-wing connections. A number of them, like Hubert Humphrey and Arthur Schlesinger Jr., were graduates of the 1940s wars on the popular front. McCarthyism they regarded with contempt, but international communism still had to be combated abroad. John F. Kennedy had spent a lifetime exposed to the doctrines of Catholic anticommunism, and if he did not locate a red enemy within, he found one on the doorstep, in Castro's Cuba. The insolent proximity of Fidel Castro made him something of a lightning rod for American anticommunist energies, diverting them from targets inside the United States. The belligerent anticommunist foreign policy of the liberal administrations of John Kennedy and Lyndon Johnson focused attention on the external dimensions of the communist threat while allowing reform policies to be pursued at home.

The disintegration of the anticommunist consensus in the late 1950s meant only that there was no longer a united front of government agencies arrayed against domestic radicalism, not that anticommunist sentiments had disappeared. SISS and HUAC remained in existence for some years, if less able to command press attention, and J. Edgar Hoover's FBI if anything stepped up its war on the Communist party. With the weakening of the communist-control laws, the FBI had to find an alternative method of combating the CP, and in 1956 it launched its COINTELPRO (Counter Intelligence Program) campaign of harassment and disruption. These operations, designed to discredit rather than prosecute their targets, through the use of rumors, smear stories, press exposures, and the "dirty tricks" of undercover agents, were later extended to the Ku Klux Klan, the Black Nationalists, and the New Left. To the depleted CP of the late 1950s, reeling from Soviet actions as well as COINTELPRO, the subscriptions of undercover FBI agents constituted a significant source of funds. But at least until the turmoil of the middle and late 1960s gave a new utility to the FBI's political surveillance, J. Edgar Hoover's crusade against domestic communism was becoming increasingly personal. His complaint about the "growing public complacency toward the threat of subversion" was a comment on his own somewhat marginalized position.

Other patriotic Americans too were becoming distressed by the emergence of a more relaxed political culture. Some signs of this could be discerned in 1958. That year saw the formation of George Lincoln Rockwell's American Nazi party and of the National States' Rights party, both of which identified "Jew-Communism" as the enemy. Racists of this kind, though predominantly anti-Semitic, were disturbed by the success of the civil rights movement, which they tended to link to Jewish and communist conspiracies. More traditional conservatives were also alarmed by the liberal tendencies of the day. In 1958 some of them formed Americans for Constitutional Action to resist the "shift toward socialism" and act as a kind of counterweight to the ADA.

But the most important of the antiradical groups founded in that year was the John Birch Society, the creation of former candy manufacturer Robert Welch, named for a young soldier who had died in an encounter with Chinese Communists soon after the Second World War, "the first American casualty in World War III." The John Birch Society for the most part avoided overt expressions of racism, attempting in principle to alert Americans of all races and creeds to the communist threat in their midst, though it tended to appeal most to upper-middle-class whites, often young, Republican-inclined, and sometimes fundamentalist. In the early 1960s several other right-wing groups surfaced to express their rejection of the liberal consensus, including the Conservative Society of America, which supported candidates of Birchite views for elective office; Young Americans for Freedom, composed of students and others who believed "the forces of international Communism" were the "greatest single threat" to individual liberties; and the Minutemen, who prepared themselves for the guerrilla warfare they believed was the only defense left to them against the communist invaders.

The emergence of these several groups, whether conservative Republican or neo-Nazi, represented not so much a swing to the right of the public mood as a revolt by rather small minorities against the prevailing centrist and liberal ethic. The collapse of the anticommunist consensus tended to strand archconservatives outside the arena of legitimate politics, rather as popular front radicals had been isolated in the late 1940s. Illustrative in this respect was the John Birch Society, which believed the Eisenhower administration was serving communist masters. A large part of the world outside the Soviet Union had already fallen to communist control, according to Robert Welch, and the United States itself was perilously close to succumbing. In one celebrated sentence—which he later attempted to retract and which, if nothing else, ensured the John Birch Society extensive publicity—Welch described Eisenhower as a "dedicated, conscious agent of the communist conspiracy." The society flourished modestly during the Kennedy and Johnson years, reaching some eighty thousand members in 1967, with centers of support in Florida, Texas, and southern California. But though it provided an outlet for those angry souls who could not distinguish liberalism from communism, its obsession with nefarious conspiracies deterred more people than it attracted. In Robert Welch's eyes, the communist conspiracy comprehended not only liberals but also the Supreme Court, the Eisenhower brothers, *Time* and *Newsweek*, and even the CIA and by 1965 had won control of 60 to 80 percent of the United States. Further, its origins could be traced to the late eighteenth-century Illuminati, a Masonic group that had attracted the suspicious attention of generations of paranoids. Such fantasies encouraged conservative Republicans like Barry Goldwater and Richard Nixon to repudiate the John Birch Society. It thus remained a fringe group, and its appeal was fading by the late 1960s when such conservatives were able to make use of public disenchantment with the Great Society and the Vietnam War to climb back to power. The revival of conservative Republicanism owed little to anticommunism of the Birchite variety, although it did owe something to that species of anticommunism that had so devastatingly embroiled American might in Vietnam.

Perhaps the main strand of continuity between the anticommunism of the 1950s and that of a later day was provided by fundamentalist Protestantism. A number of the missions that had been launched in the early 1950s continued into the 1960s and even flourished. Dr. Frederick C. Schwarz's Christian Anti-Communist Crusade managed to attract fair numbers of college-educated business and professional people and right-wing Republicans to its week-length "schools." More spectacular was the Christian Crusade of the Reverend Billy James Hargis, who broadcast daily over 270 radio stations and sent out over a million pieces of literature each month. Hargis denounced the betrayal of the United States by "liberals, welfare staters, do-gooders and one-worlders" and warned that at their present rate of advance the communists would win complete control of the country by 1974. Hargis's own ruin came in the mid-1970s when he was felled by a sex scandal, but a new breed of evangelist, exploiting the continued growth of the fundamentalist sects and the technology of television, kept alive some of the old preoccupations. Such "televangelists" as Jerry Falwell, Jim Bakker, and Pat Robertson were eloquent foes of "Godless communism." Robertson believed that Karl Marx was a "satanic priest" and that communism was "satanism." But though as determined as ever to equate communism with the devil, the anticommunism of the televangelists tended to be subordinated to a broader onslaught against "secular humanists," those liberals, atheists, academics, homosexuals, abortionists, and others who were said to be eating away at the moral fabric of American life. The permissive society had provided new targets for fundamentalist wrath, rendering the old anticommunist crusade awkwardly anachronistic.

Politicians too were wary of being tagged "McCarthyite." They might look for ways of magnifying and combating the red menace they periodically perceived in Latin America and of subtly deploying anticommunist symbols, but they sensed little political advantage in reviving the red scare at home. The Communist party itself, after all, had all but disappeared. Ravaged by the second Big Red Scare, it had been further devastated in 1956 by Khrushchev's denunciation of Stalin's crimes and by the Soviet suppression of the Hungarian uprising. Its modest 22,000 members in 1955 had fallen to 3,474 by the end of 1957. Those liberals who could be charged with popular front associations were also disappearing from the scene. In the 1960s the New Left emerged to outrage and alarm the citizens of Middle America, but it could not plausibly be linked to the machinations of a foreign power, despite the busy efforts of J. Edgar Hoover. The New Right gained political ascendancy by focusing on Democratic failures rather than on the threat of red revolution, although it did represent the discredited liberalism of the 1960s as an aberration in contrast to traditional American values. Vice President Spiro Agnew in 1970 reviled the opponents of the Nixon administration as "radical liberals," and Ronald Reagan in the 1980s reinforced his legitimacy with nostalgic memories of his Communist-hunting days in Hollywood, but such rhetorical posturings were incapable of precipitating the kind of red scare that had earlier deprived radical Americans of their lives, liberties, and livelihoods.

.

The global scene itself had changed since the period immediately after World War II when international communism had made such devastating gains in Eastern Europe and Asia. The United States had grown more accustomed to its role as a superpower, communist successes had not been repeated on the same scale, and more important, the old image of a world divided between East and West had lost its value. The Third World had emerged with a variety of ideals and demands of its own, Western Europe and Japan were no longer much beholden to the United States, and crucially the "Communist bloc" had lost the unity once imputed to it. With the disintegration of the communist monolith, the Soviet Union, like the United States, became just another country in the world, if a powerful and dangerous one. Americans still needed to maintain an armed vigilance in this uncertain world, but international communism was no longer seen as an all-conquering and ruthless force let loose on the planet and masterminded by Moscow. That American perceptions of the communist threat had changed since the darkest days of the Cold War was demonstrated when one redoubtable anticommunist politician, Richard Nixon, exploited Sino-Soviet differences by visiting China and pursuing détente with the Soviet Union, and another, Ronald Reagan, engaged in jovial nuclear arms reduction talks with the Soviet premier. The Cold War, it seemed, was ending.

While international communism was divested of some of its terror, the domestic springs of red scare politics had continued to weaken. Class conflict had evolved into different forms since the era of industrialization, and the New Left held little appeal for the taxpaying workers of the 1960s. As the United States moved into a postindustrial phase the proportion of blue-collar workers declined, the unions lost members, and the work force became more fragmented, rendering the old antilabor functions of the red scare even more redundant. The racist impulse that had often strengthened anticommunist attitudes had also faded or at least was being redirected. The political need to cultivate Third World countries abroad and racial and ethnic minorities at home had killed whatever lingering appeal Anglo-Saxon nativism may have exerted, and the dismantling of segregation laws and the rise of black voting in the South had undermined that bastion of racial antiradicalism.

American patriotic and religious instincts remained strong, and fundamentalist Protestantism in particular thrust anticommunist enmities on into the 1970s and 1980s and invaded the political arena, but it tended to locate the more immediate threat to American civilization in moral decay rather than in a revitalized Comintern. And the political and bureaucratic classes, which had been largely responsible for injecting the communist issue into modern American politics, no longer had much use for it. There were few survivors of the popular front experiments that had given the issue its sting, the CP barely functioned, and the New Left, though touched by Marxism, had collapsed by the early 1970s. Earlier red scares had done their work; the surviving anticommunist constituencies lacked a domestic enemy to rally against, and party politicians were unable to implicate their opponents in un-American conspiracies. The dynamics of class and party conflict could no longer mesh with global tensions to produce a great crusade against red enemies within.

The rise of the New Right in the 1970s and 1980s, particularly in the symbolically important presidential elections, also left domestic anticommunism with little independent purchase on American political culture. The conspicuous resurgence of patriotic, laissez-faire, and religious values afforded triumphant proof that the country had not after all succumbed to ideological subversion. In a sense the old red-hunting impulses were being subsumed in a larger repudiation of liberalism—or "secular humanism." The Democratic candidate George McGovern suffered in the 1972 election because of his perceived connection with the permissive radicalism of the 1960s, and in the 1988 campaign the Republican candidate taunted his Democratic rival with "the L word," implying that being soft on liberalism was as un-American as being soft on communism. The imagery of the anticommunist tradition still had its uses. Republican presidential candidates, as they had always done, polled well with the rich, but they also attracted impressive support from middle-income blue-collar and ethnic workers, southern whites, and born-again (and other white) Christians. The Republicans, more successfully than their rivals, were accommodating themselves to the dominant economic, racial, and religious mores of American society, drawing on traditions that at times had imparted some legitimacy to the anticommunist cause.

As the 1980s gave way to the 1990s, what President Reagan had called "the evil empire" appeared to be disintegrating. The ebbing of international communism raised the possibility that the long history of domestic anticommunism was nearing its end as a distinctive phenomenon. It would be premature to pronounce dead the American disposition to descry an internal red menace, but new domestic and international configurations would be needed to restore it to full vitality.

BIBLIOGRAPHICAL
ESSAY

•

T HIS ESSAY does not cite all the sources I consulted in writing this book, but it draws attention to those I found most useful, particularly to those secondary works that should be fairly widely available. A valuable bibliographical tool is John Earl Haynes, *Communism and Anti-Communism in the United States: An Annotated Guide to Historical Writings* (New York: Garland, 1987).

General Themes

One difficulty in approaching the subject of American anticommunism is the absence of general histories. Although McCarthyism and other episodes have attracted considerable scholarly attention, there have been few attempts to integrate such specialized studies into broader syntheses. Further, right-wing movements in American history have not given rise to as much scholarship as labor and left-wing movements, so that much of the history of American anticommunism must be approached through studies of its targets rather than of its champions. Thus, general histories of American labor tend to reveal more about domestic anticommunism than, say, general histories of American business, which, where they exist, in any case are not always very forthcoming on this sensitive issue.

An important interpretative work by a pair of social scientists is Seymour Martin Lipset and Earl Raab, *The Politics of Unreason: Right-Wing Extremism in America, 1790–1970* (New York: Harper and Row, 1970), which is not so much about anticommunism as about "the politics of backlash" resulting from the displacement of old social groups by new. More directly addressing nativism, but with a lot to say about anticommunism, is David H. Bennett, *The Party of Fear: From Nativist Movements to the New Right in American History* (Chapel Hill: University of North Carolina Press, 1988). Robert Justin Goldstein, *Political Repression in Modern America: From 1870 to the Present* (Cambridge, Mass.: Schenkman, 1978), contains a mass of useful information. John P. Roche, *The Quest for a Dream* (Chicago: Quadrangle, 1968), is an engaging—if today unconvincing—collection of essays presenting the racially prejudiced and anticommunist "Yahoos" as retreating before the advance of an urban-industrial society. Michael Parenti, *The Anti-Communist Impulse* (New York: Random House, 1969), is mainly concerned with the modern global projection of an American ideology. Michael H. Hunt, *Ideology and U.S. Foreign Policy* (New Haven: Yale University Press, 1987), contains insights relevant to domestic anticommunism. Richard M. Fried, *Nightmare in Red: The McCarthy Era in Perspective* (New York: Oxford University Press, 1990), takes a long view of its subject.

Merle Curti, *The Roots of American Loyalty* (New York: Columbia University Press, 1946), traces the evolution of patriotism. Hans Kohn, *American Nationalism* (New York: Macmillan, 1957), and Wilbur Zelinsky, *Nation into State: The Shifting Symbolic Foundations of American Nationalism* (Chapel Hill: University of North Carolina Press, 1988), explore the idea of national identity. For the American tendency to conjure an enemy within, see Richard Hofstadter, *The Paranoid Style in American Politics* (New York: Alfred A. Knopf, 1964), and David Brion Davis, ed., *The Fear of Conspiracy: Images of Un-American Subversion from the Revolution to the Present* (Ithaca, N.Y.: Cornell University Press, 1971). For much of American history, the fear of subversion was linked to nativism, the most profound study of which remains John Higham, *Strangers in the Land: Patterns of American Nativism 1860–1925* (New Brunswick, N.J.: Rutgers University Press, 1955). On WASP culture see E. Digby Baltzell, *The Protestant Establishment: Aristocracy and Caste in America* (New York: Random House, 1964). The persistence of racist ideology is traced in Thomas F. Gossett, *Race: The History of an Idea in America* (Dallas: Southern Methodist University Press, 1963); also of some value is Oscar Handlin, *Race and Nationality in American Life* (New York: Doubleday, 1957). Histories of immigration and of religion need to be consulted, of which the best general studies, respectively, are Maldwyn Jones, *American Immigration* (Chicago: University of Chicago Press, 1960), and Sidney E. Ahlstrom, *A Religious History of the American People* (New Haven: Yale University Press, 1972).

The story of American anticommunism cannot be reconstructed without the aid of business and other economic histories, although they tend to be more valuable for information on corporate structure and business values than for detail on antiradical activities. Clarence H. Cramer, *American Enterprise: The Rise of U.S. Commerce* (Boston: Little, Brown, 1973), is a general history, as is John M. Peterson and Ralph Gray, *Economic Development of the United States* (Homewood, Ill.: Irwin, 1969). Robert Sobel, *The Age of Giant Corporations* (Westport, Conn.: Greenwood, 1972), covers the twentieth century. More revealing are studies of American socialism and the labor movement. General histories of communism include the critical Irving Howe and Lewis Coser, *The American Communist Party* (New York: Praeger, 1957), and the sympathetic Paul Buhle, *Marxism in the USA from 1870 to the Present Day* (London: Verso, 1987). Casting a broader net and containing Daniel Bell's provocative essay, "Marxian Socialism in the United States," is Donald Drew Egbert and Stow Persons, eds., *Socialism and American Life*, 2 vols. (Princeton: Princeton University Press, 1952). A valuable collection of essays on American socialism is Seymour M. Lipset and John Laslett, eds., *Failure of a Dream?* (New York; Doubleday, 1974). Werner Sombart's celebrated question, *Why Is There No Socialism in the United States?* (1906; translation White Plains, N.Y.: M. E. Sharpe, 1976) has had many answers, a recent collection being Jean Heffer and Jeanine Rovet, eds., *Pourquoi n'y a-t-il pas de socialisme aux Etats-Unis?* (Paris: Ecole des Hautes Etudes en Sciences Sociales, 1988). General histories of American labor abound, among the best being Foster Rhea Dulles and Melvyn Dubofsky, *Labor in America*, 4th ed. rev. (Arlington Heights, Ill.: Harlan Davidson, 1984) and Joseph G. Rayback, *A History of American Labor* (New York: Free Press, 1966). Philip S. Foner, *History of the Labor Movement in the United States*, 4 vols. (New York: International, 1947–65), contains much useful detail. Mike Davis, *Prisoners of the American Dream* (London: Verso, 1986), essays the difficult history of the working class in the context of American politics. Welfare as well as labor histories carry some relevant material, one being Michael Katz, *In the Shadow of the Poorhouse* (New York: Basic Books, 1986). The effects of anticommunism can also be found in studies of American civil liberties, as in Zechariah Chafee, Jr., *Free Speech in the United States* (Cambridge: Harvard University Press, 1942), and Thomas I. Emerson, David Haber, and Norman Dorsen, *Political and Civil Rights in the United States* (New York: Little, Brown, 1967). For much of the twentieth century, Paul L. Murphy, *The Constitution in Crisis Times, 1918–1969* (New York: Harper and Row, 1972), is of considerable value.

Histories of those twentieth-century institutions involved on one side or the other in anticommunist episodes often contain much relevant material. The FBI has been relatively well served by scholars. A courageous early critique is Max Lowenthal, *The Federal Bureau of Investigation* (New York: Sloane, 1950); the approved version is provided by Don Whitehead, *The FBI Story* (New York: Random House, 1956). Substantial modern studies are Sanford Ungar, *The FBI: An Uncensored Look behind the Walls* (Boston: Atlantic Monthly Press, 1976), Richard Gid Powers, *Secrecy and Power: The Life of J. Edgar Hoover* (New York: Free Press, 1987), and Athan G. Theoharis and John Stuart Cox, *The*

Boss: J. Edgar Hoover and the Great American Inquisition (Philadelphia: Temple University Press, 1988). The American Legion awaits a good historian, although it has found one for part of its history in William Pencak, *For God and Country: The American Legion, 1919–1941* (Boston: Northeastern University Press, 1989). Raymond Moley, Jr., *The American Legion Story* (Des Moines: Duell, Sloan, and Pearce, 1966), is sprawling and uncritical. Rodney G. Minott, *Peerless Patriots: Organized Veterans and the Spirit of Americanism* (Washington, D.C. Public Affairs Press, 1962), is a useful study of the patriotic activities of several veterans' groups. A persistent critic of the Legion, the ACLU, has been no better served by scholars. Charles Lam Markmann, *The Noblest Cry: A History of the American Civil Liberties Union* (New York: St. Martin's Press, 1965) is poorly organized and friendly; William A. Donohue, *The Politics of the American Civil Liberties Union* (New Brunswick N.J.: Transaction Books, 1985). is tendentious and hostile.

Memoirs and biographies have been useful for this book, but they are too many to list here. Suffice it to say that very large proportions of the presidents and politicians, business and religious leaders, union chieftains and bureaucrats, publishers and newsmen, communists, socialists and other radicals whose names have figured in the preceding pages have been the subjects of biographies, and some have told their own stories. Readers are referred to the subject catalogs of good libraries.

Chapter 1

A stimulating introduction to American history in the early nineteenth century is Marcus Cunliffe, *The Nation Takes Shape, 1789–1837* (Chicago: University of Chicago Press, 1959). Arthur Schlesinger, Jr., *The Age of Jackson* (Boston: Little, Brown, 1945), remains of combative value, Edward Pessen, *Jacksonian America: Society, Personality, and Politics*, rev. ed. (Homewood, Ill.: Dorsey, 1978), is full of information, and David M. Potter, *The Impending Crisis, 1848–1861* (New York: Harper and Row, 1976), and Peter J. Parish, *The American Civil War* (New York: Holmes and Meier, 1975), address the middle decades of the century. M. J. Heale, *The Making of American Politics, 1750–1850* (New York: Longman, 1977), attempts to trace the evolution of a distinctive American polity. Robert H. Wiebe, *The Opening of American Society* (New York: Alfred A. Knopf, 1984), contains many suggestive insights. George R. Taylor, *The Transportation Revolution: Industry, 1815–1860* (New York: Rinehart, 1951), and Stuart Bruchey, *The Roots of American Economic Growth* (New York: Harper and Row, 1965) remain of value. Helpful too is Marcus Cunliffe, *Soldiers and Civilians: The Martial Spirit in America, 1775–1865* (Boston: Little, Brown, 1968).

BIBLIOGRAPHICAL ESSAY

Among the studies of American and European radicals in the young republic are Eric Foner, *Tom Paine and Revolutionary America* (New York: Oxford University Press, 1976); David Harris, *Socialist Origins in the United States: American Forerunners of Marx, 1817–1832* (New York: Humanities Press, 1966); David Herreshoff, *American Disciples of Marx* (Detroit: Wayne State University Press, 1967); Karl Obermann, *Joseph Weydemeyer: Pioneer of American Socialism* (New York: International Publishers, 1947); A. E. Zucker, ed., *The Forty-eighters: Political Refugees of the German Revolution of 1848* (New York: Columbia University Press, 1950); some of the essays in Marc Pachter and Frances Wein, eds., *Abroad in America: Visitors to the New Nation, 1776–1914* (Reading, Mass.: Addison Wesley, 1976); and Celia M. Eckhardt, *Fanny Wright: Rebel in America* (Cambridge: Harvard University Press, 1984). Uptopian communities have been extensively treated, such as by Mark Holloway, *Heavens on Earth: Utopian Communities in America, 1680–1880* (New York: Dover, 1964); Robert H. Walker, *Reform in America* (Lexington: University Press of Kentucky, 1985); and Edward K. Spann, *Brotherly Tomorrows: Movements for a Cooperative Society in America, 1820–1920* (New York: Columbia University Press, 1989). The dominant republican and democratic traditions may be approached via Gordon S. Wood, *The Creation of the American Republic, 1776–1787* (Chapel Hill: University of North Carolina Press, 1969); Alexis de Tocqueville, *Democracy in America*, 2 vols., ed. Phillips Bradley (New York: Alfred A. Knopf, 1945); and Eric Foner, *Free Soil, Free Labor, Free Men* (New York: Oxford University Press, 1970), this last book showing how the libertarian ideology of northern Republicans could be mobilized against socialism. Sean Wilentz, *Chants Democratic: New York City and the Rise of the American Working Class, 1788–1850* (New York: Oxford University Press, 1984), elucidates the emergence of class consciousness. John Ashworth, *"Agrarians" and "Aristocrats": Party Political Ideology in the United States, 1837–1846* (Atlantic Highlands, N.J.: Humanities Press, 1983), demonstrates the coexistence of both a leveling egalitarianism and a reactionary conservatism. The perceived vulnerability of republican institutions to enemies within is a theme of M. J. Heale, *The Presidential Quest: Candidates and Images in American Political Culture, 1787–1852* (White Plains, N.Y.: Longman, 1982). Among the studies of the role of religion in American political culture are Ruth Bloch, *Visionary Republic: Millennial Themes in American Thought, 1756–1800* (New York: Cambridge University Press, 1985), and Timothy L. Smith, *Revivalism and Social Reform: American Protestantism on the Eve of the Civil War* (New York: Abington, 1957), while Charles C. Cole, *The Social Ideas of the Northern Evangelists, 1826–1860* (New York: Columbia University Press, 1954), and John R. Bodo, *The Protestant Clergy and Public Issues, 1812–1848* (Princeton: Princeton University Press, 1954), emphasize the political conservatism of the revivalists. Richard Carwardine, "The Religious Revival of 1857–8 in the United States," in *Studies in Church History*, vol. 15, *Religious Motivation*, ed. Derek Baker (London: Basil Blackwell, 1978), adds interesting detail. Eugene Genovese, *The World the Slaveholders Made* (New York: Pantheon, 1969), and William J. Cooper, *Liberty and Slavery: Southern Politics to 1860* (New York: Alfred A. Knopf, 1983), are among the many books that help define the peculiar political culture of the South. David Montgomery, *Beyond Equality: Labor and the Radical Republicans, 1862–1872* (New York: Alfred A. Knopf, 1967), is richly suggestive on the political landscape of the 1860s and the limited purchase it allowed to a class-based socialism.

Chapter 2

There are many general histories of the United States in the late nineteenth century. Interpretative overviews are provided by Samuel P. Hays, *The Response to Industrialism, 1885–1914* (Chicago: University of Chicago Press, 1957), and Robert H. Wiebe, *The Search for Order, 1877–1920* (New York: Hill and Wang, 1967). Carl Degler, *The Age of Economic Revolution, 1876–1900* (Glenview, Ill.; Scott Foresman, 1967), is a lively survey, John A. Garraty, *The New Commonwealth, 1877–1890* (New York: Harper and Row, 1968), is solidly informative, and Morton Keller, *Affairs of State: Public Life in Late Nineteenth Century America* (Cambridge: Harvard University Press, 1977), is a major study of the industrializing polity. Conceptually important are Stephen Skowronek, *Building a New American State* (New York: Cambridge University Press, 1982), and Charles C. Bright, "The State in the United States during the Nineteenth Century," in *Statemaking and Social Movements*, ed. Charles Bright and Susan Harding (Ann Arbor: University of Michigan Press, 1984). The economic history of the period is detailed in Edward C. Kirkland, *Industry Comes of Age* (Chicago: Quadrangle, 1961), and Harold G. Vatter, *The Drive to Industrial Maturity* (Westport, Conn.: Greenwood, 1975), and already a classic is Alfred D. Chandler, Jr., *The Visible Hand: The Managerial Revolution in American Business* (Cambridge: Harvard University Press, 1977). Frederic C. Jaher, ed., *The Age of Industrialism in America* (New York: Free Press, 1968), and Edward C. Kirkland, *Dream and Thought in the Business Community, 1860–1900* (Chicago: Quadrangle, 1956), are helpful on business values. Herbert G. Gutman, *Work, Culture, and Society in Industrializing America* (New York: Random House, 1977), is indispensable for an understanding of the working class. Alan Dawley,

Class and Community: The Industrial Revolution in Lynn (Cambridge: Harvard University Press, 1976), while focusing on shoemakers, helps to explain why American workers embraced the political system.

The impact of the Paris Commune is explored by George L. Cherry, "American Metropolitan Press Reaction to the Paris Commune of 1871," *Mid-America* 32(January 1950): 3–12; Samuel Bernstein, "American Labor and the Paris Commune," *Science and Society* 15(Spring 1951): 144–62; and "The Impact of the Paris Commune in the United States," in *Revolution and Reaction: The Paris Commune 1871*, ed. John Hicks and Robert Tucker (Amherst: University of Massachusetts Press, 1973). For fears of the insurrectionary potential of the industrial and urban disputes of the 1870s see the labor histories and Montgomery, *Beyond Equality*, cited earlier, and Herbert G. Gutman, "Industrial Workers Struggle for Power," in *The Gilded Age*, ed. H. Wayne Morgan (1970), and Gutman, "The Tompkins Square 'Riot' in New York City on January 13, 1874," *Labor History* 6(Winter 1965): 44–70; Robert V. Bruce, *1877: Year of Violence* (New York: Franklin Watts, 1970); David B. Tyack, "Education and Social Unrest, 1873–1878," *Harvard Educational Review* 31 (Spring 1961): 194–212. Gutman's various writings are highly suggestive on the way the large city environment shaped antiradical attitudes. On the conventional economic, religious and other wisdom of the era see not only the works cited in the previous paragraph but Louis M. Hacker, *The World of Andrew Carnegie* (Philadelphia: Lippincott, 1968); Sidney Fine, *Laissez-Faire and the General Welfare State* (Ann Arbor: University of Michigan Press, 1964); Leon Litwack, *The American Labor Movement* (Magnolia, Mass.: Peter Smith, 1962); C. Howard Hopkins, *The Rise of the Social Gospel in American Protestantism, 1865–1915* (New Haven: Yale University Press, 1967). For immigration and responses to it see the previously cited works by Jones, Gossett, and Higham and also Barbara Solomon, *Ancestors and Immigrants* (Cambridge: Harvard University Press, 1956); Dirk Hoerder, ed., *American Labor and Immigration History, 1877–1920s* (Champaign: University of Illinois Press, 1983); Marianne Debouzy, ed., *A l'ombre de la statue de la Liberté: Immigrants et ouvriers dans la Republique Américaine* (Paris: Presses Universitaires de Vincennes, 1988); and Philip Taylor, *The Distant Magnet: European Emigration to the USA* (New York: Harper and Row, 1971). On Chicago and on the Haymarket Affair see Hartmut Keil and John B. Jentz, eds., *German Workers in Chicago* (Champaign: University of Illinois Press, 1988); Henry David, *The History of the Haymarket Affair* (New York: Macmillan, 1963); and Paul Avrich, *The Haymarket Tragedy* (Princeton: Princeton University Press, 1984). For the thrust of governmental coercion see Goldstein, *Political Repression*, and Daniel R. Fusfield, "Government and the

Suppression of Radical Labor, 1877–1918," in Bright and Harding, eds., *Statemaking and Social Movements*. Good treatments of the police are James F. Richardson, *The New York Police* (New York: Oxford University Press, 1970), and especially Sidney L. Harring, *Policing a Class Society: The Experience of American Cities, 1865–1915* (New Brunswick, N.J.: Rutgers University Press, 1983). Material on the militia may be found in Martha Derthick, *The National Guard in Politics* (Cambridge, Harvard University Press, 1965), and Robert Reinders, "Militia and Public Order in Nineteenth Century America," *Journal of American Studies* 11(April 1977): 81–102, and on vigilante activity in Richard Maxwell Brown, "The American Vigilante Tradition," in *The History of Violence in America*, ed. Ted R. Gurr and Hugh D. Graham (New York: Praeger, 1969); Brown, ed., *American Violence* (1970), and Robert P. Ingalls, *Urban Vigilantes in the New South: Tampa, 1882–1936* (1988). On courts and the law see Skowronek, *Building a New American State*; Arnold P. Paul, *Conservative Crisis and the Rule of Law* (1976); and Charles McCurdy, "Justice Field and Jurisprudence of Government-Business Relations," *Journal of American History* 61(March 1975): 970–1003. Several of the studies mentioned above cover the 1890s and may be supplemented by Edward Bellamy, *Looking Backward* (1888); Sylvia E. Bowman, *The Year 2000: A Critical Biography of Edward Bellamy* (New York: Twayne, 1958); Lawrence Goodwyn, *Democratic Promise: The Populist Moment in America* (New York: Oxford University Press, 1976); H. Wayne Morgan, *William McKinley and His America* (Syracuse, N.Y.: Syracuse University Press, 1963); and Wallace E. Davies, *Patriotism on Parade: The Story of Veterans' and Hereditary Organizations in America, 1783–1900* (Cambridge: Harvard University Press, 1955).

Chapters 3 and 4

The general studies by Hays and Wiebe, listed in the previous section, continue to be relevant for the 1900s and 1910s, as do the more specialized books by Higham, Goldstein, Hopkins, Skowronek, and others. Also useful for this period are Nell Irvin Painter, *Standing at Armageddon: The United States, 1877–1919* (1987), and William E. Leuchtenberg, *The Perils of Prosperity, 1914–1932* (Chicago: University of Chicago Press, 1958). A good broad treatment is Neil A. Wynn, *From Progressivism to Prosperity: World War I and American Society* (New York: Holmes and Meier, 1986). Historical perspectives on particular topics are provided by Harold M. Hyman, *To Try Men's Souls: Loyalty Tests in American History* (Berkeley: University of California Press, 1959); David Montgomery, *Workers' Control in America* (New York: Cambridge University Press, 1979), and particularly *The Fall of the House of Labor* (New York: Cambridge University Press, 1987); John Laslett, *Labor and the Left: A Study of Socialist and Radical Influences in the American Labor Movement* (New York: Basic Books, 1970); and Eldridge F. Dowell, *A History of Criminal Syndicalism Legislation in the United States* (Baltimore: Johns Hopkins University Press, 1939).

The literature on Progressivism is too extensive for full recitation, but an incisive introduction to it is John A. Thompson, *Progressivism* (Durham: British Association for American Studies, 1979). Richard L. McCormick, *The Party Period and Public Policy* (New York: Oxford University Press, 1986), is perceptive on the changing nature of the American polity. For contrasting views on the NCF see Montgomery, *House of Labor*, and James Weinstein, *The Corporate Ideal in the Liberal State* (Boston: Beacon, 1969). The reaction to the McKinley assassination is discussed in Sidney Fine, "Anarchism and the Assassination of McKinley," *American Historical Review* 60(July 1955): 777–99. The emergence of the Wobblies and the distrust they attracted are covered in the several labor histories cited earlier and in Patrick Renshaw, *The Wobblies: The Story of Syndicalism in the United States* (Garden City, N.Y.: Doubleday, 1967), and Melvyn Dubofsky, *We Shall Be All: A History of the Industrial Workers of the World* (Chicago: Quadrangle, 1969). On labor and socialism see again the works cited above; particularly Lipset and Laslett, eds., *Failure of a Dream?* including the entries on Catholic antisocialism by Marc Karson and Henry J. Browne; Ira Kipnis, *The American Socialist Movement, 1897–1912* (New York: Columbia University Press, 1952); James Weinstein, *The Decline of Socialism in America, 1912–1925* (New York: Random House, 1969); and Howard M. Gitelman, *Legacy of the Ludlow Massacre* (Philadelphia: University of Pennsylvania Press, 1988).

Particularly valuable on the roots of the Big Red Scare is William Preston, Jr., *Aliens and Dissenters: Federal Suppression of Radicals, 1903–1933* (Cambridge: Harvard University Press, 1963). The repressive impact of war is illuminated in David M. Kennedy, *Over Here: The First World War and American Society* (New York: Oxford University Press, 1980), Harry N. Scheiber, *The Wilson Administration and Civil Liberties* (Ithaca, N.Y.: Cornell University Press, 1960), and Paul L. Murphy, *World War I and the Origin of Civil Liberties in the United States* (New York: Norton, 1979). For intellectual reactions see Jacqueline Reimen, "1917–18: America's Warring Intellectuals," *Revue Française d'Etudes Americaines* 29 (May 1986): 309–24, and her "Radical Intellectuals and Repression of Radicalism during the First World War," *Revue Française d'Etudes Americaines* 2 (October 1976): 63–76. Other useful articles include O. A. Hilton, "Public Opinion and Civil Liberties in Wartime

1917–1919," *Southwestern Social Science Quarterly* 28 (December 1947): 201–24; Lorin Lee Cary, "The Wisconsin Loyalty Legion, 1917–18," *Wisconsin Magazine of History* 53(Autumn 1969): 33–50; and Hugh T. Lovin, "The Red Scare in Idaho, 1916–1918," *Idaho Yesterdays* 17(Fall 1973): 2–13. On labor and the war see Frank L. Grubbs, Jr., *The Struggle for Labor Loyalty: Gompers, the A.F. of L., and the Pacifists, 1917–1920* (Durham, N.C.: Duke University Press, 1968), and Ronald Radosh, *American Labor and United States Foreign Policy* (New York: Random House, 1969). The activities of the APL are examined in Hyman, *To Try Men's Souls;* in Joan M. Jensen, *The Price of Vigilance* (Chicago: Rand McNally, 1968); and in the revealing work of an early admirer, Emerson Hough, *The Web* (New York: Arno, 1919).

The best general study of the Big Red Scare remains Robert K. Murray, *Red Scare: A Study in National Hysteria, 1919–1920* (Minneapolis: University of Minnesota Press, 1955), which bears the mark of the McCarthyite times in which it was written. Murray Levin, *Political Hysteria in America* (New York: Basic Books, 1971), also reflects the era in which it was published and contains some useful material on the Scare. Stanley Cohen, "A Study in Nativism: The American Red Scare of 1919–20," *Political Science Quarterly* 79(1964): 52–75, is an illuminating interpretation. The Lusk committee of the New York legislature produced some awesome documentation of the perceived red menace in its *Revolutionary Radicalism: Its History, Purpose and Tactics*, 4 vols. (Albany: Senate of the State of New York, 1920). An important episode is the subject of Robert Friedheim, *The Seattle General Strike* (Seattle: University of Washington Press, 1964), and among the repercussions of the Scare are those described by Allan M. Wakstein, "The Origins of the Open-Shop Movement, 1919–1920," *Journal of American History* 51(1964–65): 460–75, and David Williams, "The Bureau of Investigation and Its Critics, 1919–1921: The Origins of Federal Political Surveillance," *Journal of American History* 68(December 1981): 560–79. The role of the attorney general is described in Stanley Cohen, *A. Mitchell Palmer: Politician* (New York: Columbia University Press, 1963). Much of the Scare took place below federal level and has been variously examined in Thomas E. Vadney, "The Politics of Repression: A Case Study of the Red Scare in New York," *New York History* 49(January 1968): 56–75; Julian F. Jaffe, *Crusade against Radicalism: New York during the Red Scare, 1914–1924* (Port Washington, N.Y.: Kennikat, 1972); David R. Colburn, "Governor Alfred E. Smith and the Red Scare, 1919–1920," *Political Science Quarterly* 88(1973): 423–44; Harold Josephson, "The Dynamics of Repression: New York during the Red Scare," *Mid-America* 59(October 1977): 131–46; Philip L. Cook, "Red Scare in Denver," *Colorado Magazine* 43(Fall 1966): 309–26; and Joey McCarty,

"The Red Scare in Arkansas," *Arkansas Historical Quarterly* 37(Autumn 1978): 264–76. For further information on American responses to the Russian Revolution see Christopher Lasch, *The American Liberals and the Russian Revolution* (New York: Columbia University Press, 1962); Peter G. Filene, *Americans and the Soviet Experiment, 1917–1933* (Cambridge: Harvard University Press, 1967); and Lloyd C. Gardner, *Safe for Democracy: The Anglo-American Response to Revolution, 1913–1923* (New York: Oxford University Press, 1984). Radical responses are detailed in Theodore Draper, *The Roots of American Communism* (New York: Viking, 1957).

Chapters 5 and 6

A robust study of the interwar years is provided by *The Age of Roosevelt* volumes of Arthur M. Schlesinger, Jr. (Boston: Houghton Mifflin), namely *The Crisis of the Old Order, 1919–1933* (1957), *The Coming of the New Deal* (1958), and *The Politics of Upheaval* (1960). William Leuchtenberg's *Perils of Prosperity* remains useful for the 1920s, as is his more substantial *Franklin D. Roosevelt and the New Deal* (New York: Harper and Row, 1963) for the 1930s. The 1920s are also treated in George Soule, *Prosperity Decade* (New York: Harper and Row, 1947), and John D. Hicks, *Republican Ascendancy, 1921–1933* (New York: Harper and Row, 1960), and the whole period is dealt with in Donald R. McCoy, *Coming of Age* (Baltimore: Penguin, 1973), and Barry D. Karl, *The Uneasy State: The United States from 1915 to 1945*, (Chicago: University of Chicago Press, 1983). Excellent on the 1930s is Anthony J. Badger, *The New Deal: The Depression Years, 1933–1940* (London: Macmillan, 1989). Relevant material may also be found in more specialized books spanning the interwar period, including Robert M. Miller, *American Protestantism and Social Issues, 1919–1939* (Durham: University of North Carolina Press, 1958); David M. Chalmers, *Hooded Americanism: The History of the Ku Klux Klan* (New York: Doubleday, 1958); Matthew and Hannah Josephson, *Al Smith: Hero of the Cities* (Boston: Houghton Mifflin, 1969); Stuart D. Brandes, *American Welfare Capitalism, 1880–1940* (Chicago: University of Chicago Press, 1976); Carol E. Jenson, *The Network of Control: State Supreme Courts and State Security Statutes, 1920–1970* (Westport, Conn.: Greenwood, 1982); Daniel Aaron, *Writers on the Left* (New York: Avon, 1961); Robert Lacey, *Ford* (New York: Ballantine, 1986); and W. A. Swanberg, *Citizen Hearst* (New York: Scribner, 1961). Irving Bernstein's histories of the American worker carry much useful information, notably *The Lean Years* (Boston: Houghton Mifflin, 1960) on 1920–33 and *The Turbulent Years* (Boston: Houghton Mifflin, 1969) on 1933–41; they may be supplemented by Robert H. Zieger, *American Workers, American Unions, 1920–1985* (Baltimore: Johns Hopkins University Press, 1986).

Some of the studies listed previously continue to be relevant to the antiradicalism of the 1920s, among them the books by Higham, Murray, and Preston. On attitudes toward Russia see also Filene, Gardner, and John L. Gaddis, *Russia, the Soviet Union, and the United States* (New York: John Wiley, 1978). Among the useful studies of the Republican administrations are Robert K. Murray, *The Harding Era* (Minneapolis: University of Minnesota Press, 1969); Ellis W. Hawley, ed., *Herbert Hoover as Secretary of Commerce* (Iowa City: University of Iowa Press, 1981); and Robert H. Zieger, *Republicans and Labor, 1919–1929* (Lexington: University of Kentucky Press, 1969). The Republicans had no monopoly on insular conservatism, as is shown by David Burner, *The Politics of Provincialism: The Democratic Party in Transition, 1918–1932* (New York: Alfred A. Knopf, 1968). For veterans see Minott, *Peerless Patriots*, and Pencak, *For God and Country*; for the Klan see Kenneth T. Jackson, *The Ku Klux Klan in the City, 1915–1930* (New York: Oxford University Press, 1967); for fundamentalism Norman K. Furniss, *The Fundamentalist Controversy, 1918–1931* (New Haven: Yale University Press, 1954); and for textbook controversies Curti, *Roots of American Loyalty*, and Jack Nelson and Gene Roberts, Jr., *The Censors and the Schools* (Boston: Little, Brown, 1963). The repressive atmosphere is explored also in Paul L. Murphy, "Sources and Nature of Intolerance in the 1920s," *Journal of American History* 51(1964): 60–76; Hugh T. Lovin, "Idaho and the 'Reds,' 1919–1926," *Pacific Northwest Quarterly* 69(July 1978): 107–15; and Edwin Layton, "The Better America Federation: A Case Study of Superpatriotism," *Pacific Historical Review* 30(1961): 137–47. For socialism and labor see the books cited previously, especially Weinstein, *Decline of Socialism*, and Theodore Draper, *American Communism and Soviet Russia* (New York: Viking, 1960). Among suggestive writings bearing on the impact of repression on reform are David P. Thelen, *Robert M. La Follette and the Insurgent Spirit* (New York: Little, Brown, 1976), and Clarke A. Chambers, *Seedtime of Reform: American Social Service and Social Action, 1918–1933* (Ann Arbor: University of Michigan Press, 1963). The most celebrated court case of the 1920s has been the subject of several studies, one of which is Louis Joughin and Edmund M. Morgan, *The Legacy of Sacco and Vanzetti* (Chicago: Quadrangle Books, 1964).

Some of the studies above also contain material on antiradicalism early in the depression, as do Carey McWilliams, *Factories in the Fields* (Boston: Little, Brown, 1939); Cletus E. Daniel, *Bitter Harvest: A History of California Farmworkers, 1870–1941* (Ithaca, N.Y.: Cornell University Press, 1981); and John H. Moore, "Communists and Fascists in a

Southern City: Atlanta, 1930," *South Atlantic Quarterly* 67(1968): 437–54. On the Hoover administration, see Edgar E. Robinson and Vaughan D. Bornet, *Herbert Hoover: President of the United States* (Stanford, Calif.: Hoover Institution Press, 1975), and Donald Lisio, *The President and Protest: Hoover, Conspiracy, and the Bonus Riot* (Columbia: University of Missouri Press, 1974). Bridging the gap between the Slump and the New Deal is Eliot A. Rosen, *Hoover, Roosevelt, and the Brains Trust* (New York: Columbia University Press, 1977). The standard studies on labor history remain indispensable, as is Harvey Klehr, *The Heyday of American Communism* (New York: Basic Books, 1984). On labor and leftist movements see also Donald R. McCoy, *Angry Voices: Left-of-Center Politics in the New Deal Era* (Lawrence: University of Kansas Press, 1958); Hugh T. Lovin, "The Fall of Farmer-Labor Parties, 1936–1938," *Pacific Northwest Quarterly* 62(January 1971): 16–26; and Jerold S. Auerbach, *Labor and Liberty: The LaFollette Committee and the New Deal* (Indianapolis: Bobbs-Merrill, 1966). The fascistic and other (right-wing) extremist groups of the 1930s have been extensively studied, among others by Morris Schonbach, *Native American Fascism during the 1930s and 1940s* (New York: Garland, 1985); Roy Campbell, "Gerald B. Winrod versus the 'Educated Devils,' " *Midwest Quarterly* 16(Winter 1975): 187–98; Charles J. Tull, *Father Coughlin and the New Deal* (Syracuse, N.Y.: Syracuse University Press, 1965); Alan Brinkley, *Voices of Protest: Huey Long, Father Coughlin, and the Great Depression* (New York: Alfred A. Knopf, 1982), which is perceptive on the antibureaucratic thrust of demagoguery; Leo Ribuffo, *The Old Christian Right from the Great Depression to the Cold War* (Philadelphia: Temple University Press, 1983); Glen Jeansonne, *Gerald L. K. Smith: Minister of Hate* (New Haven: Yale University Press, 1988); and Geoffrey S. Smith, *To Save a Nation: American Countersubversives, the New Deal and the Coming of World War II* (New York: Basic Books, 1973). Also relevant for other aspects are J. David Valaik, "American Catholics and the Second Spanish Republic, 1911 [*sic*]–1936," *Church and State* 10(1968): 13–28, and Thomas R. Maddux, "Red Fascism, Brown Bolshevism: The American Image of Totalitarianism in the 1930s," *Historian* 40(November 1977): 85–103. On the dismay of old Progressives with the New Deal see Otis L. Graham, *An Encore for Reform* (New York: Oxford University Press, 1967), and of southern intellectuals Paul K. Conkin, *The Southern Agrarians* (Knoxville: University of Tennessee Press, 1988). The larger conservative reaction to the New Deal is examined in James T. Patterson, "A Conservative Coalition Forms in Congress, 1933–1939," *Journal of American History* 52(1965–66): 757–72, and his *Congressional Conservatism and the New Deal* (1967); George Wolfskill, *The Revolt of the Conservatives: A History of* the American Liberty League, 1934–1940 (Boston: Houghton Mifflin, 1962); and Richard Polenberg, "The National Committee to Uphold Constitutional Government, 1937–1941," Journal of American History 52(1965–66): 582–98.

Chapters 7 and 8

Good introductory studies that span both the wartime and postwar years are Richard Polenberg, One Nation Divisible: Class, Race, and Ethnicity in the United States since 1938 (New York: Penguin, 1980), and John P. Diggins, The Proud Decades: America in War and Peace, 1941–1960 (New York: Norton, 1988). General studies of the period since 1945 abound. A little dated but vivid is Eric F. Goldman, The Crucial Decade and After: America, 1945–1960 (New York: Random House, 1975); William H. Chafe, The Unfinished Journey (New York: Oxford University Press, 1986), is authoritative; Lawrence S. Wittner, Cold War America; From Hiroshima to Watergate (New York: Praeger, 1974), provides a leftist perspective; and James Gilbert, Another Chance: Postwar America, 1945–1968 (Philadelphia: Temple University Press, 1981), is interestingly composed. Theda Skocpol's views may be found, among other places in "Political Response to Capitalist Crisis," Politics and Society 10(1980): 169–201. A good general text on foreign policy between 1938 and 1970 is Stephen E. Ambrose, The Rise to Globalism (New York: Penguin, 1971); Thomas G. Paterson, Meeting the Communist Threat: Truman to Reagan (New York: Oxford University Press, 1988), is a collection of essays on foreign policy. Information about public opinion can be gathered from George Gallup, The Gallup Poll: Public Opinion, 1935–1971, 3 vols. (New York: Random House, 1972). Rather surprisingly, there have been few broad studies of domestic anticommunism in the postwar era. An early interpretative thrust was provided by the essays in Daniel Bell, ed., The New American Right (New York: Criterion, 1955), which tended to present McCarthyism as a populistic revolt against liberal elites. By the 1970s a reaction had set in against this view, as is illustrated in the most comprehensive study, David Caute, The Great Fear: The Anti-Communist Purge under Truman and Eisenhower (New York: Simon and Schuster, 1978), which collects a great deal of information and places much responsibility for the many job losses on the Truman administration and Cold War liberals. Robert Griffith and Allan Theoharis, eds., The Specter: Original Essays on the Cold War and the Origins of McCarthyism (New York: Watts, 1974), is an invaluable collection of essays, several of which lay responsibility on various elites. Intellectual history provides one key to understanding Cold War political culture, and long-term perspectives are provided in

John P. Diggins, *Up from Communism: Conservative Odysseys in American Intellectual History* (New York: Harper and Row, 1975); George Nash, *The Conservative Intellectual Movement in America since 1945* (New York: Basic Books, 1976); and Allan W. Wald, *The New York Intellectuals: The Rise and Decline of the Anti-Stalinist Left from the 1930s to the 1980s* (Chapel Hill: University of North Carolina Press, 1987). One issue involved in the furor over communism was the role of government in the modern state, and useful books bearing on this are Otis Graham, *Towards a Planned Society: From Roosevelt to Nixon* (New York: Oxford University Press, 1976), and Kim McQuaid, *Big Business and Presidential Power: From FDR to Reagan* (New York: Morrow, 1982).

Material relevant to "the little red scare" can be found in several of the publications cited in the previous section, notably those by Ribuffo, Smith, Patterson, and Klehr. On the origins of HUAC see August R. Ogden, *The Dies Committee* (Washington, D.C.: Catholic University Press, 1945), and Walter Goodman, *The Committee: The Extraordinary Career of the House Committee on Un-American Activities* (New York: Farrar, Straus and Giroux, 1969). For its activities in the 1940s see Robert K. Carr, *The House Committee on Un-American Activities* (Ithaca, N.Y.: Cornell University Press, 1952). Many of the works referred to previously also cover the war years, as do Richard Polenberg, *War and Society: The United States, 1941–1945* (Philadelphia: Lippincott, 1972), and John M. Blum, *V Was for Victory* (New York: Harcourt Brace, 1976). An excellent book on the Truman administration is Alonzo Hamby, *Beyond the New Deal: Harry S. Truman and American Liberalism* (New York: Columbia University Press, 1973), although more comprehensive are Robert J. Donovan's two volumes, *Conflict and Crisis* (New York: Norton, 1977) on the first term and *Tumultuous Years* (New York: Norton, 1981) on the second. A useful collection of essays is Barton J. Bernstein, ed., *Politics and Policies of the Truman Administration* (New York: Watts, 1974); see particularly those by Athan Theoharis. Susan Hartmann, *Truman and the Eightieth Congress* (Columbia: University of Missouri Press, 1971), has some relevant material. Particularly good on the divergent strains in American liberalism in the immediate postwar years is Mary S. McAuliffe, *Crisis on the Left: Cold War Politics and American Liberals, 1947–1954* (Amherst: University of Massachusetts Press, 1978). Athan Theoharis, *Seeds of Repression: Harry S. Truman and the Origin of McCarthyism* (New York: Times Books, 1971), and Richard Freeland, *The Truman Doctrine and the Origins of McCarthyism* (New York: Alfred A. Knopf, 1972), relate the escalation of domestic anticommunism to the Truman administration's anti-Soviet rhetoric and policies. Francis H. Thompson, *The Frustration of*

Politics: Truman, Congress, and the Loyalty Issue, 1945–1953 (Cranbury, N.J.: Fairleigh Dickinson University Press, 1979), offers a somewhat unconvincing defense of Truman; better, perhaps because it preceded the anti-Truman studies, is Alan Harper, *The Politics of Loyalty: The White House and the Communist Issue, 1946–1952* (Westport, Conn.: Greenwood, 1969). On the demise of popular front politics see also the essays in Griffith and Theoharis, eds., *The Specter*, particularly that by Norman D. Markowitz, who has further probed the topic in *The Rise and Fall of the People's Century: Henry A. Wallace and American Liberalism, 1941–1948* (New York: Free Press, 1973). Useful too are Karl M. Schmidt, *Henry A. Wallace: Quixotic Crusade 1948* (Syracuse: Syracuse University Press, 1960), and Alan Yarnell, *Democrats and Progressives: The 1948 Presidential Election as a Test of Postwar Liberalism* (Berkeley: University of California Press, 1974). For the travail of the CP itself see Joseph R. Starobin, *American Communism in Crisis, 1943–1957* (Cambridge: Harvard University Press, 1972). Important for the struggle in the labor movement is Harvey Levenstein, *Communism, Anti-Communism, and the C.I.O.* (Westport, Conn.: Greenwood, 1981), and Bert Cochran, *Labor and Communism: The Conflict That Shaped American Unions* (Princeton: Princeton University Press, 1977); see also David M. Oshinsky, *Senator Joseph McCarthy and the American Labor Movement* (Columbia: University of Missouri Press, 1976), and George Lipsitz, *Class and Culture in Cold War America* (Granby, Mass.: Bergin and Garvey, 1982). For the impact of anticommunism on civil rights see Manning Marable, *Race, Reform and Rebellion: The Second Reconstruction in Black America, 1945–1982* (Jackson: University Press of Mississippi, 1984). Some of the essays in Griffith and Theoharis, eds., *The Specter*, such as that by Peter Irons, examine the conservative exploitation of the Communist issue; for the broader strategy of American businessmen see Howell J. Harris, *The Right to Manage: Industrial Relations Policies of American Business in the 1940s* (Madison: University of Wisconsin Press, 1982).

There is an enormous literature on McCarthyism. Scholarly study began with the 1955 collection by Daniel Bell, cited in the first paragraph of this section, with its emphasis on populistic or "mass politics" roots; see also Hofstadter's *Paranoid Style* under General Themes. Michael Rogin, *The Intellectuals and McCarthy: The Radical Specter* (Cambridge: MIT Press, 1967), signaled a reorientation of McCarthy scholarship by demonstrating the strength of McCarthyism in traditional Republican constituencies and the responsibility of various elites. Robert Griffith, *The Politics of Fear: Joseph R. McCarthy and the Senate*, 2d ed. (Amherst: University of Massachusetts Press, 1987), is particularly good in locating McCarthyism in the dynamics of conventional party politics. As noted in the preceding paragraph, some scholars stress the role of Truman and other liberals. Others prefer to place McCarthy in a long-term historical context of Republican and conservative politics, such as Michael Miles, *The Odyssey of the American Right* (New York: Oxford University Press, 1980); David Reinhard, *The Republican Right since 1945* (Lexington: University Press of Kentucky, 1983); and Earl Latham, *The Communist Controversy in Washington: From the New Deal to McCarthy* (New York: Atheneum, 1969), which also stresses the impact of the 1948 election on Republicans. A lively journalistic biography is Richard H. Rovere, *Senator Joe McCarthy* (New York: Harcourt, Brace and World, 1959), more authoritative are Thomas C. Reeves, *The Life and Times of Joe McCarthy* (Melbourne, Fla.: Krieger, 1982), and David Oshinsky, *A Conspiracy So Immense: The World of Joe McCarthy* (New York: Free Press, 1983). Helpful too are Edwin R. Bayley, *Joe McCarthy and the Press* (Madison: University of Wisconsin Press, 1981); Michael O'Brien, *McCarthy and McCarthyism in Wisconsin* (Columbia: University of Missouri Press, 1980); and Richard Fried, *Men against McCarthy* (New York: Columbia University Press, 1976). The principals in the Hiss case record their views in Whittaker Chambers, *Witness* (New York: Random House, 1952), and Alger Hiss, *In the Court of Public Opinion* (New York: Alfred A. Knopf, 1957); Allen Weinstein, *Perjury: The Hiss-Chambers Case* (New York: Alfred A. Knopf, 1978), concluded that Hiss was guilty, but his conclusions are disputed in Athan Theoharis, ed., *Beyond the Hiss Case: The FBI, Congress, and the Cold War* (Philadelphia: Temple University Press, 1982). The Fuchs case is briefly reviewed in M. J. Heale, "Secrets of a Special Relationship," *Reviews in American History* 16(December 1988): 630–35. The Rosenberg case also aroused scholarly controversy. Walter and Miriam Schneir, *Invitation to an Inquest* (New York: Penguin, 1973) exonerates the Rosenbergs; Ronald Radosh and Joyce Milton, *The Rosenberg File* (New York: Random House, 1983), concludes that Julius was guilty and that Ethel may not have been, and Michael Parrish, "Cold War Justice: The Supreme Court and the Rosenbergs," *American Historical Review* 82(1977): 805–42, is critical of the Court's ideological feuds and eventual rush to judgment. The Smith Act trials are studied in Michael Belknap, *Cold War Political Justice: The Smith Act, the Communist Party, and American Civil Liberties* (Westport, Conn.: Greenwood, 1977). For other legal repercussions of anticommunist politics see Stanley I. Kutler, *The American Inquisition: Justice and Injustice in the Cold War* (New York: Hill and Wang, 1982); Peter L. Steinberg, *The Great "Red Menace": United States Prosecution of American Communists, 1947–1952* (Westport, Conn.: Greenwood, and Jerold S. Auerbach, *Unequal Justice: Lawyers and Social Change in Modern America* (New York: Oxford University Press, 1976).

Chapters 9 and 10

Most of the general works cited in the first paragraph of the preceding section continue to be relevant to the 1950s and beyond. Others useful for this period include William L. O'Neill, *American High: The Years of Confidence, 1945–1960* (New York: Free Press, 1986); Paul A. Carter, *Another Part of the Fifties* (New York: Columbia University Press, 1983); and, particularly, Godfrey Hodgson, *America in Our Time* (New York: Doubleday, 1976), which ranges back in time the better to comprehend the 1960s. Also focusing on the 1960s are William L. O'Neill, *Coming Apart: An Informal History of America in the 1960s* (New York: Times Books, 1971), and Allan J. Matusow, *The Unraveling of America: A History of Liberalism in the 1960s* (New York: Harper and Row, 1984).

For the American economy in the 1950s, John Kenneth Galbraith, *The Affluent Society*, 2d ed. (New York: Houghton Mifflin, 1969), remains a revealing book. Harold G. Vatter, *The U.S. Economy in the 1950's* (New York: Norton, 1963), is informative, and helpful too is A. M. Johnson, "American Business in the Postwar Era," in *Reshaping America: Society and Institutions, 1945–1960*, eds. Robert H. Bremner and Gary W. Reichard, (Columbus: Ohio State University Press, 1982). S. Alexander Rippa, *Education in a Free Society* (New York: McKay, 1967), contains some material on the connections between business and education; Robert Griffith, "The Selling of America: The Advertising Council and American Politics, 1942–1960," *Business History Review* 57(1983): 389–412, is good on business propaganda, and also suggestive is his "Dwight D. Eisenhower and the Corporate Commonwealth," *American Historical Review* 87(February 1982): 87–122. Still useful is Martin Trow, "Small Businessmen, Political Tolerance, and Support for McCarthy," *American Journal of Sociology* 64(November 1958): 270–81. For religion in the Cold War era, in addition to Ahlstrom, *A Religious History of the American People*, see Will Herberg, *Protestant-Catholic-Jew* (Garden City, N.Y.: Anchor Doubleday, 1955); William G. McLoughlin, *Modern Revivalism* (New York: Ronald Press, 1959); Robert Wuthnow, *The Restructuring of American Religion: Society and Faith since World War II* (Princeton: Princeton University Press, 1988); Donald Crosby, *God, Church, and Flag: Senator Joseph R. McCarthy and the Catholic Church* (Chapel Hill: University of North Carolina Press, 1978); and James D. Fairbanks, "Religious Dimensions of Presidential Leadership: The Case of Dwight Eisenhower," *Presidential Stud-*

ies Quarterly 12(Spring 1982): 260–67. John Seaman, "Dilemma: The Mythology of Right and Left," *Journal of Human Relations* 17(1969): 43–57, concerns Billy James Hargis, and Arnold Forster and Benjamin R. Epstein, *Danger on the Right* (New York: Random House, 1964), contains material on right-wing fundamentalists as well as other groups. The books cited previously by Minott, Moley, and Caute contain information on veterans' groups. Several of the books on labor history cited above also cover the years of the anticommunist consensus, as do F. S. O'Brien, "The 'Communist-Dominated' Unions in the United States since 1950," *Labor History* 9(Spring 1968): 184–209, and Arthur J. Goldberg, *AFL-CIO: Labor United* (New York: McGraw-Hill, 1956). Among the studies of state and local anticommunism are M. J. Heale, "Red Scare Politics: California's Campaign Against Un-American Activities, 1940–1970," *Journal of American Studies* 20(April 1986): 5–32; James T. Selcraig, *The Red Scare in the Midwest, 1945–1951* (Ann Arbor: UMI Research Press, 1982); Don E. Carleton, "McCarthyism in Houston: The George Ebey Affair," *South-Western Historical Quarterly* 80 (October 1976): 163–76; and Walter Gellhorn, ed., *The States and Subversion* (Ithaca, N.Y.: Cornell University Press, 1952). For the South see Numan V. Bartley, *The Rise of Massive Resistance* (Baton Rouge: Louisiana State University Press, 1969); Betty C. Chmaj, "Paranoid Patriotism: The Radical Right and the South," *Atlantic* 210(November 1962): 91–97; and John A. Salmond, " 'The Great Southern Commie Hunt': Aubrey Williams, the Southern Conference Educational Fund, and the Internal Security Subcommittee," *South Atlantic Quarterly* 77(Autumn 1978): 433–52. The interlocking of antiradicalism and racism is demonstrated in Gerald Horne's books, *Black and Red: W. E. B. Du Bois and the Afro-American Response to the Cold War, 1944–1963* (Albany: State University of New York Press, 1986), and *Communist Front? The Civil Rights Congress, 1944–1956* (Cranbury, N.J.: Fairleigh Dickinson University Press, 1988).

Federal anticommunist measures under the Eisenhower administration are detailed in many of the books cited earlier, particularly those by Caute, Goldstein, and Reinhard and the several studies of McCarthy, but see also Elmo Richardson, *The Presidency of Dwight D. Eisenhower* (Lawrence: University of Kansas Press, 1979), and Stephen E. Ambrose, *Eisenhower: The President* (New York: Simon and Schuster, 1984). Hearings before HUAC are reproduced in Eric Bentley, ed., *Thirty Years of Treason* (New York: Viking, 1971). Information on the government program may be found in Eleanor Bontecue, *The Federal Loyalty-Security Program* (Ithaca, N.Y.: Cornell University Press, 1953). Edward Shils, *The Torment of Secrecy: The Background and Consequences of American Security Policies* (Chicago: Free Press, 1956), provides histor-

222

ical and comparative perspectives. Private as well as public programs are covered in Ralph S. Brown, Jr., *Loyalty and Security: Employment Tests in the United States* (New Haven: Yale University Press, 1958). J. Edgar Hoover's views are explained in his *Masters of Deceit* (New York: Holt, Rinehart and Winston, 1958), as well as in the previously cited books by Ungar and Powers, and the role of the FBI is examined in Frank M. Sorrentino, *Ideological Warfare: The FBI's Path Towards Power* (New York: Associated Faculty Press, 1985), and especially Kenneth O'Reilley, *Hoover and the Un-Americans: The FBI, HUAC, and the Red Menace* (Philadelphia: Temple University Press, 1983). Illuminating on senatorial liberals is Mary S. McAuliffe, "Liberals and the Communist Control Act of 1954," *Journal of American History* 63(September 1976): 351–76.

There is much interesting data on public opinion in Samuel A. Stouffer, *Communism, Conformity, and Civil Liberties* (Magnolia, Mass.: Peter Smith, 1955). On the conformist impulses of "the other-directed" American see David Riesman et al., *The Lonely Crowd* (New Haven: Yale University Press, 1950), and William H. Whyte, *The Organization Man* (New York: Simon and Schuster, 1955). The succumbing of the schools to the anticommunist consensus is well described in Diane Ravitch, *The Troubled Crusade: American Education, 1945–1980* (New York: Basic Books, 1983), and in Nelson and Roberts, *Censors and the Schools*; but see also Caute, *The Great Fear*, and Robert W. Iversen, *The Communists and the Schools* (New York: Harcourt, Brace and World, 1959). For higher education see David P. Gardner, *The California Oath Controversy* (Berkeley: University of California Press, 1967); Lionel S. Lewis, *Cold War on Campus* (New Brunswick, N.J.: Transaction Books, 1988); and particularly Ellen W. Schrecker, *No Ivory Tower: McCarthyism and the Universities* (New York: Oxford University Press, 1986). The purge of Hollywood and the popular media has been the subject of countless accounts. Among them are John Cogley, *Report on Blacklisting*, 2 vols. (New York: Fund for the Republic, 1956); Victor S. Navasky, *Naming Names* (New York: Viking, 1980); and Larry Ceplair and Steven Englund, *The Inquisition in Hollywood: Politics in the Film Community, 1930–1960* (Berkeley: University of California Press, 1983). For the press, see the books cited earlier by Caute and Bayley and James Aronson, *The Press and the Cold War*, rev. ed. (New York: Hastings, 1988). An interesting essay on anticommunism and culture is Jane De Hart Mathews, "Art and Politics in Cold War America," *American Historical Review* 81(1976): 762–87. Ralph L. Roy, *Communism and the Churches* (New York: Harcourt, Brace and World, 1960, is informative.

For judicial and congressional assaults on the anticommunist consen-

BIBLIOGRAPHICAL ESSAY

sus see Murphy, *The Constitution in Crisis Times*; G. Theodore Mitau, *Decade of Decision: The Supreme Court and the Constitutional Revolution, 1954–1964* (New York: Scribner, 1967); C. Hermann Pritchett, *Congress versus the Supreme Court, 1957–1960* (Minnesota: University of Minnesota Press, 1961); and Donald J. Kemper, *Decade of Fear: Senator Hennings and Civil Liberties* (Columbia: University of Missouri Press, 1965). Helping to shift opinion against government's communist control measures was the Association of the Bar of the City of New York, *Report of the Special Committee on the Federal Loyalty-Security Program* (New York: Dodd, Mead, 1956). On COINTELPRO see Athan Theoharis, *Spying on Americans* (Philadelphia: Temple University Press, 1978), and Frank J. Donner, *The Age of Surveillance* (New York: Alfred A. Knopf, 1980). Instructive if partisan on governmental dirty tricks, particularly in the 1960s, is Geoffrey Rips, *Unamerican Activities: The Campaign against the Underground Press* (San Francisco: City Lights, 1981). On right-wing groups in the late 1950s and 1960s see George Thayer, *The Farther Shores of Politics* (New York: Simon and Schuster, 1968); J. Allen Broyles, *The John Birch Society: Anatomy of a Protest* (Boston: Beacon Press, 1964); Milton A. Waldor, *Peddlers of Fear: The John Birch Society* (Newark, N.J: Lynnross, 1966); Robert A. Schoenberger, ed., *The American Right Wing* (New York: Holt, Rinehart and Winston, 1969); and Frank P. Mintz, *The Liberty Lobby and the American Right* (Westport, Conn.; Greenwood, 1985). The New Left is embraced in Todd Gitlin, *The Sixties: Years of Hope, Days of Rage* (New York: Bantam, 1987). Peter Steinfels examines *The Neoconservatives* (New York: Simon and Schuster, 1979). A well-balanced account of the rise of the New Right is Gillian Peele, *Revival and Reaction: The Right in Contemporary America* (New York: Oxford University Press, 1984).

INDEX

•

INDEX

Composed by Professional Book Compositors
in Baskerville text and display

Printed by R. R. Donnelley and Sons
on 50-lb. Cream White Sebago paper
and bound in Joanna Arrestox

Designed by Laury A. Egan